Timothy A.

W9-ALN-409

*The Female Autograph*

# The Female Autograph

THEORY AND PRACTICE OF
AUTOBIOGRAPHY
FROM THE TENTH TO THE
TWENTIETH CENTURY

*Edited by Domna C. Stanton*

THE UNIVERSITY OF CHICAGO PRESS

*Chicago and London*

The articles in this book originally appeared in *The Female Autograph,* volume 12–13 of the *New York Literary Forum,* Jeanine Parisier Plottel, Publisher. One chapter and several illustrations have been omitted from this new edition.

The University of Chicago Press, Chicago 60637
The University of Chicago Press, Ltd., London
University of Chicago Press Edition 1987
Printed in the United States of America

95 94 93 92 91 90 89 88 87    5 4 3 2 1

*Library of Congress Cataloging-in-Publication Data*

The Female autograph.

"The articles in this book originally appeared
in The female autograph, volume 12–13 of the
New York literary forum"—T.p. verso.
    Bibliography: p.
    1. Autobiography.  2. Women authors—Biography.
I. Stanton, Domna C.  II. New York literary forum.
CT25.F45     1987     920.72     87–5906
ISBN   0-226-77121-0  (pbk.)

# Contents

v

# Preface

Like all texts, the present volume is the product of method and madness, in doses that a preface invariably exposes as it retraces the purpose and contents of the work ahead. The subject of this volume—female autobiographies, memoirs, letters and diaries—represents one of those cases of maddening neglect that have motivated feminist scholarship since 1970. This body of writing about the self has remained invisible, systematically ignored in the studies on autobiography that have proliferated in the past fifteen years. Because of the exclusion of women's self-writing from both the critical and literary canons, the present volume contains essays as well as archival materials—little- or un-known, unpublished or untranslated texts—that illustrate the scope and richness of the corpus. An anthology and a work of criticism, *The Female Autograph* is, more accurately, a collage of pieces representing different disciplines and fields, different cultures and eras, different "genres" or narrative modes. To be sure, some readers may find this pluralism indiscriminate, the "impurity" irritating, but others will discern an effort to break down existing boundaries. As its title suggests, this volume does not merely aim to (begin to ) fill a blatant generic gap; it strives to undermine the generic boundaries that have plagued studies of autobiography, often resulting in extended lists of unconvincing criteria for differentiating various modes of self-inscription. Moreover, the excision of *bio* from *autobiography* is designed to bracket the traditional emphasis on the narration of "a life," and that notion's facile presumption of referentiality. These (and other) issues of substance and methodology are confronted or mediated in a diversity of ways within the parts and parcels that make up the present volume. It is not, then, to take the life out of literature that this mélange is called *The Female Autograph,* but instead, and in an ideal sense, to create a more generous and dynamic space for the exploration of women's texts that *graph* the *auto*.

Part 1 of this volume, "The Subject and the Signature: Theories of Practice," contains two essays that in divergent ways pose the question and affirm the specificity of women's writing. In "Autogynography: Is the Subject Different?," written after *A Room of One's Own*, I review recent feminist and nonfeminist autobiographic criticism in an attempt to delineate one of the possible differences of the female speaking subject. Where this essay confronts the problematic implications of valorizing the gendered signature, Sandra Caruso Mortola Gilbert and Susan Dreyfuss David Gubar's "Ceremonies of the Alphabet: Female Grandmatologies and the Female Authorgraph" examines practices that recover, re-create and mythologize woman's name. Challenging old and new views about the lack of a different woman's writing in an alphabetic, patriarchal culture, Gilbert and Gubar cite a large number of nineteenth- and twentieth-century literary and pictorial works in which fantasies about letters, hieroglyphs, and calligraphies reveal a systematic effort to authorize the female signature.

Part 2, "Toward an Archeology of Pre-Texts: The Case of Japan, England, and Spain," provides early evidence of women's propensity for autographic writing. In "The Female Hand in Heian Japan: A First Reading," Richard Bowring analyzes a group of texts—typically, diaries interspersed with poetry—that dominated the literary production of tenth-century Japan. These introspective writings, according to Bowring, elaborate a sexual grammar in which woman is the passive center, the unfulfilled text/sex waiting to be opened and read by an ever-absent, wandering man. By contrast, Janel M. Mueller's "Autobiography of a New 'Creatur': Female Spirituality, Selfhood, and Authorship in 'The Book of Margery Kempe'" traces the difficult, determined voyage of a woman seeking official recognition of her mystical calling. In demonstrating the narratological and thematic coherence of a fifteenth-century text she deems to be the first autobiography in English, Mueller underscores the specifically female refusal of the "I" to regard profound spirituality as incompatible with the roles of wife and mother, and her affirmation of an all-encompassing new 'creatur.' Religious faith as much as political strategy informs the fifteenth-century text that Amy Katz Kaminsky and Elaine Dorough Johnson, in "To Restore Honor and Fortune: 'The Autobiography of Leonor López de Córdoba,'" call Spain's first autobiography. Their introduction to the first translation of this document highlights the literariness of a text that traces the rise and fall of a powerful female speaker bent on vindicating her name.

The celebrated names that are the focus of Part 3, "Agencies of the Letter in the Seventeenth Century: Gentileschi and Sévigné," exemplify two different uses of the epistolary text—a privileged female mode of writing that Marcia J. Citron and Catharine R. Stimpson explore further in this volume. Mary D. Garrard's "Artemisia Gentileschi: The Artist's Autograph in Letters and Paintings" introduces the English-speaking reader to the letters of a successful professional artist to her patrons. These texts mark a progressive triumph over gender handicap in a masculine art world, while Gentileschi's overt and more covert pictorial self-portraits convey, for Garrard, an identification with women both as victims of oppression and heroic protagonists. In juxtaposition, Elizabeth C. Goldsmith unfolds the intimate, passionate drama of the mother-daughter relationship in "Giving Weight to Words: Madame de Sévigné's Letters to Her Daughter." Analyzing this most renowned of seventeenth-century correspondences, Goldsmith emphasizes the mother's attempts to overcome her daughter's absence by transmuting writing into spoken dialogue, an exchange that metaphorizes the economic vocabulary used by Gentileschi to communicate more pragmatic concerns.

The gap between the amateur and the professional woman, the personal and the public sphere, which the letters of Sévigné and Gentileschi illustrate, becomes the object of difficult mediations in the documents that constitute Part 4, "(Re)claiming the Symbolic: Nineteenth-Century Soldier, Minister, Musician, Lawyer." Mary Fleming Zirin's "'My Childhood Years': A Memoir by the Czarist Cavalry Officer, Nadzhda Durova" reveals the factors that led a young woman to rebel against the prescribed destiny of her sex and, as an adolescent, to enter the army disguised as a soldier. The rejection of femininity and a desire for the greater freedom of male existence are but two elements of a memoir that, as Zirin puts it, gives voice to specifically female, even feminist, perspectives and attitudes. Even more than gender, race is the distinctive and determining feature of the conversion narrative that Frances Smith Foster examines in "Neither Auction Block nor Pedestal: 'The Life and Religious Experience of Jarena Lee, A Coloured Lady.'" In her prefatory essay to the autograph of the first minister of the African Methodist Episcopal Church, Foster discusses black women's texts that neither depict the degradations of slavery nor promote the nineteenth-century ideal of femininity; instead, they describe the trials of independent working women such as Lee, who left home and family to spread the Gospel.

The hindrance and the help that male relatives represented in women's quest for professional and personal fulfillment are explored by Marcia J. Citron and Nancy F. Cott. The two letters to Felix that Citron translates in "Fanny Mendelssohn Hensel: Musician in Her Brother's Shadow" expose the growing frustration and bitterness of a trained musician who needed, but never received, approval and encouragement to publish her compositions. Failing to achieve that authority through authorship, Fanny remained a talented amateur in her illustrious family's salon. In "Women as Law Clerks: Catherine G. Waugh," Nancy F. Cott introduces a memoir that describes with wit and irony the tribulations of a young lawyer trying to establish herself in a male legal world. The text attests to women's embattled entry into the learned professions, insists Cott, an entry initially gained through the practices of their male relatives.

Over and beyond the diversity of fields represented by the texts of Part 4, Part 5, "Emblematic Places: Twentieth-Century Texts of the First and Third World," points to the heterogeneity of cultures in which woman has inscribed the self. In "The Female Sociograph: The Theater of Virginia Woolf's Letters," Catharine R. Stimpson situates the locus of a vast and variegated body of recently published letters in a middle space between the private and the public, the literal and the literary, the diary and prose fiction. Stimpson surveys the aesthetics of what Woolf identified as a woman's art, and sheds light on the shifting masks and voices of her epistolary performances. Leaving aside the theatrical metaphor, Marysa Navarro examines critically the shape and shaping of a mythology in "Of Sparrows and Condors: The Autobiography of Eva Perón." As Navarro observes, the language of humility and subordination, which cast the charismatic Evita as a sparrow to Juan Perón's condor, cohered with both her social origins and the accepted roles for women; but it also served as a covert vehicle for exalting her unique power and position. In a strikingly different political and discursive register, the tormented text that Donna Robinson Divine introduces and translates in "'Difficult Journey, Mountainous Journey': The Memoirs of Fadwa Tuqan" underscores the dual oppression of a Palestinian Arab woman. The political upheavals that have caused the oppression of her people form the background for the speaker's depiction of the struggle to find her poetic voice in a culture that perpetuates the oppression of her sex.

In the final and most contemporary section, Part 6 of *The Female Autograph* focuses on "Contemporary French Inscriptions of the Self." In "Women and Autobiography at Author's Expense," Philippe Lejeune discusses the phenomenon of "illegitimate" self-publication in a vanity press. Selecting twelve examples for analysis, Lejeune concludes tentatively, and in counterpoint to the essays of Stanton and Gilbert-and-Gubar, that there are social and cultural, but not sexual, differences between female and male inscriptions of the self. The volume closes with Julia Kristeva's "My Memory's Hyperbole," an autobiographical fragment produced expressly for *The Female Autograph* that confounds generic and generic boundaries. Writing in the first person plural, Kristeva traces the interrelated evolution of intellectual and political movements in Paris since 1965, analyzing the various scenes, acts, and dramatis personae not merely as a critical observer, but undeniably as a major protagonist.

Despite its marked diversity, or because of it, this volume displays inevitable gaps. Indeed, whatever delusions of fullness or fulfillment of a purpose may exist at the onset of a project such as this, the writing of a preface—which is more accurately an epilogue than "a saying beforehand"—constitutes the symbolic moment when the editor becomes a (re)reader, the first to perceive the work's lacunae. Aside from the cultures and eras, the authors and texts that could/should have been represented in this volume, it becomes clear, in retrospect, that issues of class, of race, and of sexual orientation have only been sporadically addressed. Like much of feminist scholarship, *The Female Autograph* exposes the need for more concerted investigation and integration of these factors in a critical practice committed to challenging existing discursive and ideological boundaries. In more limited terms, this volume also suggests two specific areas requiring further work. The first of these is more probing analyses of the (possible) differences of female autographic writing. The second, which like the first predicates continuing (re)discovery of women's texts, is the heuristic search for "an autographic literature of their own," to paraphrase Elaine Showalter's study of female novelists. The particular connections that appear in several of the texts in this volume—Julian of Norwich's *Revelations* for Margery Kempe; Sévigné's letters for Woolf; de Beauvoir's last memoir for Kristeva—are symptomatic of the overarching need for a systematic examination of the ways in which female autographs at different times, in different places, may be intertextually linked.

As a metaphorical suffix, a preface properly contains a statement of debts and credits, even if such a list is, by definition, always incomplete. My thanks to Jeanine Plottel for initially supporting this project, and publishing the collection of texts in the *New York Literary Forum*. Special thanks also go to Margaret Waller for her meticulous research in compiling the bibliography that appears at the end of the volume. Finally, however, and as the scholars who generously contributed their work would surely agree, credit for this volume ultimately lies with the women—from tenth-century Japan to late twentieth-century France—who inscribed the female self in adversity and diversity. It is those women who should be celebrated; to them *The Female Autograph* is rightly dedicated.

*The Female Autograph*

CHAPTER ONE

/

# Autogynography: Is the Subject Different?

## Domna C. Stanton

"The impulse towards autobiography may be spent." So says the "I" in *A Room of One's Own*, as she narrates autobiographically "the story" of two days she spent "combing the shelves" of libraries, reading texts and meta-texts in preparation for a discourse on women in fiction.[1] Fifty years later, the reader who would emulate Woolf's rhetorical strategy could never reach a similar conclusion about autobiography and its criticism. That reading "I," which is "only a convenient term for someone who has no real being" (p. 4), would need a figurative lifetime to consume the autobiographies on library shelves. The total far exceeds the number of titles contained in the 2,868 pages of Georg Misch's *History of Autobiography*, which closes with the Renaissance, or even in the additional 1,000 pages Misch's students compiled, which do not include the twentieth century.[2] And, leaving aside the primary texts, the autobiographical scholar would require more than two symbolic days to peruse the body of critical literature that has grown by leaps and bounds since 1968. A cursory look at the criticism published during the past fifteen years reveals a dramatic change in the discursive status of autobiography, a mode of writing traditionally considered marginal, generically inferior. Thus, where Stephen Shapiro was still trying to validate what he termed "the dark continent of literature" in 1968, in 1980, Barrett J. Mandel aptly entitled his study "Full of Life Now."[3] Even this phrase, however, does not convey the recent assertion that autobiography lies at the very center of modernist concerns. As William C. Spengemann has written: "the modernist movement away from representational discourse toward self-enacting, self-reflexive verbal structures and the critical theories that have been devised to explain this movement conspire to make the very idea of literary modernism synonymous with that of autobiography."[4]

And yet, if a female reader were to take down from the shelves the bulk of those critical volumes, she would be forced to conclude that women had written virtually no autobiographies. In traditional and "new" literary history, on both sides of the ocean, this "I"—whom I could name, after Woolf, "Mary Beton, Mary Seton, Mary Carmichael . . . any name you please, it is not a matter of any importance" (p. 5)—would find women's autobiographies conspicuous by their absence. Not a single study in Mehlman's *A Structural Study of Autobiography* (1971), Bruss's *Autobiographical Acts* (1976), Spengemann's *The Forms of Autobiography* (1980), or Lejeune's influential *L'Autobiographie en France* (1971), *Le Pacte Autobiographique* (1975), and *Je est un autre* (1980).[5] None, moreover, in the special issues on autobiography of such journals as *Genre* nos. VI 1 and 2 (1973), *Modern Language Notes* (1978), *Esprit Créateur* (1980), or *Poétique* (1983). At best, an isolated study or chapter in Butterfield's *Black Autobiography in America* (1974), Stone's *Autobiographical Occasions and Original* Acts (1982), and *Autobiography: Essays Theoretical and Critical,* edited by Olney (1980). Within this new realm of autobiographical criticism, woman still remained "the dark continent," in replication of the status that Freud ascribed to her over half a century ago.

What did that ghostly absence mean, I asked, looking as did Mary Beton, at "the blank spaces" on those shelves? (p. 54). Did it signal, once again, and despite over a decade of feminist studies, the collective repression of women? Even in phallocratic terms, it made no sense. How could that void be reconciled with the age-old, pervasive decoding of all female writing as autobiographical? One answer, I thought, turning away from those "empty shelves" (p. 54), was that "autobiographical" constituted a positive term when applied to Augustine and Montaigne, Rousseau and Goethe, Henry Adams and Henry Miller, but that it had negative connotations when imposed on women's texts. It had been used, I realized, as I moved through the stacks toward the French collections, to affirm that women could not transcend, but only record, the concerns of the private self; thus, it had effectively served to devalue their writing. Accordingly, over the centuries, the anonymous seventeenth-century *Portuguese Letters* had been called autobiographical, spontaneous, natural when ascribed to a woman, but fictive, crafted and aesthetic, when attributed to a man.[6] As with George Sand, whose fictions had been notoriously branded as autobiographical, critical reactions to Colette's work represented a dramatic case of the autobiographical wielded as a weapon to denigrate female texts and exclude them from the canon.

To be sure, women had iterated this predominant reading of their writing. Was it, perhaps, a cliché, a convention to which they subscribed to gain some currency in the marketplace?, I wondered, taking down Colette's *Break of Day:* "Man, my friend," I read, "you willingly make fun of women's writings because they can't help being autobiographical."[7] And yet, more aggressively, Beauvoir chastized the autobiographical narrowness and narcissism of female writing in *The Second Sex:* "it is her own self that is the principal—sometimes the unique subject of interest to her."[8] This view had led the future author of five remarkable volumes of memoirs to declare: "there are . . . sincere and engaging feminine autobiographies, but none can compare with Rousseau's *Confessions* and Stendhal's *Souvenirs d'égotisme*" (p. 668). Was this a provocation for women to engage in self-transcending political and philosophical questions or a reflection of the androcentrism of *The Second Sex?*

However complex the reasons for this self-devaluation, it was clearly not women who had determined the repression of autobiographies by the second sex, I countered, turning angrily to make my way to that post-Woolfian "room of our own" we call Women's Studies. Here I was sure to find the secondary sources for my text on autobiographical writing by women—what I would term *autogynography.* But my search yielded only one item in the card catalogue: Jelinek, Estelle C., ed. *Women's Autobiography: Essays in Criticism* (Indiana, 1980). Turning to the preface, I read the opening lines with growing discouragement:

> The idea for this collection came to me in 1976 when I was writing
> my dissertation on the tradition of women's autobiography. I
> found practically no criticism on women's autobiographies, except
> for that on Gertrude Stein's, and so had no way of comparing
> ideas with other critics to see if they were coming to the same or
> different conclusions I had. Working alone, I wrote that
> dissertation . . . but vowed to encourage such criticism by
> compiling this collection so that those working in the field could
> communicate with one another and individual articles would not
> be lost in journals in disparate places, but seen as a whole and as a
> distinct school of criticism (p. ix).

Three years later, the situation had hardly changed. Surely there had to be more than the few "individual articles" I too managed to locate in "disparate places." And just as surely, there had to exist a vast number of autogynographies, dating back to early periods, which those articles, written mostly on nineteenth- and twentieth-century texts, did not begin to enumerate. Yes, I decided, as I carted a highly disproportionate number of gynocentric and androcentric studies to the library desk, it was time to return to my own room and, by letter and phone, from friends and from strangers, try to unearth the primary and secondary sources I would need to write my text.

*   *   *

The search for primary sources—and here I am telescoping more than a few days—revealed the existence of important but unexplored auto-gynographies, contemporary with or even predating the earliest productions of men canonized by literary history. Scholars who claimed, for example, that English autobiography developed in the eighteenth century invariably neglected to consider the works of Laetitia Pilkington, Teresia Constantia Phillips, and Frances Anne Vane, which privileged confessions of feeling and influenced the content and form of both autobiographies and novels. In the rare instances when they were cited, these texts were dismissed as "frigidly sentimental chronicles," their authors branded as "dishonest and libertine women."9 Similarly, in a work on "English beginnings" of autobiography in the seventeenth century, Matthews mentioned the "modernism" of the Duchess of Newcastle's *True Relation of My Birth, Breeding and Life* (1656), though he treated text and author with contempt; and he ignored the *Memoirs* of Lady Ann Fanshawe, though he cited them in passing as "the first of the two lives types."10 By contrast, Mary Mason declared the *Book of Margery Kempe* (1432) "the first full autobiography in English by anyone male or female," and earlier still, Julian of Norwich, author of *A Shewing of God's Love* (c. 1300) the first Englishwoman to "speak out about herself."11 England was not an isolated instance, I discovered, as my archaeological quest progressed. Elaine Johnson and Amy Kaminsky, for example, insisted that the fifteenth-century *Written Document* of Doña Leonor López de Córdoba was not only the "first work by a known woman writer" in Spain, but that country's "first autobiography." Yes, that was more like it, I thought. But what of the non-Western world, which, critics claimed, lacked a concept and thus a literature of the individual self. Happily, I learned of Richard Bowring's research on the Heian period in Japan (794–1185). Women, who were forbidden to use Chinese, the language of the male elite, had authored a group of "introspective writings" that constituted, along with *The Tale of Genji,* the major texts of the period. From this perspective, Bowring claimed that the opening sentence of the famous *Tosa Diary* (935)—"A daily record, that preserve of men; but might not a woman produce one too, I wonder, and so I write"—penned by the male poet and grand arbiter of taste, Ki no Tsurayuki, did not involve merely a playful act of sexual substitution. Man was trying to reclaim or usurp a female literary role that was becoming entrenched, argued Bowring; thus Ki no Tsurayuki, adopting a strategy of negation or reversal, proclaimed man preeminent and woman the nascent intruder.12

Here was an emblem, provided by the East, of the strategies used by Western literary historians to efface autogynography! Indeed, this remarkable Japanese example tended to confirm Cynthia Pomerleau's contention that "the idea that oneself, one's feelings . . . were properly and innately worth writing about was essentially a female idea" (Jelinek, p. 28), one that men may have usurped and proclaimed their own by obscuring women's texts. To be sure, it was a speculative, even paranoid, reading; only the dogged pursuit of the gynarchaeological enterprise in different cultures, races, and classes would validate the theory or, in all likelihood, attenuate it. Still, it was a seed to sow in my text, perhaps in the introduction, where the need for an a-mazing journey, to use Mary Daly's demystificatory term, should be emphasized. This, however, did not resolve the matter of my text. How was I to treat the subject of autogynography when the primary and secondary sources were only beginning to emerge? Of necessity, as the Woolfian "I" had insisted, my text would contain doses of fiction and opinion (p. 4) that could have some validity but make no claim to "the essential oil of truth" (p. 25). Yes, I decided, leafing through *A Room of One's Own*, I could start by evaluating theories and studies of autobiography in those many gynoless volumes that now stood on my bookshelves before tackling the question of the specificity of women's texts in the few "individual articles" by feminist scholars. Then, perhaps, I might be able to say something, however partial and inconclusive, on the subject of autogynographical difference.

\*    \*    \*

It will surely come as no surprise that beyond their tacit agreement to exclude women's texts, critics disagreed about the specific nature and substance of autobiography. The explorations that had dramatically altered the status of autobiography had also bred controversy and confusion. Typically, Professor Y—as I chose to call the more valid critic after/against the misogynistic Professor Von X of *A Room of One's Own* (pp. 31 ff)—confronted this confusion in his opening paragraph: "As the number of people writing about autobiography has swelled," he wrote, "the boundaries of the genre have expanded proportionately until there is a virtually no written form that has not either been included in some study of autobiography or else been subjected to autobiographical interpretation" (Spengemann, p. xii). Where Professor Z—as I dubbed the less valid critic—propounded arbitrary and unconvincing criteria to differentiate "classic," "formal," or "true" autobiographies from memoirs, confessions, or diaries, Professor Y maintained that there was "no way to bring autobiography to heel as a literary genre with its own proper form, terminology and observances."[13] However, the generic fixation was not so easily exorcised; instead, it was displaced onto new thematic or discursive categories such as oratorical, dramatic, philosophical, or poetic autobiographies.[14] It transpired, too, in such formulations as "a genre without conventions" or in the expressed hope of arriving at a generic definition in the future, while speaking in the present "as if we knew what it were."[15]

More covertly, an ambivalent desire both to relinquish and to maintain generic certainty emerged in the closely related texts of Bruss and Lejeune. Although she began by proclaiming genre a nominalist fiction, Bruss also upheld it as the set of stable conventions in a community that help define what is permitted a writer and expected of a reader; and she elaborated a set of "rules" that distinguish autobiography from other illocutionary acts in a cultural context.[16] But in view of the confusion among critics, one would have to conclude that autobiography did not exist today, despite all titular or subtitular evidence to the contrary. Like Bruss, Lejeune affirmed the generic specificity of autobiography on the basis of a pact or contract between the author and the reader; at the same time, he inveighed against the essentialist and authoritarian nature of the generic impulse, which he compared to a restricted club, even a pure race, from which all deviations are branded aberrations or aborted failures.[17] Yes, this exposure of the implications of genre is salutary, I thought; but ultimately, E. S. Burt is right: "the whole project of defining autobiography generically is what needs to be abandoned."[18] That radical gesture would meet with continued resistance, however, for it would confound Professor Z's system of hierarchies and oppositions, in which the generic, as the French *genre* suggested, was inextricably linked to the genderic.

Well-intentioned, Professor Y opposed any prescriptive definitions, but his text invariably contained a minimal statement that raised troubling questions. Thus the seemingly innocuous definition, "a biography of a person written by himself,"[19] veiled the uncertain meaning and relation of the terms *person* and *himself,* and displaced the content of autobiography onto the undefined *biography.* There was, however, a difference between the autobiographic and the biographic text, which quickly came to mind: the first can never inscribe the death of the speaking subject, the terminus of life, which theoretically the second can describe. Autobiography, then, was necessarily un-ended, incomplete, fragmentary, whatever form of rhetorical closure it might contain. Of course, how much or how little of this partial *bio* an autobiography should properly contain, not even Professor Z tried to tell me. Sensitive to the variabilities and complexities of its narrative modes, Professor Y observed that autobiography might appear to privilege chronological linearity, but that it tended "toward discontinuous structures . . . with disrupted narrative sequences and competing foci of attention" (Bruss, p. 64). Indeed, an autobiography, I agreed, was a heterogeneous mixture of *discours* and *histoire,* to use Benveniste's terms,[20] the personal and the historico-cultural, the elegiac and the picaresque, the illustrative and the reflective. It might be structured around a crisis or moment of transformation; it could have explicit or implicit didactic or epistemological aims for the narratee or the narrator, but its thematic base, insisted Professor Y, was "all inclusive."[21] Inevitably, I reflected, the specific texture of an autobiography also represents the mediation of numerous contextual factors: a particular intertext, such as Rousseau's *Confessions* for George Sand and other nineteenth-century autobiographers; or a set of intertexts, such as hagiographies for Margery Kempe and conversion narratives for Quaker and Puritan women. More broadly, every autobiography assumes and reworks literary conventions for writing and reading. And its texture is ultimately determined by the ways in which meaning can be signified in a particular discursive context, an (ideo)logical boundary that always already confines the speaking subject.

Although Professor Y was largely indifferent to such matters, he did grapple with the status of the past that the speaking subject narrates, a question laden with ideological implications. Occasionally, he spoke of the recuperation or even the re-creation of the past, with the help of a selective or unconscious memory—and here he resembled Professor Z. But Professor Y also declared that the past was never a presence, only an absence; thus its textual substance necessarily involved a creation, an invention at the moment of enunciation. "The way in which the illusion of the past is presented," he said, ". . . is the 'form' the life takes."[22] In this perspective, the facts of the invented past had an undecidable status, according to Professor Y; they produced, through a set of conventions similar to those of the realistic novel, the effect or impression of a referential narrative; facts, he argued, were artifacts.[23] Such a notion of facticity, I recognized, was leading Professor Y away from Professor Z's belief in the truth-value of autobiography, which centuries of writers had claimed for their texts, or even some undefinable alloy of "design and truth," as Roy Pascal put it.[24] Yes, this theory of facticity heralded the ficticity of autobiography, I concluded, turning the page of his study to find these words: "in effect [it is] a novel written in the present with one's life as its subject. Not all fiction is autobiographical," Professor Y conceded, "but on this deeper level all autobiography is fiction."[25] Or, as Lejeune stated, internally, there is "no difference between an autobiography and an autobiographical novel."[26]

To speak of the autobiographical text as fiction did not, however, resolve the issue of the identity of the subject or its referential status, a problem that Professor Y's phrase "one's life" encapsulated. Whose life was it anyway? I wondered. Professor Y insisted that the narration by a subject of enunciation—most often, but not always, selected to be "I"[27]—about the past self or selves as object of enunciation could not, by definition, display the unity, coherence, or self-presence that mark the Western myth of subjecthood. If Professor Z objected to such views as post modernist and anachronistic to the notion of the subject in earlier times, Professor Y countered that he necessarily read with contemporary eyes and that, from his vantage point, the very nature of the autobiographical project involved a splitting of the subject. That split perdured even as the past, hetero-geneous self or selves moved discontinuously forward to the present mo-ment of enunciation in an apparent desire for self-possession and one-ness; as Lejeune observed, the autobiographical subject "becomes simple only at the moment when the narrator speaks of his own present narration."[28] Despite his insistence on a self-reflexive structure and the inscription of the myth of the self, Lejeune could not give up the referential ghost or the identity of the subject, I realized, rereading his often-cited definition of autobiography: "a retrospective narrative in prose that a real person makes of his own existence when he emphasizes his individual life, especially the story of his personality."[29] This identity between a real person, the nar-rator, and the object of narration was the basis for his autobiographical pact between author and reader. Lejeune was clearly right to privilege the reader, who served as the autobiographer's muse, said Professor Y,[30] and even, I ventured, determined the very configuration of the speaking sub-ject. But Lejeune transformed the reader into a transcendent authority, a kind of policing force who could purportedly verify the fulfillment of the contract or pronounce the work a fraud. No less troubling was the under-lying notion of a self-identical entity, which Lejeune considered an "im-mediately perceived fact" but which evoked, to his critics, the Cartesian principle of self-evidence or the spectre of Derridean phallogopresence. Thus in a disarming, autographic text, Lejeune had recently acknowledged certain imperfections or limitations of his theories and shifted his focus to the miming of a contract and the play of identity.[31]

What had not changed, however, was Lejeune's avowed belief in truth-value and the identity of the proper name, which he regarded as the "pro-found subject of autobiography."[32] Although Lejeune confused the prop-er name in the text with the authorial signature, the notion elicited ambivalent reactions, which I, as feminist reader, could not resolve. On the one hand, "author" spelled the phallic myth of authority, not to speak of the patriarchal institutions of property and law. On the other, I won-dered uncomfortably, what would the elimination of the signature mean for women autobiographers, whose texts had yet to be explored, acknowl-edged, and included in the literary and critical canons. Better to bracket that question, I decided in frustration, putting the androcentric volumes back on the shelf. Perhaps I could tackle the problem more knowledgeably once I had examined the gynocentric studies of autobiography. Yes, it was time—the days were in fact passing—to take down from my shelf that small body of work—the individual articles, the couple of books, and the unpublished texts—that friends and strangers had helped me compile, and determine, in light of the issues Professors Y and Z had raised, what heuristic claims could be made at this discursive moment for the difference of autogynography.

\*　　\*　　\*

Difference was much on her mind, I realized, as soon as I began to read the feminist scholar. Unlike Professors Y and Z, who seemed indifferent to anyone but the generic and hegemonic "he," the feminist scholar—why not call her F.S.?—strove to find genderic differences, as Jelinek's preface confirmed: "It has been gratifying," she said, "to read all the essays sent to me and to discover that the critics are substantiating our contention that there is a literary tradition in which women write autobiography that is different from that by men" (pp. xi–xii). Implicitly, however, that assertion of difference was based on a preselected corpus of male autobiographies and a preestablished set of common traits. A troubling but familiar sign of the generic fixation, I thought, now transposed to a genderic formula: Male=X, ergo Female=non-X + W. Besides, wasn't such a notion of difference premature when the archaeological quest for autogynographies had just begun to make headway? Still, any single text can suggest constructs, to be tested out on other texts, I thought, looking through the work of F.S. for discussions of formal differences. One opposition appeared repeatedly: men's narratives were linear, chronological, coherent, whereas women's were discontinuous, digressive, fragmented (pp. 17–19). This was the same narrative shape that Didier had discovered in Sand's *My Life,* a form Anaïs Nin likened to "a crazy quilt, all in bits."[33] And yet, women also wrote linear narratives, as Lynn Bloom and Orlee Holder observed in re-viewing several twentieth-century texts.[34] Moreover, narrative discontinuity was integral to Professor Y's conception of autobiography; and fragmentariness was the matrix of Beaujour's study of the "autoportrait" from Augustine to Leiris.[35] Indeed, I reflected, discontinuity and fragmentation constitute particularly fitting means for inscribing the split subject, even for creating the rhetorical impression of spontaneity and truth.

If there existed a specifically female type of narrative discontinuity, more detailed and focused analysis would have to reveal it, I concluded, turning now to the question of autogynographic content. Here, too, a binary opposition recurred that associated the female with personal and intimate concerns, the male with professional achievements[36]—a replication, it seemed, of the private/public, inner/outer dichotomies that mark genderic differences in our symbolic system. But here, too, I could object that Professor Z upheld the "personal" *Confessions* of Rousseau as the origin of modern autobiography and that Lejeune made "the history of the individual personality" central to his definition. To be sure, I could also cite autogynographies that were anything but "personal," but what precisely did the term mean: a particular type of introspective and affective analysis? a certain quantity and quality of detail? Although a domestic "dailiness," to use Kate Millet's word, often permeated autogynographies, the concept of the personal was a function of changing conventions, which determined the said and, more important, the unsaid, such as the desires and the experiences of the female body. Thus, even the violence of rape was consistently silenced in nineteenth-century female slave narratives, Francis Smith Foster had said on the phone. Reserved or "decorous communication," as Nancy K. Miller put it, any autobiography imposed decided limits on the intimate revelations of the narrating "I", which were conveyed to readers by omissions or by explicit statements, such as that of St. Theresa: "I wish I had also been allowed to describe clearly and in full detail my grave sins and wicked life . . . [but] I have been subjected to severe restrictions [by my confessors] in the matter."[37] Intrasubjectively, the self-censoring speaker invariably displayed impulses toward both exposure and concealment. Or, perhaps, what was said made room for the not-said, as Colette's *Break of Day* seemed to suggest: "[By divulging] to the public love-secrets and amorous lies and half-truths . . . she manages to hide other important and obscure secrets" (p. 62). Women's "personal" or "intimate" autographs, then, remained partial inscriptions of what Spacks called "selves in hiding."[38]

Some feminist critics defined the personal in women's autobiographies as a primary emphasis on the relation of self to others. However, this relatedness was traced to the dependence imposed on women by the patriarchal system, or then it was upheld as a fundamental female quality.[39] In the parental relation, moreover, both father and mother appeared alternatively as privileged terms. According to Spacks, the father-daughter bond dominated the works of Laetitia Pilkington, Charlotte Charke, and Fanny Burney, while the mother was depicted in negative terms that verged, in Hester Thrale's diary, on matrophobia.[40] And yet, matrilinealism prevailed in the autographs of Sand and Colette and, as Demetrakopoulous showed, in such diverse twentieth-century works as Mead's *Blackberry Winter,* Hellman's *Pentimento,* Angelou's *I Know Why a Caged Bird Sings,* and Kingston's *The Woman Warrior.*[41] To be sure, no one had yet compared the relation to the mother in female and male autobiographies, a bond that Professor Y regarded as crucial (Stone, p. 147). Still, it seemed valid that this relation would have particular meanings for the female subject, since her mother symbolized both an origin that is same and different, and subsequently, a mirror of the possibilities of becoming. Analogously, I thought, a different narrative thread must inscribe the double identification of the maternal "I" with her child, as the self she had been and the other who had been within her. However, this privileged relation also allowed authors from Anne Bradstreet to Margaret Oliphant to present their texts as records for their children and thus to legitimize or naturalize their writing. It was difficult, then, to separate a manifestation of female difference from a strategic conformity to cultural norms. Indeed, over and beyond children, the central role ascribed to husband or mate, in autographs ranging from the Duchess of Newcastle's *True Relation* to the memoirs of Hellman and Beauvoir, could signal either a special female relatedness and/or an acquiescence to the dominant sex through which the female is meant to define and confine the self in our symbolic order.

More than the ambiguous inscription of multiple personal relations, the autogynographical narrative was marked by conflicts between the private and the public, the personal and the professional. As F.S. observed, there was a systematic tension between the conventional role of wife, mother, or daughter and another, unconventional self that had ambition or a vocation. This dual and contradictory impulse, which Professor Z had first located in Lady Ann Fanshawe's seventeenth-century text, was displayed much earlier in the "two equally demanding identities" of wife-mother and pilgrim-mystic that structured the *Book of Margery Kempe*.[42] That "divided consciousness" and the "rhetoric of uncertainty" that conveyed it, as Spacks put it, recurred in various forms throughout the centuries, down to the autographs of Eleanor Roosevelt and Golda Meir.[43] A similar tension underlay Elizabeth Cady Stanton's *Eighty Years and More,* in which, as Jelinek showed, the "I" kept returning to the public career, even though the stated intention was to present "the story of my private life as wife and earnest reformer, as an enthusiastic housekeeper, proud of my skill in every department of domestic economy, and as the mother of seven children (pp. 71–72). So doing, the speaking subject strove and failed to present the unitary and ordinary self of wife and mother.

Beyond professional aspirations there was, I believed, a fundamental deviance that pervaded autogynographies and produced conflicts in the divided self: the act of writing itself. For a symbolic order that equates the idea(l) of the author with a phallic pen transmitted from father to son places the female writer in contradiction to the dominant definition of woman and casts her as the usurper of male prerogatives.[44] Internalized, this generic "horizon of expectations," to paraphrase Jauss,[45] generated a particular self-consciousness about the fact of writing often manifested in a defensive or justificative posture. "Because I am a woman, ought I therefore to believe that I should not tell you of the goodness of God?", asks the "I" in Julian of Norwich's *Showings,* proceeding to use the insignificant hazelnut as a metaphor for God's perfection and the value of her own narrative.[46] As this example also revealed, however, the speaking "I" constituted the reading "you" as the representation of society's view of women and thus as the personification of the writing interdiction. Analogously, although the eighteenth-century *Narrative of the Life of Mrs Charlotte Charke* was defiantly dedicated to the self, the reader was still encoded as the amused critic of the eccentric female speaker: "those that like to laugh I know will encourage me; and, I am certain, there is none in the World MORE FIT THAN MYSELF TO BE LAUGHED AT. I confess myself an odd Mortal, and believe I need no Force of Argument, beyond what has already been said, to bring the whole Globe terrestrial into that Opinion."[47] Forgoing such self-mockery, the female "I" could resort to more conventional means of attenuating the deviance or, in Fanny Burney's case, the sin of writing: she could cast her text in the ethical frame of a spiritual journey, a search for virtue and goodness, or the fulfillment of a duty,[48] semes that found a latter-day expression as therapy for the speaker in the diaries of Anaïs Nin.

Although the injunction against writing had somewhat lifted for some women in some contemporary places,[49] autogynography, I thought, had a global and essential therapeutic purpose: to constitute the female subject. In a phallocentric system, which defines her as the object, the inessential other to the same male subject—that *The Second Sex* had proved beyond a doubt—the *graphing* of the *auto* was an act of self-assertion that denied and reversed woman's status. It represented, as Didier had said of Sand's *My Life,* the conquest of identity through writing (p. 562). Creating the subject, an autograph gave the female "I" substance through the inscription of an interior and an anterior. And yet, the symbolic specificity of woman as the inessential other also helped explain why the female self was textually constructed through the relation to mother and father, mate and child. This "delineation of identity by way of alterity," as Mason put it, was nowhere more clearly illustrated than in the *True Relation* of the Duchess of Newcastle:

> I hope my readers will not think me vain for writing my life, since there have been many that have done the like, as Caesar, Ovid and many more, both men and women, and I know no reason I may not do it as well as they: but I verily believe some censuring Readers will scornfully say, why hath this Lady writ her own life? since none care to know whose daughter she was or whose wife she is, or how she was bred, or what fortunes she had, or how she lived, or what humour or disposition she was of? I answer that it is true, that it is to no purpose to the Readers, but it is to the Authoress, because I write for my own sake, not theirs; neither did I intend this piece for to delight, but to divulge; not to please the fancy but to tell the truth, lest after-ages should mistake, in not knowing I was daughter to one Master Lucas of St. Johns, near Colchester, in Essex, second wife to the Lord Marquis of Newcastle; for my Lord having had two wives, I might easily have been mistaken, especially if I should die and my Lord marry again.[50]

In this remarkable passage, the "I" asserted that she "writ her own life" "for [her] own sake," out of a need to differentiate the self from others, only to show that its constitution and individuation predicated reference and relatedness to others: father and husband, and beyond, less "censuring Readers" of "after-ages." It was no mere coincidence, then, that three centuries later, Beatrice Webb's *The Partnership* began with a chapter entitled "The Other." Beyond the surface theme of marital happiness, the title suggested both the affirmation of the female as subject and the recognition that one cannot exist without the other.[51] The female "I" was thus not simply a texture woven of various selves; its threads, its life-lines, came from and extended to others. By that token, this "I" represented a denial of a notion essential to the phallogocentric order: the totalized self-contained subject present-to-itself.

BECAUSE of woman's different status in the symbolic order, autogynography, I concluded, dramatized the fundamental alterity and non-presence of the subject, even as it asserts itself discursively and strives toward an always impossible self-possession. This gendered narrative involved a different plotting and configuration of the split subject, which the androcentric Professor Y wholly ignored, although he had begun to consider the problematics of subjecthood. Indeed, I reflected, surveying my differing bookshelves, Professor Y seemed ready, in a few instances at least, to undermine the notion of identity, whereas F.S., at this discursive moment, appeared determined to affirm and maintain it. What scenarios underlay those contrasting tendencies? I wondered, leaning back in my chair. One possible explanation was that Professor Y was feeling paralyzed by the identity that the symbolic order bestowed (or imposed) upon him, whereas F.S. was still struggling, in that recently constructed room of her own, to assert an identity that was denied her. To be sure, there were exceptions, most notably among women with French connections, who considered the unitary subject inimical to the feminist enterprise. By and large, however, F.S. did not seem willing to accept Gertrude Stein's pronouncement that identity "destroys creation", whereas masterpieces derive from "knowing there is no identity and producing while identity is not."[52] Moreover, in contrast to Stein's *Autobiography of Alice B. Toklas,* a text that openly rejects the "autobiographical pact" of identity between a real person, the subject, and the object of enunciation, the valorized notion of female identity in most readings by F.S. was conjoined with an explicit or implicit belief in the referentiality and truth-value of autogynographies as "honest records of the moment," or of women's "inner lives."[53] It was almost as if—and here I was speculating again—the feminist scholar's own identity depended on the referential reality of the woman in the text, as if that woman was the same and different other through whom F.S. needed to construct and relate her self. Still, I thought, glancing at the corpus I had now finished reading, the notion of romances, of fictions, of "imagined selves" had appeared in a couple of "disparate places"[54] and there was no predicting the future shape of our room.

It was nonetheless clear that F.S. was not going to help me confront the question of the status and the significance of the female signature. And yet, I thought anxiously, as I put the gynocentric studies back on the shelf, I cannot end my text without shifting focus from the *auto* in the *graph* to its author, and exploring, however ambivalently or abortively, the importance of her/his gender and referentiality. To broach these issues, I would have to look beyond autobiographical criticism, since Professor Y, with his generic he, was oblivious to their problematics. In the one pertinent article I had found, Professor Y envisaged the death of the author, after Derrida and most especially Foucault, who declared that this relatively recent manifestation of the system of private property served to constrain the proliferation of new meanings and readings.[55] Yes, I said, the name of the female author has consistently generated restricted and distorted readings,[56] when her texts were not, as autogynographies had been, simply banned from consideration; in that sense, Foucault was right, although he never spoke of women. Because of that gender-bound discursive situation, however, in which I was engaged, I had to privilege and promote the female signature, make it visible and prominent, or else endure and insure more of the phallocentric same. The elimination of the signature, Nancy K. Miller had warned in a debate with Peggy Kamuf (who assumed a Foucaultian stance), could even spell a return to female anonymity.[57] In this perspective, I could argue that at this symbolic moment the female signature, unlike the generic fixation, had liberating rather than constraining effects, although there was always the risk of reconfirming, as Kamuf emphasized, the very systems and institutions we wished to undermine.

More problematic by far was the question of the referential status of the signature. To be consistent with my textual, nonreferential approach to the female subject, I should view the signature as a name that comprised various semes of gender, ethnicity, or class and that evoked various cultural and literary associations. Did it matter, after all, on the signifying plane, whether the name affixed to *Life's Adventure* (Woolf, p. 98) was Mary Carmichael or Mary McCarthy? And yet, as the names George Sand and Pauline de Réage illustrated, a signature could always be counterfeit.[58] Given that uncertainty, I could take the signature at its face value and promote, with Peggy Kamuf and Mary Jacobus, Derridean and Kristevan notions of the "feminine" as a modality open to both men and women;[59] but that I resisted, for it involved recourse to abstract and essentialist predefinitions, rather than the heuristic exploration of sexual/textual differences. Even less satisfactory as a solution, however, was a return to Lejeune's pact and to a policing reader who could purportedly confirm anatomical truth. Yes, I realized, pacing the room in frustration, I was at an impasse. My text would leave an unresolved contradiction. But why not?, I asked, sitting back at my desk; contradictions were emblematic of broad discursive problems; and I was, it appeared, in good company. Jacobus, for instance, rejected the idea of the gendered signature, but she also unconsciously used it when she contrasted Mary Shelley to all the rivalrous male authors she cited. And although Foucault said with Beckett that it does not matter who is speaking, he also promoted certain male writers as "founders of discursivity" (p. 154), thus confirming by his own practice, that the author had not, and perhaps could not, at present be eliminated. At the very least, then, I should clearly mark the contradiction in my text—no less overtly than the divided female subject in the autograph—before I exposed my illogical belief that the gender of the author did make a difference, at this discursive point in time.

"What should that difference be?", asked the "I" in *A Room of One's Own,* just before she proceeded to imagine and affirm the distinct difference of the sentence, sequence, theme, and sensibility of Mary Carmichael's *Life's Adventure* (pp. 81 ff). And yet, I realized, reading Woolf's last chapter a last time, Mary Beton had ultimately retreated into an incandescent vision of androgyny, an ideal that, in our system, would guarantee the female anonymity she decried. To be sure, although I had not reached any inspired conclusions, I had something to say about the different subject of and in the female autograph, a tentative, exploratory idea that other readings by F.S. and, perhaps even Professor Y would revise. I would want to cast my own text in the interrogatory mode, I decided, taking out a blank sheet of paper and writing: *Autogynography: Is the Subject Different?* And instead of a formal closure, I would leave my text unended, open it to a critical reading by appropriating a passage from Woolf: "Lies will flow from my lips, but there may perhaps be some [valid statement] mixed up with them; it is for you to seek out [this statement] and to decide whether any part of it is worth keeping. If not, you will, of course, throw the whole of it into the waste paper basket and forget all about it" (p. 4).

## NOTES

1. Virginia Woolf, *A Room of One's Own* (New York: Harcourt, Brace and World, 1929), p. 83. A first draft of this essay was presented at the colloquium on New Directions in Women's Biographies and Autobiography sponsored by the Project on Women and Social Change, Smith College, June 12–17, 1983.

2. Georg Misch, *Geschicte der Autobiographie,* 4 vols. (Frankfurt am Main: Schulte und Bulmke, 1946–69).

3. Stephen A. Shapiro, "The Dark Continent of Literature: Autobiography," *Com-*

*parative Literature Studies* 5 (1968), 421–54; Barrett J. Mandel, "Full of Life Now," *Autobiography: Essays Theoretical and Critical,* ed. James Olney (Princeton: Princeton Univ. Press, 1980), pp. 49–72.

4. William C. Spengemann, *The Forms of Autobiography: A Collection of Critical Essays* (Englewood Cliffs, N.J.: Prentice-Hall, 1981), p. xiii.

5. See, however, Lejeune's article in this volume. And, in a recent conversation, Lejeune told me he is undertaking a systematic survey of women's autobiographies of the nineteenth and twentieth centuries.

6. See Peggy Kamuf, "Writing Like a Woman," *Women and Language in Literature and Society,* ed. Sally-McConnell-Ginet, Ruth Borker, and Nelly Furman (New York: Praeger, 1980), pp. 284–99.

7. Colette, *Break of Day,* trans. Enid McLeod (New York: Farrar, Straus and Cudahy, 1961), p. 19.

8. Simone de Beauvoir, *The Second Sex* (New York: Vintage Books, 1974), p. 655.

9. Wayne Shumaker, *English Autobiography: Its Emergence, Materials and Form* (Berkeley: Univ. of California Press, 1954), pp. 23–24. See also Jelinek, pp. 2–5.

10. William Matthews, "Seventeenth-Century Autobiography," paper read at the William Andrews Clark Memorial Library. Los Angeles: Univ. of California, 1973, p. 14.

11. Mary G. Mason, "The Other Voice: Autobiographies of Women Writers," in Olney, op. cit., pp. 207, 209.

12. See the texts of Bowring, Kaminsky and Johnson in this volume.

13. James Olney, "Autobiography and the Cultural Moment: A Thematic, Historical and Bibliograpical Introduction," in Olney, op. cit., p. 4.

14. See Spengemann, op. cit., and William Howarth, "Some Principles of Autobiography," in Olney, pp. 83–114.

15. Michael G. Cooke, "'Do You Remember Laura?,' or the Limits of Autobiography," *The Iowa Review,* 9, No. 2 (1978), 68; Georges May, *L'Autobiographie* (Paris: Presses Universitaires de France, 1979), p. 12.

16. Elizabeth W. Bruss, *Autobiographical Acts: The Changing Situation of a Literary Genre* (Baltimore: Johns Hopkins Univ. Press, 1976).

17. Philippe Lejeune, *Le Pacte Autobiographique* (Paris: Seuil, 1975), passim, but especially pp. 311–45.

18. E. S. Burt, "Poetic Conceit: The Self-Portrait and Mirrors of Ink," *Diacritics* 12, No. 4 (Winter 1982), 19.

19. Jean Starobinski, "The Style of Autobiography," in Olney, p. 73.

20. Emile Benveniste, *Problèmes de linguistique générale,* vol. 2 (Paris: Gallimard, 1974), pp. 237–50.

21. Howarth, op. cit., p. 87.

22. Mandel, op. cit., p. 64.

23. Louis A. Renza, "The Veto of the Imagination: A Theory in Autobiography," in Olney, p. 269.

24. Roy Pascal, *Design and Truth in Autobiography* (Cambridge: Harvard Univ. Press, 1960).

25. Burton Pike, "Time in Autobiography," *Comparative Literature* 28 (1976), 337.

26. Lejeune, "Le Pacte Autobiographique," *Poétique,* 14 (1973), 147.

27. See, however, Lejeune's "Autobiography in The Third Person," *New Literary History* 9, No. 1 (Autumn 1977), 26–50, and Julia Kristeva's first person plural autograph in this volume.

28. Lejeune, "Le Pacte Autobiographique," *Poétique,* 14 (1973), 157.

29. Lejeune, *Le Pacte Autobiographique* (Paris: Seuil, 1975), p. 139.

30. Renza, in Olney, p. 293.

31. See Michael Ryan, "Self-Evidence," *Diacritics*, 10, No. 2 (Summer 1980), 2–16; and Lejeune, "Le Pacte Autobiographique (bis)," *Poétique*, 56 (November 1983), 416–34.

32. Lejeune, ibid., and *Poetique*, 14 (1973), 153.

33. Béatrice Didier, "Femme, identité, écriture: A Propos de *L'Histoire de ma vie* de George Sand," *Revue des Sciences Humaines*, 168, No. 4 (1977), 561–76; Anaïs Nin is quoted in Albert R. Stone, *The American Autobiography: A Collection of Critical Essays* (New Jersey: Prentice Hall, 1981), p. 192; see also Annette Kolodny, "Towards a Theory of Form in Feminist Autobiography: Kate Millet's *Flying* and *Sita*, Maxine Hong Kingston's *The Woman Warrior*," in Jelinek, pp. 221ff.

34. Lynn Bloom and Orlee Holder, "Anaïs Nin's *Diary* in Context," in Jelinek, pp. 208ff; see also Patricia Meyer Spacks, *Imagining a Self: Autobiography and Novel in Eighteenth-Century England* (Cambridge: Harvard Univ. Press, 1976), pp. 151ff.

35. Michel Beaujour, *Miroirs d'encre: Rhétorique de l'auto-portrait* (Paris: Seuil, 1980).

36. See Jelinek's "Introduction: Women's Autobiography and the Male Tradition," and Patricia Meyer Spack's "Selves in Hiding," both in Jelinek, pp. 10, 113.

37. Nancy K. Miller, "Women's Autobiography in France: For a Dialectics of Identification," *Women and Language in Literature and Society*, op. cit., p. 268; Saint Theresa is quoted in Renza, op. cit., p. 284.

38. Spacks, "Selves in Hiding," op. cit., pp. 112–32.

39. Ibid., p. 122 and Spacks, *Imagining a Self*, op. cit., p. 73; Stone, op. cit., p. 196.

40. Spacks, *Imagining a Self*, pp. 74–78, 164; "Reflecting Women," *Yale Review*, 63 (1973), 33. On matrophobia, see also Mary Fleming Zirin's contribution to this volume.

41. Stephanie Demetrakopoulos, "The Metaphysics of Matrilinealism in Women's Autobiography . . . ," in Jelinek, pp. 180–205. See also Lynn Z. Bloom, "Heritages: Discussions of Mother-Daughter Relationships in Women's Autobiographies," *The Lost Tradition: Mothers and Daughters in Literature*, ed. Cathy N. Davidson and E. M. Broner (New York: Ungar, 1980), pp. 281–302.

42. See Matthews, op. cit., p. 14; Mason in Olney, pp. 211, 221.

43. Spacks, "Reflecting Women," op. cit., p. 37; "Selves in Hiding," op. cit., pp. 112–32.

44. See Sandra Gilbert and Susan Gubar, *The Madwoman in the Attic* (New Haven: Yale Univ. Press, 1979).

45. Hans-Robert Jauss, "Littérature médiévale et théorie des genres," *Poétique*, 1, No. 1 (1970), 91.

46. See Mason in Olney, p. 215.

47. Quoted in Spacks, *Imagining a Self*, p. 82.

48. Ibid., pp. 59ff.

49. See Elizabeth Winston's analysis of some English and American women's autobiographies after 1920 in "The Autobiographer and Her Readers: From Apology to Affirmation," in Jelinek, pp. 93–111.

50. Mason in Olney, p. 231; Margaret, Duchess of Newcastle, "A True Relation of My Birth, Breeding and Life," *The Lives of William Cavendish, Duke of Newcastle, and of his Wife, Margaret Duchess of Newcastle*, ed. Mark Antony Lover (London: John Russell, 1892), pp. 309–10.

51. Beatrice Webb, *Our Partnership* (Cambridge: Cambridge Univ. Press, 1975). For a woman-centered manifestation of this idea see Luce Irigaray, "And the One Doesn't Stir Without the Other," trans. Hélène Wenzel, *Signs: Journal of Women in Culture and Society*, 7, No. 1 (Autumn 1981) 60–67.

52. Quoted in James E. Breslin, "Gertrude Stein and the Problems of Autobiography," in Jelinek, p. 150.

53. Demetrakopoulos, in Jelinek, p. 208; Mary G. Mason and Carol H. Green, eds., *Journeys: Autobiographical Writings by Women* (Boston: G. K. Hall, 1979), p. vii.

54. E.g., Didier, Miller, Spacks, *Imagining a Self,* all op. cit., and Germaine Brée "George Sand: The Fictions of Autobiography," *Nineteenth-Century French Studies,* 4, No. 4 (Summer 1976), 438–49.

55. Michael Sprinker, "Fictions of the Self: The End of Autobiography," in Olney, pp. 322ff. Michel Foucault, "What is an Author?", *Textual Strategies,* ed. Josue V. Harari (Ithaca: Cornell Univ. Press, 1979), pp. 141–60.

56. See Jonathan Culler, "Reading as a Woman," *On Deconstruction: Theory and Criticism after Structuralism* (Ithaca: Cornell Univ. Press, 1982), pp. 43–64.

57. Peggy Kamuf and Nancy K. Miller, "Dialogue," *Diacritics,* Summer 1982, pp. 42–53.

58. See Jacques Derrida, "Signature Event Context," trans. Jeffrey Mehlman and Samuel Weber, *Glyph,* 1 (1977), 172–96.

59. Kamuf, op. cit., pp. 42–47; Mary Jacobus, "Is There a Woman in This Text?" *New Literary History,* 1982, pp. 117–41.

CHAPTER TWO

# Ceremonies of the Alphabet: Female Grandmatologies and the Female Authorgraph

*Sandra Caruso Mortola Gilbert*
*Susan Dreyfuss David Gubar*

The alphabet is made up of *elements*, out of which the whole human speech is compound. These elements . . . stand for the elements out of which the universe is compounded; and their order, the row . . . in which they stand, is the world order. By the might of the elements you have power to control the universe. . . .

Jane Ellen Harrison, "Alpha and Omega"

"Ought women to learn the alphabet?" asked Thomas Wentworth Higginson in a fiercely profeminist 1859 *Atlantic Monthly* essay. "There," he added, "the whole question [of women's liberation] lies. Concede this little fulcrum, and Archimedea will move the world before she has done with it: it becomes merely a question of time."[1] Ironically meditating on "this little fulcrum," Emily Dickinson's sometime mentor was himself ostensibly responding to the French satirist Sylvain Maréchal's "Plan for a Law prohibiting the Alphabet to Women" (1801), a misogynist proposal consisting, reports Higginson, "of eighty-two clauses, and . . . fortified by a 'whereas' of a hundred and thirteen weighty reasons."[2] Opposed as these two thinkers were, however, both would very likely agree with a most unlikely third party—the contemporary French theorist Hélène Cixous, who has recently proclaimed that "with a few rare exceptions, there has not yet been any writing that inscribes femininity." Despite Cixous's radical critique of masculinism, both might agree, as well, with her complementary assertion that "the logocentric project [has] always been . . . to *found* (fund) phallocentrism, to insure for masculine order a rationale equal to history itself[.]"[3]

Are Higginson, Maréchal, and Cixous correct? What *is* the historical relationship of women to the alphabet and to the arts that that ancient *aleph-beth* implies, those multifarious inscriptions of the *logos* that Yeats once called "gradual Time's last gifts, a written speech/Wrought of high laughter, loveliness, and ease?"[4] To explore the inextricable, even tautological relationship between literature and letters, we might begin by noting that a consideration of both the nature and the culture of alphabetic writing would seem to support the intimation of female literary exclusion that these three otherwise very different theorists have in common. On the one hand, because, as Jacques Derrida has observed, the letters of the alphabet are signifiers signifying nothing but elemental sounds, which are themselves also signifiers, such writing has distinguished itself from speech precisely because it constitutes a system of abstraction in which "the circulation of signs is infinitely facilitated," marking "the progress of analytic rationality."[5] On the other hand, because, as Derrida has also noted, the letters of the alphabet constitute the most nearly "phonographic" script we have, they are most capable of representing the authoritative presence of the voice of authority. Whether abstract or phonographic, however, the public character of the alphabet would seem to exclude women's historically privatized experiences: because woman is traditionally associated with what is, in Sylvia Plath's words, "blood-hot and personal," the abstraction of the alphabet might eradicate her even while, because she is also traditionally associated with the silence and submissiveness of what Shirley Ardener calls "muted groups," the phonographic authority of the alphabet might subordinate her.[6]

What we have called the culture of the alphabet, moreover, would seem to have reinforced both women's exclusion from the "ease" of "written speech" and her subordination to the "high laughter" of its hierarchical authority. To be sure, as Lévi-Strauss has suggested, writing may always have been associated with class oppression, but as feminist theorists from Woolf to Beauvoir have argued, the situation of woman goes beyond class: no matter what their socioeconomic status, those who reproduce the species have never controlled the production of culture.[7] Even in their abstraction, after all, our Roman letters preserve in themselves the archaic traces of the patriarchal glyphs and graphs from which they evolved, as if to remind us that they themselves are relics of a society in which women were as much chattels as cattle were. Our *A,* philologists tell us, is originally the Phoenician pictographic symbol 𐤀 (*aleph,* meaning "ox") turned on its side; similarly, our *B* is the Phoenician 𐤁 (*beth,* meaning "house") revised and transformed; arising from a patriarchal culture, symbols of patriarchal history, both letters, like most of their fellows, have been filtered through the classical and classically misogynistic cultures of Greece and Rome, as if, again, to remind us that they were designated and designed to serve what Adrienne Rich calls "the oppressor's language."[8] More specifically, the fact that writing in general, and especially alphabetic writing, with its phonographic flexibility, has long been associated with hierarchization, with the imperial power of priests, princes, and merchants, and even with, in Lévi-Strauss's words, "the enslavement of . . . human beings," would of course further connect it with the oppression or at least the subordination of the "second sex," the paradigmatic other in patriarchal culture.[9] Most specifically, the fact that the development of writing made possible not only the widespread pronouncement but also the long-term perpetuation of power would inevitably associate the alphabet with the ineradicable lineaments of a history that has always silenced and excluded women.

"In Books lies the *soul* of the whole Past Time," declared Thomas Carlyle in *On Heroes, Hero-Worship, and the Heroic in History* (1841), explaining that because of his command over such linguistic preserves the "*Man* of Letters" (italics ours) is in effect the true ruler of eternity.[10] As if to expand on this point, moreover, Carlyle's American contemporary Henry David Thoreau distinguished in *Walden* (1854) between speech and writing by defining, on the one hand, a "transitory . . . almost brutish" dialect that "we learn . . . unconsciously, like the brutes, of our mother"—"a mother tongue"—and by describing, on the other hand, a "reserved and select expression, *too significant to be heard by the ear*" (italics ours), which he called "our father tongue."[11] The implication behind the assertions of both these nineteenth-century men of letters is clear: as Lévi-Strauss more recently put it, the group that writes "can accumulate a body of knowledge that helps it to move ever faster toward the goal that it has assigned itself," whereas the group that does not, cannot, write must "remain the prisoner of a history worked out from day to day, with neither an origin nor the lasting consciousness of a plan"—a situation that leaves the "second sex" in a classic double bind.[12] Without the alphabet, women would seem to be without a history of their own; yet history itself would seem to have been constituted by precisely that alphabet that has denied women a place in history.

If we focus for a moment on a particular problem of the "female autograph"—on the issue of proper and improper names—we can see in even more detail just how this double bind has functioned. Any human subject, as Jacques Lacan tells us, is in a sense "the slave . . . of a discourse . . . in which his place is already inscribed at birth, if only by virtue of his proper name."[13] At the same time, though, the (male) linguistic preserve of history begins with empowering, rather than enslaving, preservation of (male) names: some of the earliest translations of hieroglyphic and cuneiform as well as alphabetic inscriptions showed, after all, that those enigmatic marks on "monuments of unaging intellect" were the names of kings, princes, priests, and generals, suggesting that the first records of literate life were patrilineal in intent and patriarchal in essence and supporting Derrida's claim that "the birth of writing . . . was nearly everywhere and most often linked to genealogical anxiety."[14] For woman in our culture, however, a proper name is at best problematic; even as it "inscribes" her into the discourse of society by designating her role as her father's daughter, her patronymic effaces her matrilineage and thus erases her own position in the discourse of the future. Her "proper" name, therefore, is always in a way *im*proper because it is not, in the French sense, *propre,* her own, either to have or to give. With what letters, then, can a woman of letters preserve herself, as Carlyle's men of letters have from the beginning of recorded time? How can she employ the alphabet to perpetuate the most elementary trace of her identity—a meaningful auto-graph?

Two twentieth-century works by women writers suggest both the parameters and the persistence of this problem even while they hint at the outlines of a solution that, we will argue, literary women have explored for some centuries in order to do precisely what Maréchal, Higginson, and Cixous seem to agree they have not done—produce a writing that "inscribes femininity." First, Zora Heale Hurston recounts in *Their Eyes Were Watching God* (1937) the history of a heroine nicknamed "Alphabet 'cause so many people had done named me different names,'" a point that reflects not only the primary dispossession of all women from "proper" nomenclature but also the double dispossession of black women, who have been exiled from their African heritage as well as from their female matronymic.[15] Becoming "Alphabet," moreover—or so Hurston implies—this woman would seem to have no chance to become anything more than a term in the discursive economy of society, a character (like the letters of the alphabet) who signifies nothing for herself while facilitating the "circulation of signs" that reinforces communication among men.[16]

More recently, and even more explicitly, Ruth Stone mourns the lost names of her matrilineage in a poem named "Names":

My grandmother's name was Nora Swan.
Old Aden Swan was her father. But who was her mother?
I don't know my great-grandmother's name.
I don't know how many children she bore.
Like rings of a tree the years of woman's fertility.
Who were my great aunt Swans?
. . . As anemone in mid-summer, the air
cannot find them and grandmother's been at rest for forty years.
. . .[17]

If a woman is not a signifier in an alphabet possessed by men ("Old Aden Swan was her father"), speculates Stone, she would seem to be no more than a sort of function of the landscape. For instead of being graphed by distinguished inscriptions, women leave indistinguishable traces, natural accretions like the "rings of a tree" whose very presence attests to the absence of cultural identity. After all, "Who can bother naming all those women churning butter,/leaning on scrub boards, holding to iron bedposts/sweating in labor?"

Paradoxically, however, the terms in which Hurston and Stone put woman's linguistic problem begin to provide significant solutions that allow for female self-signification. The variety of "Alphabet's" social experience, for instance—represented by the range of her names—finally enables her to renounce the two husbands whose pleasure she has served in the name of respectability and to take for her own pleasure a young lover (with the interestingly domestic name of "Tea Cake") through whose muselike intervention she learns "de maiden language all over" (172). ". . . [N]ew thoughts had tuh be thought and *new words said*" (italics ours), she explains, describing the way this relationship has transformed the terms of her connection with society, and at the end of the novel, empowered by the saying of such words to tell her own story, she has become a sort of goddess who pulls "in her horizon like a great fish-net. [Pulls] it from around the waist of the world and [drapes] it over her shoulder" (286).

Similarly, though using a rather different strategy, Ruth Stone empowers herself in "Names" by imagining an alternative to patriarchal naming:

> . . . My grandmother knew the names of all the plants on the
> mountain. Those were the names she spoke of to me. Sorrel,
> lamb's ear, spleenwort, heal-all never go hungry, she said, when
> you can gather a pot of greens.

Thus, though Stone doesn't know "who . . . the women [are] who nurtured her for me," though "the air/cannot find" their names,

> In me are all the names I can remember—pennyroyal, boneset,
> bed-straw, toad-flax—from whom I did descend in perpetuity.

What this poet recovers are names of power, regal autographs drawn from a feminized nature. Where Hurston prophesies a new ("maiden") language that postdates the inscriptions and descriptions of patriarchy, in other words, Stone dreams of an archaic language that predates the patronymics of culture. Both, however, are gaining strength through fantasies of either an original or an originary linguistic matrilineage, a "grandmatology" that they implicitly set against the patrilineal linguistics of the grammatology that has historically subordinated them and their ancestresses.

Hurston's and Stone's fantasies are paradigmatic because, as we shall show here, women of letters have for centuries defended themselves against the intimations of linguistic mortality conveyed to them by the nature and the culture of the alphabet through fantasies about names, letters, ideograms, hieroglyphs, characters, and calligraphies, fantasies that consistently (though sometimes covertly, sometimes overtly) mythologize the female sign even as they signify the female signature and authorize womanly orthographies and women's autobiographies. To be sure, as we will see later, male writers have also meditated in various ways on such matters. We believe, however, that the alphabet poses an especially urgent problem for women. For with the pioneering feminist anthropologist Jane Ellen Harrison, literary women recognize the magic of letters even while they fear the (male) mystification of letters. Harrison's essay on "Alpha and Omega" describes and analyzes the "ceremony of the alphabet" in which a Roman Catholic bishop consecrates a cathedral by tracing the characters of the Greek and Roman alphabets in a sacred pattern on the church floor. The "ceremony of the alphabet," she notes, gives its hierophant the illusion that s/he has the "power to control the universe" despite the fact that it is a form of "hocus pocus," for "tracing alphabets does *not* help us to command the universe"[18] (italics ours). Implicit in Harrison's meditation are two antithetical but equally important positions: on the one hand, a rejection of the Omega of "eikonic" theology, the patriarchal "letter that killeth" whose place in an inexorable sequence represents for women an unsatisfactory "world order"; on the other hand, an attraction to a revisionary and "aneikonic" Alpha, which women subversively associate with matriarchal spiritual origins. Finally, therefore, in their struggle to reinvent "the elements" of writing, to reorder the sequence of the letters, and to revise the characters of power so as to spell new words or word new spells, women of letters have long inscribed "femininity" while they described their efforts to deform the alphabet of patriarchy in order to re-form "the world order."

On the most literal level, the new words as well as the transformative new meanings of women artists have traditionally been expressed by the new names they have conferred on themselves. To be sure, from James MacPherson ("Ossian") to Samuel Clemens ("Mark Twain"), men have also employed *noms de plume,* but their motives for doing so have had neither the same consistency nor the same urgency as those that impelled literary women. Certainly, as we all now recognize, by the mid-nineteenth century the male pseudonym was quite specifically a mask behind which the female writer could hide her disreputable femininity, as Charlotte Brontë ("Currer Bell"), Mary Ann Evans ("George Eliot"), Aurore Dupin Dudevant ("George Sand"), Mary Chavelita Dunne ("George Egerton"), Katharine Bradley and Edith Cooper ("Michael Field"), Violet Paget ("Vernon

Lee"), and Ethel Florence Lindesay ("Henry Handel Richardson") did. But a changing attitude toward female names was evident at the turn of the century and was very likely related to the self-consciously revolutionary theories of feminists and suffragists who either kept their maiden names after marriage or used three names, a tradition that instantly became popular for women writers, especially in America. While such Victorian Englishwomen as Mrs. Gaskel, Mrs. Humphrey Ward, and even Mrs. Braddon had established their allegiance to marital respectability by acquiescing in the couverture of "Mrs.," Charlotte Perkins [Stetson] Gilman, Mary E. Wilkins Freeman, Elizabeth Cady Stanton, Elizabeth Stuart Phelps Ward, and Edith Summers Kelly defined themselves through an accumulation of names that reflected compound identities and in some cases preserved a matrilineage that would otherwise be lost. From a male point of view, in fact, the power of such female genealogies was infuriating enough to instigate the sort of "jokes" Nathanael West records in *Miss Lonelyhearts*. Complaining about the number of female writers ("they've all got three names . . . Mary Roberts Wilcox, Ella Wheeler Catheter . . ."), a group of male reporters agree: "what they all [need is] a good rape."[19]

Even while women writers used accretions of real names to enlarge their identities, however, the pseudonym began to function more prominently as a name of power, the mark of a private christening into a second self, a rebirth into linguistic primacy. Olive Schreiner, for instance, married a man who took her maiden name as his own last name. But at the same time she published several works under the name of "Ralph Iron," employing "Ralph" as a tribute to Ralph Waldo Emerson and "Iron" as a signifier of an invulnerable new spirit achieved in the forge of transformation. To be sure, some twentieth-century women writers were still concerned with maintaining an anonymous or anomalous gender identity: Lulu McCullers was happier with the androgynous family name "Carson," just as Mary O'Connor opted for "Flannery," and "Willa" Cather was so circumspect about her given name that, even after her death, Leon Edel had great difficulty establishing the fact that it was originally "Wilella."[20] But, like "Fanny Fern" or "Sarah Grand" in the late nineteenth century, a number of modernist women sought to make their names into icons of female artistry. Born Cicely Fairfield, Rebecca West named herself after the feminist heroine of Ibsen's *Rosmersholm*, while Karen Dinesen went through the names Tanne, Karen Blixen, Isak Dinesen, and, most impressively, The Lioness. Laura Gottschalk, née Riechenthall, used the name "Laura Riding" until she began to sign her work "Laura (Riding) Jackson," and just this year she found herself defending her full name against a reviewer who insisted on calling her "Laura."[21] Winifred Ellerman renamed herself "Bryher" after an island in the North Atlantic. What all these redefinitions have in common is an effort on the part of women to rid themselves of the patronymic, an effort perhaps most dramatically enacted in the transformation of the Anglo-American Pauline Tarn into the French poet "Renée Vivien."

Born in the United States and raised in England, the woman artist called "Renée Vivien" renounced not only her familial but also her national origins when she took up residency in Paris and began to write *fin de siècle* verse in a French as foreign to her native tongue as her lesbianism was to the hegemonic heterosexual idiom. Her metamorphosis gains particular resonance in her 1906 poem "Viviane," a portrait of the female "Sovereign of fantasy" who is figured with the accoutrements this poet repeatedly identified with sapphic erotic power: a magic forest or garden, a mirroring pond, a mist of veils, a crown of stars, violets, twilight, and, finally, "Gliding along her bare arms, green serpents."[22] A sinister but sensuous figure, "more powerful than fate," Viviane carries "sleep and death in her hand," yet she is "born anew"—"Elle renaît," in the original—because, like Vivien herself, "Elle a changé de nom, de voix et de visage" (She has changed names, voice, and visage). Indeed, obstinately remaining a single woman who refuses to have her maiden name obliterated, exchanged, or subsumed. Vivien, like Viviane, embodies the prize of maidenhood, for she will be maiden (*née*) again and again (*re-née*), as she is reborn (*renée*) vivid Vivien.

But the name Vivien is also of course associated with the reworking of Arthurian legend in Tennyson's *Idylls of the King,* where a beautiful maiden named Vivien seduces the magician Merlin to gain a book that contains a charm that blinds and binds, a charm that enables her to cast the male sage into a hollow oak and deprive him of "name and fame."[23] Illustrating this passage, Burne-Jones's painting *The Beguiling of Merlin* (Figure 1) seems also to illustrate Vivien's "Viviane": the Pre-Raphaelite artist's triumphantly statuesque Vivien appears, carrying the book of power, in a magic forest, insinuatingly dressed in a mist of veils, with violets at her feet and a snakey net hardly restraining her auburn hair as she gazes scornfully down on the greatest enchanter of his time, now himself enchained and enchanted. Significantly, moreover, the book Vivien steals from Merlin was originally inscribed for a king who sought to keep his queen "all his own" by transforming her into a sleeping beauty. Thus, usurping a charm that has traditionally enthralled and pacified women, Vivien appropriates the seductive arts of the alphabet to turn men into sleeping uglies, while gaining for herself the power to break the male sexual monopoly and become herself a charmer of women in her lesbian poetry.

While Pauline Tarn stole the charm of male language in order to create her own "authorgraph" as "Renée Vivien," another twentieth-century poet—Hilda Doolittle—would seem to have acquiesced in an identity be-

1. Edward C. Burne-Jones, *The Beguiling of Merlin*. Lady Lever Gallery, Port Sunlight, Liverpool.

stowed by patriarchal power, for, understandably hesitant about using her surname, she accepted the camouflage Ezra Pound provided when he baptized her "H.D., *Imagiste*." Yet the power of names and the names of power were as crucial in H.D.'s life as they were in Vivien's. She was quite clear, for instance, about her fascination with a name composed of initials, explaining in *Tribute to Freud* that, "I have used my initials H.D. consistently as my writing signet or sign-manual, though it is only, at this very moment, as I check up on the word 'signet' in my Chambers's English Dictionary that I realize that my writing signature has anything remotely suggesting sovereignty or the royal manner."[24] Initials are, of course, an emblematic hieroglyph, not unlike the hieroglyphs of the Freudian unconscious, the alphabet of knocks in spiritualist table-tapping, the astrological signs on horoscopes, the Kabbalistic signatures of the Sephiroth, and the pictorial icons of the Tarot, all of which fascinated H.D. throughout her career. But in particular, she was obsessed with the significance of her own signature. As Adalaide Morris has noted, for instance, she meditates continually on the letter "H," which signals not only her own name, Hilda, but her mother's name, Helen, as well as the names of many of her heroes and heroines: Helmsman, Huntress, Hermione, Hippolytus, Hippolyta, Hermes, Helios, Heliodora, and Helen of Egypt.[25] In addition, however, she broods on the mirror imagery of "H.D." and "D.H.," which indicates to her that the novelist/poet D. H. Lawrence is her male counterpart, and on the doubling of "H.D." and "H.D.," which tells her that Hugh Dowding, England's chief air marshal in World War II, is her reincarnated consort.[26] Finally, she mythologizes the letters "H.D." so that they stand for the Hermetic Definitions that she makes out of the longer epic powers that extricate her art from Pound's diminution of her as "*Imagiste*."

"Names are in people, people are in names," proclaims Hermione, the eponymous heroine of H.D.'s most autobiographical novel.[27] But the exact relationship of person and name continued to be problematic for H.D. herself and for the women writers who were her descendants. From Sylvia Plath and Anne Sexton to Adrienne Rich, Ai and Alta, contemporary women poets dwell on the terms of naming as they struggle to define the terminology of the self. Plath relinquishes her name, symbolic of a mistaken identity, with intense relief: "I am nobody . . . I have given my name and my day-clothes up to the nurses," she declares in "Tulips." Alluding to Christopher Smart, Sexton invents in "O Ye Tongues" an imaginary "Christopher" to compound the reality of "Anne," and, as Sexton, smartly sets the two names into a series of Psalms outlining a private myth of origins. In "In the Secret Room, East of the Sun, West of the Moon" Diane Wakoski "feeling the loneliness/of my cold name," confesses that "I live in a secret place" and complains that "my life/is unspoken."[28] Adrienne Rich goes further still, first defining herself as "The

Stranger," "the androgyne," and noting mysteriously that "the letters of my name are written under the lids/of the newborn child," then in "Reforming the Crystal" claiming that "my/name on the marriage-contract was not mine" and imagining herself back in

> the cratered night of female memory, where delicately and with intense care the chieftainess inscribes upon the ribs of the volcano the name of the one she has chosen.

Finally, in one of her "Twenty One Love Poems," she rechristens herself with a single name—"Adrienne, alone"—a strategy also employed by recent poets like "Alta" and "Ai" to circumvent the problem of the patronymic.[29]

For contemporary ethnic and lesbian writers, both groups confronting what we earlier, in discussing Hurston's "Alphabet," called a double dispossession, names that are or are not "in people" are especially troublesome. Whether, like Naomi Long Madgett they decide to "keep the name my father gave me," or whether, like Toni Cade Bambara, they take the name from a signature on a sketchbook in a great-grandmother's trunk, or whether they assume "native" names, like Ntozake Shange, women of color may be haunted by nameless or foreign-named ancestors, as Maxine Hong Kingston is in *The Woman Warrior* by "No Name Woman," or they may fetishize names, as Pilate does in Toni Morrison's *Song of Solomon,* when she folds her heraldic and heretical name in a brass box and hangs it from her ear. For with Morrison's significantly named "Milkman Dead," all believe that "under the recorded names [are] other names . . . Names that [have] meaning. . . . Names that [bear] witness," and with Audre Lorde, all wonder "what name shall we call ourselves now/our mother is gone?"[30] Similarly, lesbians who follow Judy Grahn's prescriptions for "Murdering the King's English" may emulate the artists who have struggled for erotic self-definition by renaming themselves as "the Carpenter," "Dykewoman," or "Riverfinger Woman."[31] Illegitimate as the names Ruth Stone "can remember—pennyroyal, boneset,/bedstraw, toad-flax"—such emblems of identity nevertheless legitimate the alternative lineages that Jane Ellen Harrison might associate with the origin and history of a new female consciousness, a new ordering of the relationship between Alpha and Omega.

IN 1969 a placard at an art show announced that "*Judy Gerowitz* hereby divests herself of all names imposed on her through male social dominance and freely chooses her own name, *Judy Chicago*"[32] (italics ours). Redefining herself with the name of a "second city" that recalls the "second sex," however, the woman who became "Judy Chicago" also began what composition experts would now call a "writing process" that metamorphosed into a painting process representative of many of the fantasies women have had about alphabets, hieroglyphs, autographs, and calligraphies. For even women who do not write seem to speculate in many art forms about the power of script and the inscription of power. In paintings named after names like "Virginia Woolf" or "George Sand," for instance, Chicago herself creates a cursive text that frames a central image of flowering female genitals so as to illustrate the nature of desire blocked, stamped, or stumped in the lives of women. In words like "Transformation—Painting—Great Ladies Transforming Themselves into Butterflies" and "Peeling Back" (Figure 2), moreover, her print continually glosses her visual imagery. Finally, in *The Dinner Party,* her calligraphic needlepoint runners emblematize the women throughout history whose greatness won them a service at a meal consecrating female creativity.[33]

Like "Judy Chicago," other female artists and craftswomen—many of them, significantly, now nameless—have drawn upon specifically female arts in order to illustrate the significance of the female autograph as a work of art. Medieval tapestries like the famous "Tapestrie de la Reine Mathilde" in Bayeux traditionally preserved what the eighteenth-century English poet Anne Finch called the "interwoven name[s]" and histories of the women who made them, a fact that interested the American novelist Willa Cather as much as it fascinated Finch.[34] More recently the stitchery of two lesser-known contemporary American needlewomen typifies the way in which countless crafty women have sewn their genealogies, with what Emily Dickinson once called "ecstasies of stealth," into the fabric of their life's work. Whether she is portraying her husband's dry goods shop or the Double Springs Baptist Church, for example, Ethel Wright Mohamed, of Belzoni, Mississippi, creates what she calls a "family picture album" in her needlework. Similarly, Pecolia Warner, of Yazoo City, Mississippi, sews the initials of her name into her "P quilt" (Figure 3): "I was just sitting around and didn't have anything else to do," she explains, "so I said, 'I just believe I'll make me a piece that will be the start of my name.' It's a P quilt, I call it. I want to make more letters, just like I made that P. I bet I could even do a whole alphabet."[35]

Like many other mute, inglorious domestic artists, Mohamed and Warner are employing the conventions of the sampler, which was used to teach generations of girls how to sew, and which almost always included a representation of the alphabet, the first nine numbers, and either a monogram or an autograph. But of course the very nature of the sampler, with its samplings of the elements of female identity, reminds us that when women have not used a needle as a pen, they have needed to needle the world with their pens, expressing the urgencies of signature even as far back as the twelfth century, when a nun named Guda signed

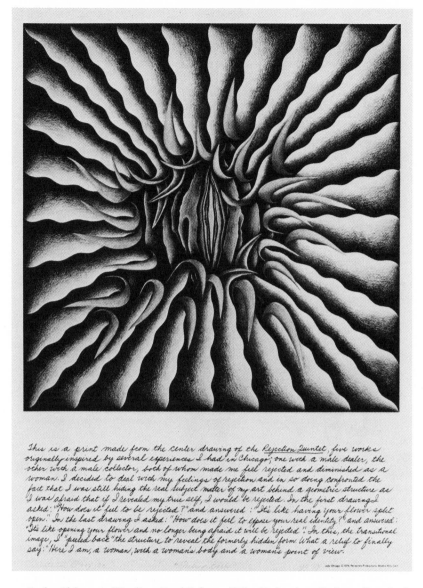

This is a print made from the center drawing of the Rejection Quintet, five works originally inspired by several experiences I had in Chicago; one with a male dealer, the other with a male collector, both of whom made me feel rejected and diminished as a woman. I decided to deal with my feelings of rejection and in so doing confronted the fact that I was still hiding the real subject matter of my art behind a geometric structure as I was afraid that if I revealed my true self, I would be rejected. In the first drawing I asked: "How does it feel to be rejected?" and answered: "It's like having your flower split open." In the last drawing I asked: "How does it feel to expose your real identity?" and answered: "It's like opening your flower and no longer being afraid it will be rejected." In this, the transitional image, I "peeled back" the structure to reveal the formerly hidden form. What a relief to finally say: "Here I am, a woman, with a woman's body and a woman's point of view."

2. Judy Chicago, "Peeling Back" from "The Rejection Quintet." © Judy Chicago, 1974. Prismacolor on rag paper, 29″ × 23″. Courtesy San Francisco Museum of Modern Art. Photograph by Michele Maier.

her name and drew her self-portrait inside her copies of initial letters (Figure 4) and another sister, named Herrade of Landsberg, illustrated *The Garden of Delights* with what Karen Petersen and J. J. Wilson call "a kind of class picture" of the women from her convent, each represented with her name (Figure 5).[36] From the inscriptions of medieval nuns working as

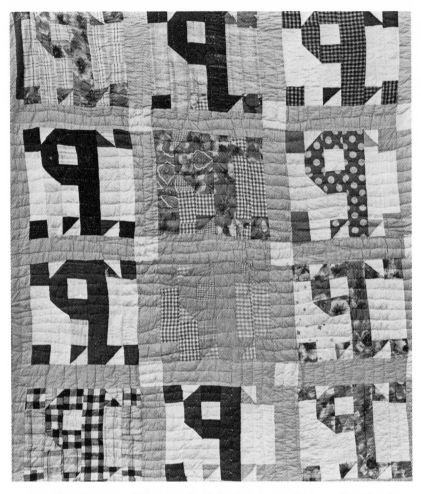

3. Pecolia Warner, "The P Quilt." Courtesy Center for Southern Folklore.

scribes to the elaborations of eighteenth- and nineteenth-century embroiderers to the illustrations of contemporary craftswomen, therefore, visions of writing have served women as empowering fantasies of self-certification even while they functioned as ceremonies of initiation into creativity.

Significantly, however, as if some women were half-consciously attempting to evade the inexorable sequences and phonographic authority of the alphabet, a number of these visions—and not just those of graphic artists or craftswomen—have been dreams of nonalphabetic script. In her 1877 novel, *The Story of Avis,* for example, Elizabeth Stuart Phelps [Ward] describes a woman painter's hallucination of the Sphinx. Glowing on her bedroom wall like an enigmatic hieroglyph of power, this ancient emblem betokens the riddle of female artistry that Ward's heroine resolves (unsuc-

et etia laceras : sine ulla priua[ca]
cione manebit etia securitas : si
ne aliq miseria eccedit etna felici
tas. p xpm drim nrin. Sermo sea
n io ... his epi : de dd v ...

los
sos arangeret ..., ..., ..., ... ...
tos. plurimos ..., ..., de quay...
rio eligeret rege. rectore ipoiet
duce pplo pfecisset. inueiut dd ...
iuiui onsiui n potuit. cui o cestiu...
nui reddidit dicens. Inuem dd uiu...

4. Guda, self-portrait from *Homeliary*, Frankfurt am Main, Staatsbibliothek.

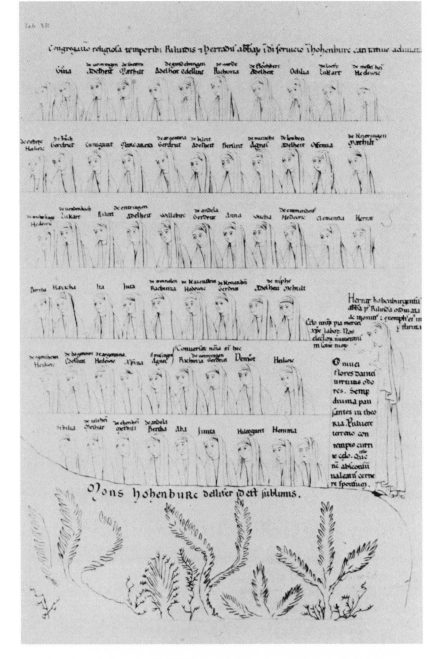

5. Herrade von Landsberg, Abbes of Hohenburg, *Hortus Deliciarum*.

cessfully, as it turns out) to solve in her life and work.[37] More famously, H.D. records in her *Tribute to Freud* the crucial moment when, first, she herself and, then, her companion "Bryher" witnessed "writing on the wall" that magically graphed woman's linguistic and aesthetic ambition. Beginning with an image of a mysterious "soldier or airman," moving through images depicting the oracular Delphic tripod, symbol of female prophecy, and the victoriously winged Niké, symbol of female potency, and culminating in a vision of the union of Niké with her divine male counterpart Helios, the luminous script that the two friends "read" in an apparently irrational series of mystic glyphs constitutes a subversive text that they collaboratively set against the traditional masculinist order of Alpha and Omega as if it were "the other side" of the mirror of the male alphabet. Reporting her own sensations, H.D. confesses that she felt, while "reading," "as if I were searching under water for some priceless treasure, and if I bobbed up to the surface the clue to its whereabouts would be lost forever."[38] Indeed, it may be said that, as she risks drowning in the "otherness" of what Rich calls "the cratered night of female memory," this woman poet is seeking (as both Rich and Ward's Avis do) the secret of the "chieftainess's" signature.

Similar visions of nonalphabetic writing haunt literary women from Charlotte Perkins Gilman to Virginia Woolf, Willa Cather, and Margaret Atwood. With its "lame uncertain curves," "outrageous angles," and "unheard-of contradictions," Gilman's "Yellow Wallpaper" is, after all, a text that that famous story's narrator must "read," if only so that she can liberate herself (and the woman "behind" the script) into lunacy. More positively, Woolf's Katharine Hilbery articulates her joy in life and love at crucial moments in *Night and Day* through enigmatic fantasies of "algebraic symbols, pages all speckled with dots and dashes and twisted bars" while her sympathetic suitor, Ralph Denham, expresses himself in drawings of "blots fringed with flames meant to represent—perhaps the entire universe." Again, in *Mrs. Dalloway,* the shellshocked Septimus communicates through pictographic "writings" that consist of "Diagrams, designs, little men and women brandishing sticks for arms, with wings—were they—on their backs, circles traced round shillings and sixpences—the suns and stars . . . and little faces laughing out of what might perhaps be waves: the map of the world." It is as if Woolf, who dreamt in *A Room of One's Own* of "a woman's sentence" that could counter the "man's sentence," which was as alien to woman's mind as "the older forms of literature were to her imagination," was trying in some part of herself to annihilate the alphabetic basis and bias of "sentences" altogether, while Gilman was trying to excavate the truth of woman's condition by going behind or beneath the enigmatic "writing on the wall" of her heroine's destiny.[39]

Comparable acts of annihilation and excavation are implicit, though more subtly, in works by Willa Cather ranging from *The Song of the Lark* to *My Antonia* to *The Professor's House* to *Death Comes for the Archbishop,* whose protagonists must learn to "read" the significance of tracks and traces scrawled on landscapes, ruins, and relics. Whether, like Jim Burden in *My Antonia,* these characters try to decipher the meaning of a prehistoric Indian circle that graphs the land "like strokes of Chinese white on canvas" or whether, like Kit Carson in *Death Comes for the Archbishop,* they "read" the apparently unreadable countryside itself because they have "got ahead of books, gone where the printing-press [cannot] follow" them, their preoccupation with natural or cultural pictography suggests that Cather herself, even through the medium of male minds, is trying to imagine a nonalphabetic "maiden language" that would predate or postdate patriarchal history.[40] Finally, inheriting a tradition of such imaginings, Margaret Atwood creates in *Surfacing* a nameless narrator who traces her own history and her father's fate by analyzing her childhood illustrations and his mysteriously pictographic drawings.[41]

For Atwood, however, as also for Woolf and Doris Lessing, alphabetic writing itself becomes a crucial issue on which narrators and characters alike frequently brood. The multiply-named heroine of Atwood's *Lady Oracle,* for instance, who identifies herself variously as "Joan Crawford," "Louise K. Delacourt," and "Joan Foster," is obsessed with the curious code created by an Italian typewriter without the letter *k.* More crucially, she describes entranced literary journeys, trips like H.D.'s through "the other side" of the mirror, which yield uniquely female automatic writings in familiar yet strange words out of which she makes the poems that constitute her subversively self-defining volume called "Lady Oracle."[42] Elsewhere, in a poem entitled "It is dangerous to read newspapers," Atwood explains this woman's need to reappropriate and redeem patriarchal language, observing that "Each time I hit a key/on my electric typewriter . . . another village explodes."[43] Her linguistic anxiety, as well as her sense of linguistic estrangement, illuminates not only her own covertly revolutionary procedures for underground revisions of alphabetic writing but also those of key characters in Doris Lessing's novels—Mark and Dorothy in *Four-Gated City,* for example, or Anna Wulf in *The Golden Notebook*—all of whom try to decipher the relationship between oppression and "sentencing" by papering rooms with newspaper clippings, letters, and charts, or by reordering their lives in notebooks defined not just with words but with symbolically significant colors. In addition, Atwood's obsession with the problem of language helps explain the foregrounding of handprinted letters throughout Charlotte Salomon's *Charlotte: Life or Theatre?,* an autobiographical "play" composed in gouaches that was completed by a German-Jewish artist before her death in Auschwitz in 1943.

Renaming herself with a name of power—Charlotte Kann—Salomon comes to terms not only with the tragedies of her own family history but also with the historical tragedy of the Holocaust, and she does so by setting print on, in, and around her paintings as if simultaneously to examine the tyrannical invasion of life by death sentences and the stubborn resistance of life's sentences to dead letters.[44]

Surely, however, the grandmother of such female grandmatologies is Virginia Woolf, who mediates throughout her career on the meaning of alphabetic writing even while she considers pictographic alternatives to such script. As early as *The Voyage Out,* after all, Rachel Vinrace—falling ill with an unnamed tropical disease whose symptoms significantly recapitulate Woolf's own spells of madness—hears her lover reading the words of Milton's *Comus* and thinks that "it was painful to listen to them; they sounded strange; they meant different things from what they usually meant." Later, in *Jacob's Room,* Woolf's narrator resolves to "consider letters," implicitly setting the "unpublished" letters "of women, written by the fireside in pale profusion" against the magisterial authority of the male linguistic preserves represented, say, by Miltonic verse. Words, she complains, as if protesting against the historicity of the alphabet itself, "have been used too often, touched and turned, and left exposed to the dust of the street"; but, she adds, anticipating the natural "maiden" languages of Hurston, Cather, and Stone, "The words we seek hang close to the tree. We come at dawn and find them sweet beneath the leaf." Even later, in *The Waves,* just after young Susan complains that "I am tied down with single words" while the girl's male counterpart, Bernard, rises up "higher, with words and words in phrases," the author herself vouchsafes the two children a glimpse of Elvedon, "an unknown land" where a magic-seeming "lady sits between . . . two long windows, writing" what may well be a new, female script. Finally, in *Between the Acts,* Woolf allows her mysterious Miss La Trobe to imagine "words of one syllable" rising from mud, "words without meaning—wonderful words."[45] Like the fantastic texts and entranced transcriptions of female artists as various as Judy Chicago, Pecolia Warner, H.D., and Margaret Atwood, such visionary words gloss woman's desire for a sentence of her own even while they disentangle the "mother tongue" from what Thoreau thought was the "brutishness" of speech. "Too significant to be heard by the ear," they inscribe "femininity" as a powerfully inaudible authorgraph.

BESIDES fantasizing about what we might call the *gestalt* of writing manifested in names, sentences, and pictographs, however, female artists have long meditated on what Jane Ellen Harrison calls the elements of writing—meditated, that is, on the implications of the alphabet itself much as

Harrison does in "Alpha and Omega." Are alphabetic characters necessarily ambiguous or engimatic? Is the "analytic rationality" of the alphabet, with its apparently inexorable sequence, essentially coercive or corrupt? Most important, can the alphabet be, in Denise Levertov's phrase, "relearned"? From the fifteenth-century feminist Christine de Pisan to Harrison's great admirer, Virginia Woolf, to such contemporary writers as Sylvia Plath, Denise Levertov, and Monique Wittig, women of letters have struggled to come to terms with what Higginson called the "little fulcrum" of the alphabet by answering these questions.

To be sure, male thinkers have also meditated on the same issues, and not always (like Maréchal and Higginson) in connection with women. As John Irwin demonstrates in *American Hieroglyphics,* for instance, writers of the American Renaissance like Poe, Melville, and Hawthorne were obsessed with the relationship between the hieroglyphs of nature and the hieratic graphs of culture. Like Wordsworth, who reads the "Characters of the Great Apocalypse,/The types and symbols of Eternity,/Of first, and last, and midst, and without end" at a climactic moment of *The Prelude,* these artists brooded on both epistemology and eschatology as they strained to trace the traces of origins and to glimpse the glyphs of Apocalypse. Poe's Arthur Gordon Pym strives to "read" a polar landscape in much the same way that Cather's Kit Carson "reads" the western wilderness. Hawthorne's scarlet letter famously emblematizes the ambiguity of alphabetic emblems, while the letter's human incarnation, little Pearl, is herself described as "a living hieroglyph," and Melville's tattooed Queequeg, like his enigmatically inscribed Moby Dick, is "in his own proper person . . . a riddle to unfold."[46]

More recently, moreover, male thinkers as strikingly dissimilar as Arthur Rimbaud and Wallace Stevens, Rudyard Kipling and Jacques Derrida, Ezra Pound and Roland Barthes, have toyed with letters as if, both playfully and seriously, to investigate the nature and culture of the alphabet. In "Voyelles," for instance, Rimbaud defines the colors of vowels ("A noir, E blanc, I rouge, U vert, O bleu") in order to tell their secret origins ("naissances latentes"), while Stevens, whose primordial artist is "The Comedian as the Letter C," muses on the "murderous alphabet" in "The Man with the Blue Guitar," on "a fusky alphabet" in "Phosphor Reading by His Own Light," and on "The ABC of being [and] The vital, arrogant, fatal, dominant X" in "The Motive for Metaphor."[47] Seeking the same origins that Rimbaud explores, Rudyard Kipling writes two "Just So" stories about the invention of the alphabet, significantly, by a prehistoric father/daughter couple.[48] Similarly, in *Glas,* his meditation on Hegel and Genet, Derrida deconstructs and reconstructs *écriture* as Stevens does, fashioning an L-shaped body of text in order to consider the connection between the originary body of "elle" and Jean Genet's transcription of the mother's character.[49] Finally, as if to fuse hieroglyphs with alphabetic phono-graphs, Pound reinforces *The ABC of Reading* with the pictographic authority of "ideograms" while Barthes meditates on the semiotic relationship between the slashing shape of Z, "the letter of mutilation," and the fully normative curve of S, and the contemporary American poet David Young in "A Lowercase Alphabet" transforms the Roman alphabet itself into just what Pound thought it wasn't, a system of ideograms (for instance, "x dancer, hourglass . . . y the root begins to sprout," and so forth).[50]

What differences are there, if any, between the alphabetic fantasies produced by these male artists and those proposed by women of letters? To begin with, it seems clear that—whatever their dissatisfactions with phonetics, or their anxieties about *écriture*—most literary men define themselves as inheritors of both the authority and the inexorability of the traditional alphabet. If they seriously or playfully protest or revise its "first, and last, and midst, and without end," therefore, their struggle is usually a form of the Oedipal battle Harold Bloom describes as he outlines his theory of the "anxiety of influence."[51] Remaking or rereading the alphabet, these men appropriate the power of the precursor, even while they acquiesce in the inevitability of a history that their great-grandfathers originated and that their great-grandsons will inherit. From a female point of view, however, not only the alphabet's origins but its shapes, its sequences, and its inheritance often appear ambiguous, even bizarre, suggesting that they experience what we have elsewhere called an "anxiety of authorship" even more debilitating than the male "anxiety of influence."[52]

A kind of ironic dyslexia, for instance, sometimes informs the writings of women like Gertrude Stein, Virginia Woolf, Sylvia Plath, Sue Owen, and Ruth Stone, who sardonically distance themselves from the elements of the alphabet through various imaginative strategies. In "Marry Nettie," for instance, a poem whose title constitutes a resistant revision of the name of the protofascistic Italian futurist Marinetti, Stein complains that "I do not like to have it said that it is so necessary to hear the next letter."[53] As for Woolf, even while she envisions strange pictographic writings and fantasizes visionary words or sentences, this crucial feminist modernist famously describes in *Mrs. Dalloway* a skywriting airplane that emits an enigmatic trail of smoke that might mean "Glaxo," "Kreemo," "toffee" or "KEY." Still more famously, she records in *To the Lighthouse* the way Mr. Ramsay's "splendid mind" struggles to explore "thought" that, "like the alphabet," is ranged in twenty-six letters all in order": "he had not genius," she slyly, wryly remarks, "but he had, or might have had, the power to repeat every letter of the alphabet from *A* to *Z* accurately in order. Meanwhile he stuck at *Q*. On, then, on to *R*."[54] Clearly, in such a passage, the alphabet functions for her—the way it rarely does for her male contemporaries—as a parodic emblem of the "analytic rationality" that makes women feel stupid at the same time that, from a female point of view, it seems to stupefy patriarchal consciousness.

As if echoing Woolf (for whom she felt a great "kinship"), moreover, Sylvia Plath has her Esther Greenwood write in *The Bell Jar* about the problem of reading "the alphabet soup of letters" that marks the "fall" in *Finnegans Wake*. Indeed, where Joyce, like Rimbaud or Stevens or Derrida, played with the magical properties and phonographic proprieties implicit in "names" like "HCE" and "ALP," Plath's Esther finds herself, as Woolf's narrator did in *To the Lighthouse,* alienated and excluded. "Why should there be a hundred letters?" she asks at first, then confesses that when "[h]altingly, I tried the word aloud, it sounded like a heavy wooden object falling downstairs," and at last reveals that when she went on reading "[t]he letters grew barbs and rams' horns [and] associated themselves in fantastic, untranslatable shapes, like Arabic or Chinese."[55] Similarly, and expressing the same sense of linguistic marginality, Sue Owen observes in her recent *Nursery Rhymes for the Dead* that "THE DEVIL// Will build his kingdom/with a capital letter./He will claim the first/letter of the alphabet//because it is susceptible./Then he will start to write/in longhand on anger."[56] Finally, for Ruth Stone, whose meditation on "Names" was paradigmatic earlier in this essay, the conventions of the alphabet present a series of problems in alienation. A Stone poem significantly entitled "Poetry" relates, for instance, that "I sit with my cup/to catch the crazy falling alphabet," and goes on through an estranged description of "High rise L's, without windows" and "Subway G's, Y's, twisted,/collapsing underground" to worry that "no one, no one at all,/is sifting through the rubble."[57] From the perspective of women like Stein, Woolf, Plath, Owen, and Stone, it appears, Stevens's "murderous" or "fusky" alphabets both might be and should be "rubble": whether they annihilate or are annihilated by women, their cryptic elements are both distant and questionable in ways that they never could be for men of letters.

At the same time, however, even while these literary women ironically isolate themselves from the patriarchal "first, and last, and midst, and without end" of dead letters, they and many of their colleagues struggle to excavate what Plath once called "pristine alphabets" from beneath the "rubble." Where male writers, in other words, struggle to certify themselves by appropriating the potency of Thoreau's "father tongue," these female thinkers try to transcend the alphabetizings of history and the history of the alphabet to dream about—in Elinor Wylie's phrase—"The immaculate bosom of the mother-tongue," which, as Wylie also notes, is expressed through a mythical "alphabet with astral fire seasoned."[58] Some, like the German poet Nelly Sachs, even dream of regenerating the ruins of a history shattered by the Holocaust through a mystical redemption achieved through "the alphabet womb." Thus, the complex process of reinventing, relearning, or reviewing the alphabet becomes for these writers a crucial act of both self-definition and self-assertion.

Most simply, graphic artists like Sonia Delaunay and Jenny Snider commemorate the role of letters in their own lives, and their own roles (and the roles of all women) in the teaching of letters, by producing canvases devoted to individual letters or *Pencil Picture Dictionaries* (Snider).[59] Similarly, writers from Christina Rossetti ("An Alphabet") to Gertrude Stein (*Alphabets and Birthdays*) to Djuna Barnes (*Creatures in an Alphabet*) create either alphabets for children or childlike alphabets to express their feeling that, as Stein puts it in "Lifting Belly," "Any letter is an alphabet" and that, again as Stein says in the same poem, "In the midst of writing there is merriment."[60] More subtly, writers like Vita Sackville-West, Monique Wittig, Sande Zeig, and Olga Broumas use the alphabet to commence and configure antipatriarchal, lesbian erotic arrangements. In a parodically ordered epistle from Egypt to Virginia Woolf, for instance, Sackville-West confesses that she can only deal with that strange land "alphabetically." But though she begins sedately enough—"Amon . . . alabaster . . . beggars . . . camels, crocodiles, colossi, cooks," she ultimately revises the archaic heterosexual sequence so that she can put Virginia in her place under *V,* and "steal [her] away, and put her in the sun among the objects mentioned alphabetically above."[61] Similarly, Wittig and Zeig reorganize the world in their *Lesbian Peoples/Material for a Dictionary* by allowing the ancient sequences of the alphabet to guide them toward new definitions of such words as "alphabet" ("invented" by Carmenta, Thetis, Kali), "Amazons" ("companion lovers"), "Love" ("an exchange of tattoos") and "word" ("to write one's life with one's blood").[62]

Again, as if echoing Wittig's reiteration of *O* throughout *Les Guérillères* or critiquing Pauline Réages's use of that letter in *The Story of O,* Broumas writes as "Artemis" in *Beginning with O* about a mystically "curviform alphabet/that defies//decoding" and "appears/to consist of vowels, beginning with *O,* the *O-*/mega, horseshoe, the cave of sound"—the simultaneously phonographic and pictographic cave of female desire.[63] Revising myths of linguistic origin in order to valorize female originality, all these writers seem to be working in a tradition of visionary feminist alphabetizing that goes back at least as far as Christine de Pisan's *City of Ladies,* which was founded, its author asserts, "on the field of letters," and which memorialized, among other women worthies, the Roman prophetess Carmentis, who, Christine insists, invented the alphabet and educated her people in its uses and usages.[64]

It is in Denise Levertov's "Relearning the Alphabet" (1970), however, that woman's desire not just to learn but to *re*learn the alphabet becomes most passionately manifest. As if responding to Higginson's century-old question—"Ought women to learn the Alphabet?"—Levertov creates in this work her own "ceremony" of letters, a ritual in which she reappropriates and resanctifies the ancient elements of writing so that they can function to express her own, distinctively female feelings. Feelings, indeed, rather than analytic rationality, are for Levertov the key to her relearned alphabet's revolutionary articulations, for though her letters are phonographic, the elemental sounds they inscribe are not (as Derrida insists such vocalizings must be) merely signifiers: *A* represents for Levertov a sound that has its own intrinsic meaning—"the ah! of knowing in unthinking/joy"—and *B* signifies "To be. To love another only for being." At the same time, again even though they are phonographic, Levertov's mystical letters do not represent the authoritative presence that Derrida would see as the "phallogocentric" voice of authority. Rather, "lost in the alphabet" of tradition, Levertov re-creates her alphabet as a maze for amazing voyages of self-discovery, a mirror, not of someone else's authority, but of her own desire. Thus, as the questor who seeks instead of the lady who is traditionally sought, she sets out from the authentic "ah!" of *A* and the absolute "to be" of *B* toward the *V* of vision, past the will of *W*, through *Y*'s yearnings, to the "blazing addresses" of "wing-tipped" *Z*, its "different darkness."[65] Supple and flexible, her sequence of letters becomes a graph of her self—a self of power, a self whose range of sighs and sounds suggests that in her womanliness she can both conceive and command the primordial Alpha and the ultimate Omega.

Finally, with the young Chicana writer, Margarita Cota-Cardena, Levertov might claim

> letters of the alphabet
>     we are
> sisters         we
>         germinate man
>         conjugate his all[66]

yet the sisterhood she and Cota-Cardena imagine would not be one of helpless inscription, of signs interminably circulating in an infinite system of Lévi-Straussian exchange, but rather a sisterhood of potent self-signification. Clearly, in the female tradition the nexus of letters, literature, and gender consistently inspires defiant and self-defining fantasies like the vision of a bowl of alphabet soup that the contemporary Spanish writer Teresa de León records in her *Memoria de la Melancolia*:

> Letters that float pursued by the spoon where they were going to die. Did they ever compose my name in the bowl? "Femme de lettres." I have never felt more reverence for the state of my uneasiness, for this daily itch within my flesh which writing gives me.[67]

Halfway through "Ought Women to Learn the Alphabet?" Thomas Wentworth Higginson observes that "the empire of the past has belonged to man," then prophecies that "the present epoch"—the era in which women will learn the alphabet—is one for which "the genius of woman has been reserved." What the lingustic fantasies of female artists from Guda and Herrade to Cather, Woolf, Levertov, and Cota-Cardena imply, however, is that women have always "known" the alphabet—known it subversively, known it periodically, known it poetically, known it mystically—and they have consistently employed it to set the female authorgraph into a revisionary, alternative history. True, they have had to struggle against what Rich calls "the oppressor's language" but that long struggle, we would argue, has been more fruitful than Maréchal, Higginson, or even Cixous suppose. "Earth waits for her queen," as Higginson reminds us, "was a favorite motto of Margaret Fuller Ossoli."[68] But the complex female ceremonies of the alphabet that we have reviewed here suggest that the queen Fuller and Higginson so eagerly awaited has long since put on her royal robes, not just to indict male penmanship but also, more significantly, to indite her own powerful character.

## NOTES

We are indebted throughout this essay to Karen Petersen and J. J. Wilson for invaluable suggestions about women's alphabetic arts and illustrations.

Epigraph: Jane Ellen Harrison, "Alpha and Omega," in *Alpha and Omega* (London: Sidgwick & Jackson Ltd., 1915), p. 182.

1. Thomas Wentworth Higginson, "Ought Women to Learn the Alphabet?" reprinted in *Women and the Alphabet* (Boston & New York: Houghton Mifflin, 1900), p. 3.

2. Quoted by Higginson, pp. 1–2.

3. Hélène Cixous, from "Sorties," in *La Jeune née,* trans. Ann Liddle, *New French Feminisms,* ed. Elaine Marks and Isabelle de Courtivron (Amherst: Univ. of Massachusetts Press, 1980), p. 92.

4. W. B. Yeats, "Upon a House Shaken by the Land Agitation," *Collected Poems* (New York: Macmillan, 1956), p. 93.

5. Jacques Derrida, *Of Grammatology,* trans. Gayatri Chakravorty Spivak (Baltimore and London: Johns Hopkins, 1976), p. 300.

6. Sylvia Plath, "Totem," in *Ariel* (New York: Harper, 1966), p. 75; and Shirley Ardener, "Introduction," *Perceiving Women* (London: J. M. Dent & Sons Ltd., 1977), pp. xi–xvii.

7. On the oppressive qualities of writing, see most notably, Lévi-Strauss, "A Writing Lesson," in *Tristes Tropiques,* trans. John Russell (New York: Atheneum, 1965), pp. 286–97; for a different perspective on the same subject, however, see also Derrida's meditation on Lévi-Strauss's "Writing Lesson" in "The Violence of the Letter: From Lévi-Strauss to Rousseau," *Of Grammatology,* pp. 101–40. For feminist socioeconomic theories see Virginia Woolf, *A Room of One's Own* (New York: Harcourt, 1928), passim, and Simone de Beauvoir, *The Second Sex,* trans. H. M. Parshley (New York: Knopf, 1953), passim.

8. For a useful summary of the evolution of the Phoenician alphabet into the Roman alphabet see A. C. Moorhouse, *Writing and the Alphabet* (London: Cobbett, 1946), esp. pp.

41–43; for "the oppressor's language," see Adrienne Rich, "The Burning of Paper Instead of Children," in *Adrienne Rich's Poetry,* ed. Barbara Charlesworth Gelpi and Albert Gelpi (New York: W. W. Norton, 1975), p. 50.

9. Lévi-Strauss, *Tristes Tropiques,* p. 292.

10. Thomas Carlyle, *On Heroes, Hero-Worship, and the Heroic in History,* ed. Carl Niemeyer (Lincoln: Univ. of Nebraska Press, 1966), p. 160.

11. Henry David Thoreau, "Reading," *Walden, or Life in the Woods,* in *The Norton Anthology of American Literature,* ed. Gottesman, Holland, Kalstone, Murphy, Parker, Pritchard (New York: W. W. Norton, 1979), pp. 1594–95.

12. Lévi-Strauss, *Tristes Tropiques,* p. 291.

13. Jacques Lacan, "The Agency of the Letter in the Unconscious. . . ," *Ecrits,* trans. Alan Sheridan (New York: W. W. Norton, 1977), p. 148.

14. Derrida, *Of Grammatology,* p. 124.

15. Zora Neale Hurston, *Their Eyes Were Watching God* (Urbana: Univ of Illinois Press, 1978), p. 21. All references hereafter will be included in the text.

16. For woman as a signifier of "conspicuous consumption," see Thorstein Veblen, *The Theory of the Leisure Class* (New York and London: Macmillan, 1899), passim; for woman as, essentially a "signifier," see Lévi-Strauss, *The Elementary Structures of Kinship,* trans. Bell, Sturmer, and Needham (Boston: Beacon, 1969), passim.

17. Ruth Stone, "Names," *Kentucky Poetry Review,* 16, 2/3 (Summer/Fall 1980), p. 14.

18. Harrison, *Alpha and Omega,* p. 183.

19. Nathanael West, *Miss Lonelyhearts* (New York: New Directions, 1933), p. 14; to be sure, even such an attempt to preserve a matrilineage is utopian, for the mother's name is really, after all, her father's.

20. See Leon Edel, "Homage to Willa Cather," in *The Art of Willa Cather,* ed. Bernice Slote and Virginia Faulkner (Lincoln: Univ. of Nebraska Press, 1974), p. 193.

21. Jane Marcus, "Laura Riding Roughshod," *The Iowa Review,* XII, 2/3 (Spring/Summer 1981), pp. 195–99.

22. Renée Vivien, "Viviane," *At the Sweet Hour of Hand in Hand,* trans. Sandia Belgrade (Tallahassee: The Naiad Press, Inc., 1979), pp. 47–49.

23. Alfred Lord Tennyson, "Merlin and Vivien," from *Idylls of the King, in Poems of Tennyson,* ed. Jerome H. Buckley (Boston: Houghton Mifflin, 1958), p. 388.

24. H. D., *Tribute to Freud* (New York: McGraw-Hill, 1974), p. 66.

25. Adalaide Morris, "Reading H.D.'s 'Helios and Athene,'" in *The Iowa Review,* XII, 2/3 (Spring/Summer 1981), p. 55.

26. For one of H.D.'s more crucial meditations on "D.H.," see H.D., *Tribute to Freud,* p. 141; many of her most revealing meditations on Dowding are contained in as yet unpublished manuscripts, such as "Thorn Thicket" and "The Sword Went Out to Sea," which are held at the Beinecke Library, Yale University.

27. H.D., *Hermione* (New York: New Directions, 1981), p. 5.

28. For a closer examination of these passages, see Sandra M. Gilbert, "'My Name Is Darkness': The Poetry of Self Definition," *Contemporary Literature,* Vol. 18, No. 4 (Autumn 1977); on naming, see also Pamela Annas, "A Poetry of Survival: Unnaming and Renaming in the Poetry of Audre Lorde, Pat Parker, Sylvia Plath, and Adrienne Rich," *Colby Library Quarterly,* Vol. 18, No. 1 (March 1982).

29. Adrienne Rich, "The Stranger," in *Adrienne Rich's Poetry,* p. 65; "Re-Forming the Crystal," in *Contemporary American Poetry,* ed. A. Poulin, Jr. (Boston: Houghton Mifflin, 1980), pp. 396–97; "XVIII" in "Twenty-One Love Poems," *The Dream of a Common Language* (New York: W. W. Norton, 1978), p. 34.

30. Naomi Long Madgett, "Nomen," in *Black Sister,* ed. Erlene Stetson (Bloomington:

Indiana Univ. Press, 1981), p. 129; Dexter Fisher explains the origins of Toni Cade Bambara's name in her headnote to "Maggie on the Green Bottles," in *The Third Woman: Minority Women Writers of the United States,* ed. Dexter Fisher (Boston: Houghton Mifflin, 1980), p. 196; Ntozake Shange was born Paulette Williams in New Jersey; Maxine Hong Kingston, "No Name Woman," *The Woman Warrior: Memoirs of a Girlhood among Ghosts* (New York: Vintage, 1976), pp. 1–20; Toni Morrison, *Song of Solomon* (New York: Signet, 1977), p. 333 and epigraph; Audre Lorde, "Harriet," *The Black Unicorn* (New York: W. W. Norton, 1978), p. 21.

31. Judy Grahn, "Murdering the King's English," *True to Life Adventure Stories,* is quoted by Jan Clausen in *A Movement of Poets: Thoughts on Poetry and Feminism* (New York: Long Haul Press, 1982), p. 22.

32. Judy Chicago, *Through the Flower: My Struggle as a Woman Artist* (New York: Doubleday, 1975), p. 63.

33. See the illustrations in *Through the Flower,* and Judy Chicago, *The Dinner Party* (New York: Anchor, 1970).

34. Cather discusses Queen Mathilde's tapestry at Bayeux—"alongside the big pattern of dramatic action [there was] the little playful pattern of birds and beasts that are a story in themselves"—in *The Professor's House* (New York: Vintage, 1973), p. 101; see also Anne Finch, "A Description of One of the Pieces of Tapestry at Long-Leat," in *The Poems of Anne Countess of Winchelsea,* ed. Myra Reynolds (Chicago: Univ. of Chicago Press, 1903), p. 47.

35. Emily Dickinson, J 1651 ("A Word Made Flesh Is Seldom"), *The Complete Poems of Emily Dickinson,* ed. Thomas H. Johnson (Boston: Little, Brown, 1960); Ethel Wright Mohamed, "H. Mohamed Dry Goods" and "Double Springs Sacred Harp Sing," in the Center for Southern Folklore, 1216 Peabody Avenue, P.O. Box 4081, Memphis, TN 38104; Pecolia Warner, Yazoo City, Mississippi, in Center for Southern Folklore, 1216 Peabody Avenue, P.O. Box 4081, Memphis, TN 38104.

36. Karen Petersen and J. J. Wilson, *Women Artists: Recognition and Reappraisal from the Early Middle Ages to the Twentieth Century* (New York: Harper Colophon, 1976), pp. 12 and 16–17.

37. Elizabeth Stuart Phelps Ward, *The Story of Avis* (Boston: James R. Osgood, 1877).

38. H.D., *Tribute to Freud,* pp. 44–56; "priceless treasure," p. 53.

39. Charlotte Perkins Gilman, *The Yellow Wallpaper* (New York: The Feminist Press, 1973); Virginia Woolf, *Night and Day* (New York: Harcourt, 1919), pp. 300, 487. *Mrs. Dalloway* (New York: Harcourt, 1925), p. 122; *A Room of One's Own* (New York: Harcourt, 1928), p. 79.

40. Willa Cather, *My Antonia* (Boston: Houghton Mifflin, 1954), p. 62; and *Death Comes for the Archbishop* (New York: Vintage, 1971), pp. 76–77.

41. Margaret Atwood, *Surfacing* (New York: Popular Library, 1972), pp. 69, 136, 142, 170.

42. As a literary technique, automatic writing is usually associated with nineteenth- and twentieth-century male writers, most notably the French surrealists, led by André Breton; Atwood, however, exploits its connection with the trances and researches of women spiritualists like, e.g., George Yeats, whose automatic writings were the ostensible source of her husband's *A Vision.* See Margaret Atwood, *Lady Oracle* (New York: Simon & Schuster, 1976), pp. 194, 220–23.

43. Margaret Atwood, *Selected Poems* (New York: Simon & Schuster, 1976), p. 60.

44. See Charlotte Salomon, *Charlotte: Life or Theater?* (New York: Viking, 1981), passim.

45. Virginia Woolf, *The Voyage Out* (New York: Harcourt, 1915), p. 326. *Jacob's Room* in *Jacob's Room and the Waves* (New York: Harcourt, 195?), pp. 91, 93; *The Waves,* pp. 185–86; *Between the Acts* (New York: Harcourt, 1941), p. 212.

46. William Wordsworth, *The Prelude,* Book VI, lines 638–40; for commentary on Poe, Melville, and Hawthorne see John T. Irwin, *American Hieroglyphics* (New Haven: Yale Univ. Press, 1980), passim.

47. Arthur Rimbaud, "Voyelles," in *Oeuvres Complets* (Paris: Gallimard, 1972), p. 53; Wallace Stevens, *Collected Poems* (New York: Knopf, 1955), pp. 27, 179, 267, 288.

48. Rudyard Kipling, "How the First Letter Was Written" and "How the Alphabet Was Made," in *Just So Stories* (New York: Doubleday, 1912).

49. See Derrida, *Glas* (Paris: Editions Galilée, 1974). See also Geoffrey Hartman, *Saving the Text* (Baltimore: Johns Hopkins Univ. Press, 1980), pp. 74–76.

50. Ezra Pound, *The ABC of Reading* (New York: New Directions, 1960), pp. 21–23; Roland Barthes, *S/Z,* trans. Richard Miller (New York: Hill & Wang, 1974), pp. 106–7; and David Young, *The Names of a Hare in English* (Pittsburgh: Univ. of Pittsburgh Press, 1979), pp. 32–33.

51. See Harold Bloom, *The Anxiety of Influence* (New York: Oxford, 1973), especially p. 11, which situates "Battle between strong equals, father and son as mighty opposites, Laius and Oedipus at the crossroads" at the heart of literary history.

52. See Chapter 2 in our *The Madwoman in the Attic* (New Haven: Yale Univ. Press, 1979), pp. 45–92.

53. Gertrude Stein, "Marry Nettie," in *The Yale Gertrude Stein,* ed. Richard Kostelanetz (New Haven: Yale Univ. Press, 1980), p. 72.

54. Virginia Woolf, *Mrs. Dalloway,* pp. 29–32; *To the Lighthouse* (New York: Harcourt, 1927), pp. 53–55.

55. Sylvia Plath, *The Bell Jar* (New York: Bantam, 1972), pp. 101–2.

56. Sue Owen, "The Devil," *Nursery Rhymes for the Dead* (Ithaca: Ithaca House, 1980), p. 41.

57. Ruth Stone, "Poetry," *The Iowa Review,* Vol. 12, No. 2/3 (Spring/Summer 1981), 322.

58. Elinor Wylie, "Dedication," *Collected Poems* (New York: Knopf, 1932), pp. 109, 110. Nelly Sachs, *O the Chimneys: Selected Poems,* trans. by Michael Hamburger, Christopher Holme, Ruth and Matthew Mead, and Michael Roloff (New York: Farrar, Straus and Giroux, 1967), p. 125 ("And unwarps, as though it were linen sheets").

59. Sonia Delaunay, "The Alphabet ABC," Collection Sonia Delaunay, and Jenny Snider, *Pencil Picture Dictionary* (New York: Head, Hand, Heart and Tooth Publications, 1973).

60. Gertrude Stein, "Lifting Belly," *The Yale Gertrude Stein,* pp. 48, 54.

61. Vita Sackville-West, *The Letters of Vita Sackville-West to Virginia Woolf,* edited by Mitchell Leaska and Louise DeSalvo (New York: William Morrow; London: Hutchinson), forthcoming September 1984. We are indebted to Mitchell A. Leaska and Nigel Nicolson for permission to quote from the Alphabet letter.

62. Monique Wittig and Sande Zweig, *Lesbian Peoples/Material for a Dictionary* (New York: Avon, 1979), pp. 4, 5, 100, 166.

63. Olga Broumas, "Artemis," *Beginning with O* (New Haven: Yale Univ. Press, 1979), p. 23. In this connection, it is also interesting to consider the possibility of a relationship between the *O* in *Les Guerrillères* (1969) and *O* in *The Story of O* (1954).

64. Christine de Pisan, *The Book of the City of Ladies,* trans. Earl Jeffrey Richards (New York: Persea, 1982), pp. 16 and 71–73.

65. Denise Levertov, "Relearning the Alphabet," in *Relearning the Alphabet* (New York: New Directions, 1966), pp. 110–20.

66. Margarite Cota-Cardena, "Spelling out the Cosmos," in *The Third Woman,* ed. Fisher, p. 398.

67. Maria Teresa León, *Memoria de la melancolia* (Barcelona: Laia/Picazo, 1977), p. 308.

68. Higginson, *Women and the Alphabet,* p. 26.

# The Female Hand in Heian Japan:
# A First Reading

*Richard Bowring*

*When my brother . . . was a young boy learning the Chinese classics, I was in the habit of listening to him and I became unusually proficient at understanding those passages which he found too difficult to grasp. Father, a most learned man, was always regretting the fact: "Just my luck!" he would say. "What a pity she was not born a man!"*[1]

Murasaki Shikibu Diary

It could be anywhere, any age, but the reference to Chinese gives the game away. In fact we are in Japan and the year is 1010. Classical Chinese, the language of government, decree, and "knowledge" for some centuries, was jealously guarded as the exclusive domain of the male. Women were thereby effectively excluded from participation in the power structure, linguistically cut off from the source of authority. To perpetuate this state of affairs the useful fiction was generated that it was unbecoming for the female to learn Chinese. We know from diaries and other sources that women did not always acquiesce to this fiction,[2] but there is no doubt that the acquisition of Chinese by women was made intentionally difficult and was seen as a threat, a subversive act of considerable, if undefined, moment.

So far there should be no surprises; it is a familiar story. But the picture begins to change when we discover that the lady whose diary has just been quoted is known as Japan's greatest novelist and that the Heian period (794–1185) in general is remarkable for the way in which women dominated the field of Japanese prose. A list of major works by women from the tenth and eleventh centuries would include *The Gossamer Years, The Pillow Book of Sei Shōnagon, The Tale of Genji, The Murasaki Shikibu Diary, The*

*Izumi Shikibu Diary,* and *The Sarashina Diary.*[3] Nothing that we can identify as being male authorship comes close to rivaling this list in quality and
quantity.

With the exception of *The Tale of Genji,* a highly complex and subtle
fiction, these works form a distinguished group of female introspective
writings. They are among the earliest examples of the attempt by women
living in a male-dominated society to define the self in textual terms. Indeed it is largely because of these works that classical Japanese becomes of
more than parochial interest; and it is because of the existing linguistic
situation that women became the texts through which we now tend to
define the whole period. In retrospect it is a form of sweet revenge. The
Heian period will always bear for us a strong female aspect; to a great
extent it is the women who have become our historians, and it is they who
define the parameters within which we are allowed to approach their
world, themselves, and their men.

There are a number of reasons why men lost control, as it were, of their
own language. Men were under considerable pressure not to use Japanese
and to prove their fitness for office, ultimately their masculinity, by their
command of Chinese. This pressure, coupled with a Confucian-inspired
distrust of fiction as an unworthy pursuit, served to divorce men from
their tongue and condemn them to working in a foreign language, which,
of necessity, guided their thoughts and expression along non-native paths.
The case of poetry is somewhat more complex and cannot be discussed
here in detail. But there is evidence that by the mid-tenth century men had
begun to realize that prose had to a certain extent slipped from their grasp,
had become marked as "female," and hence was in need of reappropria-
tion.

About the year 935 Ki no Tsurayuki (the grand old man of Japanese
poetry) wrote a work entitled *The Tosa Diary.* Although a low-ranking
courtier not politically favored in any real sense, Tsurayuki had done more
than anyone else to rehabilitate native poetry after a period of decline and
had compiled the first imperial anthology of such poetry, the *Kokinshū* of
905–10. His *Tosa Diary* opens with the following famous sentence: "A
'daily record,' that preserve of men; but might not a woman produce one
too, I wonder, and so I write." What is signified by this foregrounding of
sexual difference? What kind of deception lies behind this act of substitution in which a man pretends to be a woman usurping a male role?

The usual interpretation of this piece of role playing is that in 935 the
low status of Japanese prose meant that a man could not use it openly.
Tsurayuki had to pretend to be a woman. But Tsurayuki had already established himself as *the* arbiter of taste and of the two *Kokinshū* prefaces one
was written in Japanese. Another theory has it that this role playing was a

wholly "literary" move, an effective way of establishing the fictionality of what followed.[4] But the matter can also be seen in a more radical light: an attempt to usurp a female role, before it became too well entrenched, by suggesting the exact opposite. It is not, then, a stratagem to avoid a charge of effeminacy, but a device to neutralize a general female threat. Very few texts remain from this early period, so proof that women were already in control of prose by 935 is hard to come by, and this particular interpretation must remain speculative. But the autobiographical works under discussion began to appear soon after this date, and prose was to remain in female hands for the next century and a half. Tsurayuki's attempt can hardly be said to have succeeded. When women finally lost their "dominant" literary position in twelfth-century Japan, it was due to the general decline of court culture and the rise of a warrior culture rather than a specifically male victory over the female within the court itself.

W H A T kind of works were these female texts that, in retrospect, swept the stage? How did women textualize themselves during the period? In part, because they acquiesced to the view that writing fiction was demeaning, they make no reference to women authors being in charge; nor should one expect them to do so, for this "dominance" appears only with the help of hindsight. The image of woman that emerges is by no means one of female triumphant. Man is at the very center of the world, and women define themselves almost exclusively in relation to this all-powerful other. *The Gossamer Years,* for instance, an autobiographical work covering the years 954–974, written by a woman known to us only as "the mother of Michitsuna," is famous for the bitterness with which the woman views her fate. It is largely a chronicle of frustration and jealousy that damns both man and self:

> My house and garden were going to ruin. It apparently did not occur to the Prince how it hurt me to have him come and go without offering to help, indeed without seeming to notice that anything was wrong. He said he was busy, and perhaps he was; perhaps his duties outnumbered the weeds in my garden (*The Gossamer Years,* p. 60).

Common to all these works is a series of rules that govern the literary expression of sexual relations, a sexual grammar that remains remarkably constant throughout the period. Woman, the passive center of the narrative, cannot initiate passion, but rather generates it in the other. Male and female always live apart, and woman is the object of desire whose thoughts are concentrated on the man's next visit.

The Sixth Month came, and counting back I found that he had not visited me in the evening for more than thirty days, and in the daytime for more than forty. . . . I could not keep my mind fixed on anything, but would spend my time gazing listlessly at the garden, or, ashamed to have anyone see me, lie with my face pressed gainst the floor to hide my tears (*The Gossamer Years*, p. 82).

In such a passive role, woman is defined in terms of waiting, pining for the other:

I lived forever in a dream world. The height of my aspirations was that a man of noble birth, perfect in both looks and manners, someone like Shining Genji in the Tale, would visit me just once a year in the mountain village where he would have hidden me like Lady Ukifune (*As I Crossed a Bridge of Dreams*, pp. 71–72).

The reference is to *The Tale of Genji*, where such fantasies assume their most famous fictional form and where women are always the visited. They live indoors, behind screens that are there to be penetrated. A move through a curtain signifies capitulation. The very act of seeing in such a haremlike environment becomes identified with violation. The *locus classicus* for this topos of visual rape, known as *kaimami* or "seeing through a gap in the hedge," appears in the first section of *The Tales of Ise* (mid-tenth century), usually considered a "male" text.

Once a man who had come of age went hunting on his estate at Kasuga village near the Nara capital. In that village lived two very beautiful sisters. He saw them through a gap in the hedge. Amazed to find such an incongruity in the old capital he lost his head. Ripping off the hem of his hunting cloak he wrote down a poem and sent it in. The fabric was a purple print called "wild passion":

> Ah young purple fern
> Of Kasugano,
> This printed cloak,
> The wild disorder of my passion
> Knows no limit.[5]

In this passage from *The Tales of Ise*, a text consisting of a series of poems with extended prefaces, the act of poetic creation is explicitly tied to the onset of sexuality. The young male must learn that the production of poetry and the tight control over emotional expression that it signifies is the *sine qua non* of the cultured man. When passion rather than sexual hunger strikes, it is encoded as occupation by the other; love is a loss of self-control, a spiritual possession in inverse proportion to the physical. Man, condemned to live outdoors, the constant aggressor in constant motion, is the eternal visitor, the eternal traveler from curtain to curtain. There is no concept of home, of family, of fathering a generation for this furtive visitor who must come in the dark and leave at dawn in the best of taste. For instance, after a long disquisition on how a lover should act, Sei Shōnagon in her *Pillow Book* demands that "a good lover will behave as elegantly at dawn as at any other time. . . . Indeed, one's attachment to a man depends largely on the eloquence of his leavetaking" (pp. 29–30). Clearly this privileging of aesthetics may be read as a defense mechanism, but the stature of women in these texts is closely related to their capacity to express sympathy for the male who cannot remain behind.

In such a world of physical separation it is hardly surprising to find an overwhelming emphasis on communication as the means of bridging the gap between self and other. Language represents a way of ratifying one's very existence, and the ability to express oneself in poetry becomes a necessary part of being desirable, for either sex. Narration often proceeds in the form of ritual repartee, an exchange of poems (*zōtōka*) that stands for a civilized form of coupling and recoupling. Fully half the *Izumi Shikibu Diary*, for instance, consists of such exchanges. And given the rule that space must be maintained between the partners, it is to a large extent written poetry with the hand-carried letter as its medium. The letter is, of course, a substitute, a sign of absence; and by that token the physical object, its form, its accompaniments, its "hand," its carrier, becomes a fetish. Thus, when a letter is sent, great care is taken to choose the paper that matches the mood of the occasion, as the "I" of the *Murasaki Shikisu Diary* indicates:

> I was in the middle of composing a reply to a note sent by Lady
> Koshōshō when all of a sudden it became dark and started to rain.
> As the messenger was in a hurry, I finished it off with: "and the sky
> too seems unsettled." I must have also included a rather lame verse,
> for the messenger returned that evening with a poem written on
> dark purple cloud-patterned paper (p. 75).

Even more important, the "hand" reveals sex, age, status, and taste; as such, it triggers sexual passion. Relationships often begin solely on the basis of handwriting, and graphology becomes an essential talent, an integral part of sexual mores. So strong is the mystique of the written sign that it becomes *the* mark of certain identity. In this body of literature there are many examples of physical substitution, of intentional mistakes in the dark, but on no occasion does writing become the agent of deception. The written cannot lie, and mistakes occur only when the letter fails to reach its destination. Writing seems to be privileged over presence itself.

The old Japanese word for letter, for writing, is *fumi,* a "print" or "trace." Script is often referred to as being the tracks of a bird on sand; it is what remains. And yet the culture imbues these signs with certainty. The letter is proof of absence, yes, but at the same time it testifies, it contains within it the essence of the absent party. However, it is not the written *word* that constitutes proof but the writing itself. The message is often deliberately obscure and couched in vague terms on the grounds that words can betray, but the "hand," the graphic sign in and of itself, cannot. As one might expect in a culture that had only recently evolved its own script by deforming one belonging to a language built on entirely different principles, the link between sign and word is by no means accepted as axiomatic.[6]

It is in this sense that one can speak metaphorically of woman seeing herself as a text to be read by man when he chances by. In the frustration of waiting, women begin to read, and moreover, write themselves. As man is always the reader and woman the read, she exists to generate male interest and can have no power of her own until read. Indoors, forever waiting, she can become a force only when seen and opened, for without the male reader the female text is barren. The unopened, unread letter, then, comes under the rubric of "depressing things" for the cataloguer Sei Shōnagon:

> One has written a letter, taking pains to make it as attractive as possible, and now one impatiently awaits the reply. "Surely the messenger should be back by now," one thinks. Just then he returns; but in his hand he carries, not a reply, but one's own letter, still twisted or knotted as it was sent, but now so dirty and crumpled that even the ink-mark on the outside has disappeared (p. 21).

Once activated, however, the predominant trait turns out to be jealousy, a passion that tries to take revenge on any other text that threatens to lure the man away.

> It began to appear that the lady in the alley had fallen from favor since the birth of her child. I had prayed, at the height of my unhappiness, that she would live to know what I was then suffering, and it seemed that my prayers were being answered. She was alone, and now her child was dead. . . . The pain must be even sharper than mine had been. I was satisfied (*The Gossamer Years*, p. 44).

Whatever satisfaction the pain of the other waiting woman might provide, the rules stipulate that female passion be invariably self-destructive.

The corollary to this unfulfilled waiting female is man the eternal traveler. He is never allowed to read the female text at leisure, but can open only the first few pages, an act to be endlessly repeated in future visits. The form of these introspective narratives in turn reflects this sexual grammar; they are diaries rather than full-fledged autobiographies; they suggest chronicles rather than historical narratives; hence they lack much interest in teleological motion. For both male and female reading means suspension, rather than resolution, and it is the opening of the book, not its closing, that constitutes the obsessive gesture. The fragmented nature of sexual experience in these texts is paralleled by a constant undermining of narrative coherence. In part, this is due to the pervasive presence of poetry, which is used as a mode of dialogue, but which creates a sense of rupture, of interruption by continually introducing tangential intertexts. In part, this incoherence is also due to the fact that the women never situate their writings in a concrete, historical context. There are few dates, few names, no references to political realities. It is as if the women have consciously cut away that part of the world over which they have no power, to concentrate entirely on private fears and sorrows. The effect is disturbing not only because women present themselves in a permanent vacuum but because there is apparently no hope or even desire for what nature defines as order, just an endless repetition of seasonal cycles, and visits by the reader.

## Notes

1. *Murasaki Shikibu Diary,* p. 139. For details see note 3.

2. For instance, the passage that immediately follows the above quotation reads: "But then gradually I realized that people were saying, 'It's bad enough when a man flaunts his learning; she will come to no good,' and ever since then I have avoided writing even the simplest character. My handwriting is appalling. And as for those classics, or whatever they are called, that I used to read, I gave them up entirely. Still I kept on hearing those malicious remarks. Worried what people would think if they heard such rumors, I pretended to be unable to read even the inscriptions on the screens. Then Her Majesty asked me to read to her here and there from the Collected Works of Po Chü-i, and, because she evinced a desire to know more about such things, we carefully chose a time when other women would not be present and, amateur that I was, I read with her the two books of Po Chü-i's New Ballads in secret."

3. A bibliographic note. English translations of these works are available as follows: E. Seidensticker, trans., *The Gossamer Years* (*Kagerō nikki*) (Tokyo and Rutland, Vermont: Tuttle, 1964); I. Morris, trans., *The Pillow Book of Sei Shōnagon* (*Makura no sōshi*) (New York: Columbia Univ. Press, 1967); E. Seidensticker, trans., *The Tale of Genji* (*Genji monogatari*) (New York: Knopf, 1976); R. Bowring, trans., *Murasaki Shikibu: Her Diary and Poetic Memoirs* (*Murasaki Shikibu nikki*) (Princeton: Princeton Univ. Press, 1982); E. Cranston, trans., *The Izumi Shikibu Diary* (*Izumi Shikibu nikki*) (Cambridge, Mass.: Harvard Univ. Press, 1969); I. Morris, trans., *As I Crossed a Bridge of Dreams* (*Sarashina nikki*) (New York: The Dial Press, 1971). Other works of interest in this regard are: I. Morris, *The World of the Shining Prince* (Oxford: Oxford Univ. Press, 1964); W. McCullough, "Japanese Marriage Institutions in the Heian Period," *Harvard Journal of Asiatic Studies* 27 (1967); W. and H. McCullough, trans., *A Tale of Flowering Fortunes* (*Eiga monogatari*) (Stanford: Stanford Univ. Press, 1980); T. Rohlich, trans., *A Tale of Eleventh-Century Japan* (*Hamamatsu Chūnagon monogatari*) (Princeton: Princeton Univ. Press, 1983); and R. Willig, trans., *The Changelings* (*Torikaebaya monogatari*) (Stanford: Stanford Univ. Press, 1983).

4. See Konishi Jin'ichi, *Tosa nikki hyōkai* (Tokyo: Yūseidō, 1951), pp. 18–19.

5. Adapted from H. McCullough, trans., *Tales of Ise* (Tokyo: Tokyo Univ. Press, 1968), p. 69.

6. The same equivocal relationship between sign and word runs deep in the language today. Characters in Chinese are logograms, but in Japanese they are transformed into a complex of semantograms, phonograms, and rebus constructions. When they are used in conjunction with the syllabary the result is a form of writing under constant erasure. The juxtaposition of these systems and their interlineal struggle for domination in Japanese produces a degree of surface "noise" and interference that radically undermines referentiality and makes Japanese a fruitful example for those interested in such questions.

CHAPTER FOUR

# Autobiography of a New 'Creatur': Female Spirituality, Selfhood, and Authorship in "The Book of Margery Kempe"

## Janel M. Mueller

Since its discovery in manuscript in 1934, *The Book of Margery Kempe* has engaged the interest of students of late medieval literature and spirituality. But this interest has tended, until recently, to obscure the narrative and thematic coherence of the *Book's* autobiographical design. It is remarkable enough that the work is the first autobiography in English, and the auto-biography of a woman. It emerges as a still more remarkable creation from the sidelights afforded on Margery's authorial struggles. In the preface and in the reflections linking Book I with Book II, we learn that Margery, an illiterate laywoman of over sixty, had nearly completed an account of twenty-five years or so of her experience when, in 1436, the man who had been writing at her dictation and reading back to her for checking sud-denly died. After this scribe's handwriting proved undecipherable to oth-ers, Margery obtained another man's help. He made a new, somewhat fuller transcript for her in 1438; this is the version of her *Book* that sur-vives.[1]

More secular currents of interest in Margery have mainly run in two channels: in that of social history, her robust self-esteem and broad travel experience invite comparison with a literary antecedent, Chaucer's Wife of Bath; and in the channel of language history her *Book* contributes to docu-menting the widespread resumption of English as a written medium in the fifteenth century.[2] For their part, students of late medieval spirituality have worked at identifying affinities between *The Book of Margery Kempe* and other mystical works, especially those of two close female contempo-raries: Julian of Norwich's *Showings of Divine Love* and St. Birgitta's *Reve-lations*. Margery herself indicates that possible female affinities are not exhaustive, for she refers to works by St. Bonaventure, Richard Rolle, and

Walter Hilton that a priest read aloud to her.[3] Nonetheless, Margery's firsthand experience gives special pertinence and strength to the links with Julian and Birgitta. Margery's spirituality, like that of Julian, whom she tells of having visited to obtain spiritual counsel (Book I, chapter 18), centered on the Sacred Manhood and the Passion of Christ—a dominant strain in popular devotion of the period. Also, like Birgitta, whose canonization was confirmed in ceremonies at Rome, which she witnessed (I.39), Margery was called to become a bride of God—even though she, unlike Birgitta, was no widow at the time and did not proceed to formal religious vows.

Margery parts company with others, men and women, in the controlling and apparently distinctive feature of her spiritual life: her calling to a mystical spousal while remaining in the world and, indeed, remaining bound to a living husband in certain evolving ways. These, we shall see, are vital to the autobiographical design of her *Book*. But before we examine the peculiar nature and implications of Margery's calling, we must take some notice of the difficulty experienced by her first amanuensis with regard to another aspect of her spirituality. In a rare obtrusion of his own voice (I.62), he interrupts a series of anecdotes illustrating the hostility and ostracism to which Margery was subjected because of her violent "wepyng & sobbyng" in public places. He confesses that he at first had "fled & enchewyd" her under the influence of a censorious friar and that he had begun writing down Margery's story for her before he had a "ryth cler mende of the sayd mater" of her tears. "Therefor he wrot the lesse thereof" and "les seryowslech & expressiowslech" than he eventually came to do.[4] This scribe explains that he sought to understand Margery better by reading in Bonaventure's *Stimulus amoris* and in Rolle's *Incendium amoris* how these two mystics report themselves to have run in the streets, crying out and calling upon the Lord. But he remained disturbed about the lack of fit he found between Margery's weeping and Bonaventure's and Rolle's crying—a lack of fit we can partially ascribe to the influence of a potent (and male) scriptural precedent, David the king and psalmist, upon the behavior of the latter (Psalms 17:1, 6; 22:2, 6–7; 27:6–11; cf. 2 Samuel 6:14–16). In further searching, the scribe tells us, he could find only one relevant analogue for "terys of pyte & compassion" as a whole "maner of levyng" in "plentyuows grace." This was the biography of the saintly Marie d'Oignies (1177–1213) written by her spiritual director, the Augustinian canon Jacques de Vitry. Through reflecting on Marie's *Life*, Margery's first amanuensis came to *bona fide* acceptance of the two women's shared mystical 'gift of tears' and thence to willing cooperation with Margery in setting down an account of her life and spirituality in her own words.[5]

It would be hard to overrate the importance of Margery's 'gift of tears'—a trait manifested copiously every day for ten years, and at less frequent intervals over an additional fifteen (I.27, 82, 85). The prominence of her devout fits of weeping as a compositional element in her *Book* stems directly from their indispensability to her: they validate her personal witness to God's unfailingly tenderhearted love for the whole of mankind. Thus, any examination of the autobiographical design of Margery's *Book* must begin with the vital equivalence between her tears, on the one hand, and the truth of feeling and being a "creatur" of God, on the other, which she everywhere reaffirms. As the associative, loosely sequential progression of her story establishes itself, no fewer than three early chapters rehearse assurances from Jesus, Our Lady, and Julian of Norwich that Margery's tears mark her as a special recipient of divine love and favor. First, Jesus tells Margery "in her mende" that "terys of compunccyon, devocyon, & compassyon arn the heyest & sikerest ʒyftys that I ʒeve in erde" (I.14). Almost immediately thereafter, Julian urges upon Margery this view of her tears: "Whan God visyteth a creatur wyth terys of contrisyon, devosyon, er compassyon, he may & owth to levyn that the Holy Gost is in hys sowle" (I.18; *BMK,* pp. 31, 42–43; B-B, pp. 23, 34). Next, after Our Lady assures Margery that her tears attest the flowings of Jesus' grace, to make the world wonder at her and love the Son for Margery's sake (I.29), the *Book* attains a level of confidence that never recedes, despite intermittent doubts and challenges. Margery identifies her very life and selfhood with what she calls her "welle of teerys" (I.32, 41, 57; II, concluding prayers). So complete is this identification that when she finds herself "bareyn fro teerys," her consciousness goes numb with anguish. She cannot function religiously or socially (I.82) until her capacity to weep is restored (*BMK,* pp. 81, 99, 141, 199, 249; B-B, pp. 70, 86, 129, 182, 227). In alleging a singular spiritual counterpart for the weeping Margery in Marie d'Oignies, the *Book's* first scribe points to an external of social behavior as the sign of a characteristic sensibility—a mode of expression and a way of life—that appears to be female; his search turned up no male analogues. However, this scribe's preoccupation with the likenesses between Marie and Margery keeps him from remarking what to us is an equally essential difference. Margery's female spirituality impelled her, as it did not impel Marie, to the joint self-awareness and self-realization demonstrated in compiling an autobiography. Not only did the interworkings of female spirituality, selfhood, and authorship issue in the transmissible record known as *The Book of Margery Kempe;* they also etched that record with its unique autobiographical design.[6]

One major aspect in which female spirituality, selfhood, and authorship come together is in the formation of blocks or sequences of narrative that address the question of giving credence to Margery, to what she says and does. The authorial imperative she faces at the outset of her *Book*—in rhetorical terms, the necessity to use *ethos* effectively in self-presentation—is exactly the challenge Margery presents herself as having to face in life. Certainly it was anomalous, not to say scandalous, that she experienced her calling to become a bride of God when she had a living husband and had recently borne a child. The precedent of the virginal Marie d'Oignies could in no way cover the latter circumstance. St. Birgitta, too, had received her calling to mystical spousal only after she was widowed. The utter incongruity of Margery's situation with her newly announced calling causes the otherwise well-disposed Richard Caister, vicar of St. Stephen's, Norwich, to exclaim in sheer bemusement: "What? Cowd the woman ocupyn an owyr er tweyn owyrs in the lofe of owyr Lord?" (I.17; *BMK,* p. 38; B-B, p. 30).

Inevitably, the first steps in the spiritual reorientation that Margery seeks for her life entail breaking with various settled conceptions and demands to which she as a woman is subject—those of her husband most immediately, later those of religious and civil authorities as well as society at large. Having to strain toward her new identity against these settled conceptions and demands creates the constitutive narrative tension of several important sequences of chapters set in England, where Margery is a known entity and also commands her native tongue for use in self-definition and self-defense. In the first such sequence, chapters 9 through 25 of Book I, Margery's prime objective is to secure her husband's consent to her newly spiritualized understanding of her wifehood in the form of a mutual vow of sexual continence.[7] After almost three years she wins his cooperation and support, demonstrated in his accompanying of her on a less successful quest—a quest for permission from ecclesiastical superiors in York, Canterbury, Lincoln, and Norwich that Margery be allowed to wear the white garments of a bride of God. The long withholding of this permission figures prominently in the design of her *Book.* In the second relevant sequence, chapters 43 through 55 of Book I, the narrative tension rises as Margery, now attempting to negotiate official recognition of her special spiritual identity without her husband's help, is arraigned for questioning at Worcester and then actually prosecuted for heresy (Lollardy) at Leicester, York, and Beverley.

As author, Margery works deftly to shape and sustain these blocks of narrative that convey the notion that she had no selfhood, no existence worthy of naming, before her protracted struggle to clarify and confirm her religious calling both to herself and to others. Thus, she introduces herself in the most minimal terms at the opening of her *Book* by leaving anonymous the two male figures, father and then husband, whose dependent she successively was. Her husband is cited only as "a worchepful burgeys" and her father as "sum-tyme meyr of the town N. and sythyn . . . alderman of the hey gyld of the Trinyte in N." (I.1, 2; *BMK,* pp. 7, 9; B-B, pp. 1, 3), while she consistently styles herself, here and throughout, as "this creatur"—a locution that encapsulates her sense of radical dependency on God for her ongoing creation. In the ensuing blocks of narrative, which detail society's grudging acknowledgment of the claims of Margery's spirituality, the calculated unspecificity of the style raises one question—namely, Who is this woman?—and the tension of social dealings transmutes it into another question: What possible place or meaning can her life have? The purposiveness of autobiographical design in *The Book of Margery Kempe* emerges in the answers it offers to these questions.

Although Margery's first steps toward reorienting herself and her sexual and social roles under the imperative of divine love take disjunctive form—the new as a break with the old—she is soon instructed that true female spirituality proceeds otherwise. Its nature consists in an embrace of nonexclusive, coexisting relations and functions that may well strike us readers as cognate with the most enduring historical role of women as characterized by Elise Boulding.[8] To Margery, however, the lesson in the comprehensiveness that her spirituality must attain comes as the will of her Lord, and her initial advance in such consciousness provides the crux of the first sequence of chapters in her *Book*. Near its end (I.21, 22), Margery voices perplexity and abashment at being singled out as a special recipient of her Lord's love, because she does not belong to either privileged category—maiden or widow. Her Lord reassures her that he finds her "a synguler lover" and beloved in a range of roles; he calls her "a mayden in thi sowle," "dowtyr," "myn owyn derworthy derlyng," "myn owyn blyssed spowse" (*BMK*, pp. 52–53; B-B, p. 42). The initial insight to be gained by the spiritually instructed Margery and communicated to her husband is this: there is no inherent incompatibility between becoming a bride of God and being acknowledged as the wife of John Kempe, burgess of Lynn, and the mother of his fourteen children (cf. I, 15).

Society at large, however, clings to either/or thinking with respect to Margery, especially in England where, if anywhere, she has her place. The crux of the second extended narrative sequence is Margery's pertinacity in seeking the public confirmation of her special spiritual status, which would come with permission to wear white wool clothing and a gold ring engraved *Jesu est amor meus;* in this regard she must persuade males other than her husband who have authority over her. Hence, the issue of her clothing is more complicated in the sense of being more social than the vow of continence was. Margery is also as intensely concerned with her clothes as she is with her tears; she treats both as an extension of herself, a measure of the recognition accorded her in the public domain. Perhaps her concern with her clothes indicates an emergent feature of female authorial consciousness.[9] Yet it is well to be cautious about any such inferences, for Rolle had set a famous precedent in English mysticism by devising a new dress for his religious calling from his sister's garments; and, nearer in time to Margery, a general mindfulness of sumptuary considerations marks other, quite disparate vernacular works in fifteenth-century England.[10] At any rate, it is indicative of the strength of her difficulties at home that Margery first reports wearing her white clothes and gold ring in a discontinuous group of chapters on her travels to Zurich, Constance, Bologna, Venice, Jerusalem, and Rome, which intervenes between the first and the second narrative sequences dealing with England.

When Margery is abroad, her weeping creates as much disturbance and antipathy as it does at home. But otherwise, when she is abroad, she emerges in her text as a far more tenuous and peripheral presence—a woman remarked at best in passing, for the most part slighted and disregarded, isolated too by her inability to speak any language but English. It is against this desultory and disorienting backdrop that Margery strikes a bargain with her Lord: if she is brought safely to Rome, she will fulfill His longstanding injunction that she wear white clothes (I.30). She keeps her bargain (I.31) and has the self-possession to defy an English priest in Rome who commands her to shed her hypocritical holiness (I.33). Next, however, she obeys a German priest who tells her to resume wearing her black clothes (I.34). Yet what looks like vacillation proves to be the last shedding of Margery's diffidence regarding the rightness of a mystical spousal for one in her marital state. In direct succession follows one of the most arresting chapters in the *Book* (I.35): Margery's account of her wedding to the Godhead in the Church of the Holy Apostles in Rome on the feastday of St. John Lateran. This experience, in which God the Father plights to Margery's soul the bridegroom's "for richer or for poorer" troth before the other Persons of the Trinity and a large company of saints and angels, reconfirms dramatically the lesson of nonexclusivity in her roles and relations that she had earlier been taught as a precept. This experience also climaxes the pilgrimage of nearly two years on which Margery had embarked just after she and John had together vowed sexual continence. Quite simply, it makes her able to return home.

A rapid narrative transition signals that any further development of the ramifications of Margery's status, selfhood, and spirituality, as externalized in the issue of her clothing, must await her arrival in England. The development begins as soon as she disembarks in Norwich and regains the use of her tongue in her native speech community (I.43). To a monk who confronts her with the rumor that she had borne an illegitimate child abroad, she declares "how it was owr Lordys wyl that sche xulde be clad in white clothyng." This declaration seems to be vindicated forthwith; "a worshepful man in Norwich" makes her a present of a white gown, kirtle, hood, and cloak, and John, her husband, arrives to conduct her back to Lynn (I.44; *BMK,* pp. 103, 104; B-B, pp. 90, 91). Before she can go her way, however, Margery has to answer to the bishop of Worcester for calling some of his retainers "the Develys men" because they wore slashed and pointed clothes (I.45; *BMK,* p. 109; B-B, p. 96) much like those she describes herself as having worn in her unregenerate youth (cf. I.2). To her surprise, the bishop receives Margery hospitably, white clothes and all, insisting that she dine with him because he recognizes her as John of Brunham's daughter, from Lynn. In this solitary instance social identification promotes rather than hinders acceptance of Margery's singular spirituality.

Much more typical and much more highlighted in the narrative design of the *Book* are the negative reactions to her spirituality and selfhood that Margery proceeds to encounter at Leicester, York, and Beverley. In the next sequence of chapters, every interrogation ends by pitting the power of society against Margery's dual spousal, the operative assumption of the authorities being that once they determine who she is, they will know what she cannot be. Thus the mayor of Leicester reviles Margery as "a false strumpet, a fals loller, & a fals deceyver of the pepyl" when she lays claim to the identity of a bride of God. Indeed, she makes matters worse and seems more outrageous when she offers on behalf of her claim the credentials of her present male connections:

> "Syr," sche seyd, "I am of Lynne in Norfolke, a good mannys dowtyr of the same Lynne, whech hath ben meyr fyve tymes of that worshepful burwgh and aldyrman also many yerys; & I have a good man, also a burgeys of the seyd town, Lynne, to myn husbond" (I.46; *BMK,* pp. 111–112; B-B, p. 98).

By contrast, the steward of Leicester refuses to believe Margery's protestations that she is "a mannys wife" because she is unaccompanied. When she resists his sexual advances by laying claim to the protection of divine love, the steward's bafflement erupts in this disjunction: "Eyther thu art a ryth good woman er ellys a ryth wikked woman" (I.47; *BMK,* p. 113; B-B, p. 100). Later, as events in Leicester build to a hearing on heresy charges before the abbot and dean, Margery struggles to articulate her understanding of the embracing consciousness enjoined on her as her proper spirituality. Confessing herself, on the one hand, "bowndyn" to the husband by whom she was "born xiiij childryn," she asserts, on the other, that "there is no man in this worlde that I lofe so mech as God, for I lofe hym a-bovyn al thyng." She then phrases the inclusiveness of her feeling in her state of dual spousal in this way: "Ser, I telle yow trewly I lofe al men in God & for God." The only response she records from Leicester officialdom to all this comes from a man who frankly sees her example as a threat to the social order: "I will wetyn why thow gost in white clothys, for I trow thou art comyn hedyr to han a-wey owr wyvys fro us & ledyn hem wyth the" (I.48; *BMK,* pp. 115, 116; B-B, pp. 102, 103).

The pattern of incomprehension and recoil that unfolds in such detail at Leicester continues at York. There Margery, clad in white, circulates like a preaching friar among the people, reprehending vice in folk fables—for example, that of the bear and the flowering pear tree—which she herself devises (I.50, 52). Although she is branded a "wolf" in her white wool clothing and warned by the archbishop not to "techyn ne chalengyn the pepil in my diocyse" any longer, she refuses to swear an oath to this effect; for, she says, Christ in the Gospel gave women warrant to witness of Him (*BMK*, pp. 120, 125–126; B-B, pp. 107, 113). At Beverley, questions about Margery's identity predominate. First she is accused of being Lord Cobham's daughter and a member of an outlawed communications ring (I.53); later she is taken for the woman who counseled Lady Greystoke, John of Gaunt's granddaughter, to forsake her husband (I.54). Finally, the disruptive force that she is perceived as being finds recognition even in the friendly advice given to Margery by countrymen of the Beverley region: "Forsake this lyfe that thu hast, & go spynne & carde as other women don, & suffyr not so mech schame & so meche wo" (*BMK*, p. 129; B-B, p. 117).

Throughout the narrative of her experiences at Leicester, York, and Beverley, Margery's mounting confidence regarding her spirituality, selfhood, and authorship takes shape in a distinct but complex design. To some extent the sequence reads typologically, for it utilizes the familiar conventions of female and male saints' lives: it develops Margery's identity through identification with her Lord, a prophet without honor in his own country (Matthew 13:57; Mark 6:4; John 4:44) who was repeatedly called to account by the civil and religious authorities of his time.[11] Nevertheless, the dominant overlay in the design of the narrative sequences of Margery's *Book* remains circumstantial, experiential, autobiographical. We are repeatedly reminded that the selfhood and the spirituality in question are a woman's, and that it is she, rather than a third party, who stands to vouch to the authorities for what she has learned about divine love: its embrace transcends all human compartmentalizations. Thus, a deep thematic resonance emits from the narrative resolution (I.55) in which Margery finally obtains permission to dress in public as a bride of God after her husband has accompanied her to Lambeth palace and made appeal with her to the archbishop of Canterbury.

Just how constitutive this autobiographical design is in the composition of *The Book of Margery Kempe* can be traced likewise in the shaping of the materials of its second book, a comparatively brief addition made in 1436, at a four-year remove from the original account. Margery may have been motivated to resume her life story by a revelation from her Lord that her authorial efforts pleased Him (I.89). In the second book the aging Margery continues to learn how she is to accommodate her human involvements as a mother and mother-in-law to her Lord's spiritual imperatives.

Since the issue of her selfhood is cast once again as a quest fraught with opposition and misgivings, it is a noteworthy advance that "this creatur" is able, for the first and only time in her *Book,* to make a full reference to herself as "Mar. Kempe of Lynne" (II.9) in a context where she is being maligned and misreported. From start to finish, we find her tirelessly absorbed in what she conceives as setting the record straight about herself.[12]

Beyond its function as a catalyst in the narrative, Margery's apprehension of specific imperatives of divine love for her as a female contributes vitally to the emotional and thematic substance of her story. This apprehension has a continuing referent in the mode of behavior enjoined upon Margery when she acts the role of Our Lady's maidservant in her revelations; the mode is summed up in the set phraseology of the word-pairs *mekenes & pacyens, mekely & paciently.*[13] Although these wordpairs are reserved for the characterization of Margery's role as maidservant, they obviously have no exclusive bearing on female comportment. Another phrase, however, develops more and more exclusively female associations as Margery learns through conversations with her Lord that divine love must manifest itself in her life by familiarity, intimacy, openness of the self to an other, especially in acts of tendance and nurture. The locution for such love in Margery's *Book* is one shared with Julian's *Showings:* "to be homely."[14] But in Margery's *Book,* unlike Julian's *Showings,* the homeliness of divine love becomes a direct function of mystical spousal. Her Lord tells Margery: "For it is convenyent the wyf to be homly wyth hir husbond. . . . Ryght so mot it be twyx the & me, for I take non hede what thu woldist be. . . . Therefore most I nedys be homly wyth the." In turn and equally, the homeliness of divine love, ranging through the reaches of the husband-wife relationship, is to activate simultaneously in Margery the entire spectrum of female responses and roles. Thus her Lord exhorts her:

> "Take me to the as for thi weddyd husbond, thy derworthy
> derlyng, & as for thy swete sone, for I wyl be lovyd as a sone
> schuld be lovyd wyth the modyr & wil that thu love me, dowtyr, as
> a good wife owyth to love hir husbonde" (I.36; *BMK,* p. 90; B-B,
> p. 77).

Such exhortations embolden Margery, in a remarkable continuation of this passage, to invite the reader's reflection on all the reasons a woman might have to open her arms or to share her bed with another in the course of her experience. By these homely images of her own, she evokes the manifold responsiveness that divine love demands of her soul.

As Margery progresses on the contemplative plane, she finds herself able to empathize equally with the love felt for Jesus by his mother Mary, by the passionately devoted Mary Magdalene, and by the bereaved disciples—all personages with whom she has vivid and prolonged visionary contact. What is more, she learns to integrate her visions with her experiences in the world, at first simply as an observer who has as ready a devotional response to mothers with their boy babies, or to seemly youths, or to a beating in the street as she has to a consecrated Host, images of Our Lady and Christ, or the sacred places of Jerusalem.[15] But a still more significant stage in Margery's maturing sense of self as loving and beloved of God involves putting her tenderheartedness to the test in day-to-day conduct. A priest in Rome inducts her in this vein by assigning her, as a penance, the care of a destitute old woman for six weeks (I.34); immediately thereafter, she is brought to recognize her creaturehood as wedded to the Godhead of the Father, and His will and purposes, not simply engrossed in love and affection for the Manhood of Christ (I.35). The consequent redirecting of Margery's energies into difficult and even repellent tasks becomes a measure of her growth in understanding and responding to the absoluteness of divine love. The measure is at its fullest late in Book I, where a series of chapters carries the ramifications of spirituality and selfhood to the greatest experiential extremities and autobiographical insights in Margery's *Book*.

Margery describes her ministrations to various sick persons in Lynn, particularly the affectionate care that she—like Marie d'Oignies—gave to street lepers whom others reviled and refused to touch, as she, too, formerly had done (I.72, 74, 75). Then, by one of the associative, loosely temporal transitions so characteristic of her *Book*,[16] Margery proceeds to relate the most taxing but finally illuminating imperative laid upon her by divine love: her six years spent in nursing her senile, incontinent husband after a near-fatal fall (I.76). With extraordinary candor she rehearses her Lord's injunction—"I bydde the take hym hom & kepe hym for my lofe"—and her objection to doing what she considered a severe hindrance to her mystical spousal. "Nay, good Lord," Margery rejoins, "for l xal then nat tendyn to the as I do now." But her Lord insists that she fix her thoughts on the all-embracingness of spirituality, which is her peculiar lesson and the overarching theme of her *Book*:

> "Yis, dowtyr," seyd owr Lord, "thu xalt have as meche mede for to
> kepyn hym & helpyn hym in hys nede at hom as yf thu were in
> chirche to makyn thi preyerys. And thu has seyd many tymes that
> thu woldist fawyn kepyn me. I prey the now, kepe hym for the lofe
> of me, for he hath sumtyme fulfillyd thi wil & my wil bothe, and
> he hath mad thi body fre to me that thu xuldist servyn me & levyn
> chast & clene, and therefor I wil that thu be fre to helpyn hym at
> hys nede in my name" (*BMK*, p. 180; B-B, p. 165).

In the event, as she describes it, Margery draws heavily upon the range of female roles she has acted in life to persevere in caring for her husband. Her candor and authorial self-consciousness come to the fore again in her remarkable admission that, only by making herself remember the "many delectabyl thowtys, fleshly lustys, & inordinat lovys to hys persone" that she had entertained "in hir yong age," could she steel herself to the endless washing and wringing entailed when John "in hys last days . . . turnyd childisch a-gen" and "as a childe voydyd his natural digestyon in hys lynyn clothys ther he sat, be the fyre er at the tabil, whethyr it wer, he wolde sparyn no place" (*BMK*, p. 181; B-B, pp. 165–166). Clearly, the implicit typology of this episode derives from the parable in Matthew 25:31–46; its moral is that any ministering done to the least of one's fellow human beings is done to Christ. And yet this moral translates literally in Margery's life as a resumption of earlier diapering and laundering to keep pace with John's lapse into second childhood. But the at-once-enjoined and voluntary character of the resumption makes all the difference: Margery undertakes it on her Lord's assurance that such service will not separate her from her devotion to Him; rather, it will confirm her devotion all the more.

The third from last chapter (I.86) in the original ending of Margery's *Book* is particularly conclusive for understanding the meaning and purpose of her life as she presents them. Here her Lord emphasizes that she did not repudiate her earlier sexual and social roles through mystical spousal, but, instead, was granted a means to their more encompassing exercise. He interprets the pattern of her marital experience for her as follows:

> "Dowtyr, yf thu knew how many wifys ther arn in this worlde that
> wolde lovyn me & servyn me ryth wel & dewly, yf thei myght be as
> frely fro her husbondys as thu art fro thyn, thu woldist seyn that
> thu wer rygth meche beheldyn on-to me. . . . And for the gret
> homlynes that I schewe to the . . . thu art mekyl the boldar to
> askyn me grace for thi-self, for thin husbond, & for thi childryn, &
> thu makyst every Christen man & woman thi childe in thi sowle for
> the tyme & woldist han as meche grace for hem as for thin owyn
> childeryn" (*BMK*, p. 212; B-B, p. 192).

In reporting her Lord's words thus, Margery signals the fulfillment of her spirituality and selfhood through an expansion of her wifely and maternal concerns to encompass all the souls of Christendom in homely love. Such a transvaluation of the sexual and social roles into which she was born made an autobiographer of her as well, for she resolved that the implications she perceived in her experience should be preserved in the *Book* that keeps alive for us her name and her story.

## NOTES

1. Margery's reflections on her authorial role, both on her inward sense (shared with Julian of Norwich) that she should await understanding before recording her experience and on the time and effort that authorship took away from her life of devotion, are to be found in the latter part of the preface and in Book I, chapters 87 and 88. See *The Book of Margery Kempe,* ed. Sanford B. Meech, with annotation by Hope Emily Allen, EETS orig. ser. 212 (London: Humphrey Milford, 1940), pp. 3–6, 214–16, 219–20; cited hereafter as *BMK.* For discussion of aspects of the cooperative process by which Margery's *Book* came into being, see M. C. Seymour, "A Fifteenth-Century East Anglian Scribe," *Medium Aevum* 37 (1968), 166–73; and John C. Hirsh, "Author and Scribe in *The Book of Margery Kempe,*" *Medium Aevum* 44 (1975), 145–50.

2. See, in the former connection, H. S. Bennett's essay on Margery in *Six Medieval Men and Women* (Cambridge, Eng.: Cambridge Univ. Press, 1955), pp. 124–50; and Joseph Crawford, "Independent Women in a Medieval World," *Spritual Life* 20 (1973), 199–203. In the latter connection, see especially Shozo Shibath, "Notes on the Vocabulary of *The Book of Margery Kempe,*" in *Studies in English Grammar and Linguistics: A Miscellany in Honor of Takanobu Otsuka,* ed. Kazao Araki (Tokyo: Kenkysha, 1958), pp. 209–20; Alfred Reszkiewicz, *Main Sentence Elements in The Book of Margery Kempe: A Study in Major Syntax* (Wroclaw-Warszawa-Krakow, 1962); and Robert Karl Stone, *Middle English Prose Style: Margery Kempe and Julian of Norwich* (The Hague: Mouton, 1970). For listings of other studies, see the "Margery Kempe" section in *A Bibliographical Index of Five English Mystics,* comp. and ann. by Michael E. Sawyer (Pittsburgh: The Clifford E. Barbour Library of Pittsburgh Theological Seminary, 1978), pp. 97–103.

3. See *BMK,* I, chapters 17, 58, 62. For discussions of Margery's spirituality, see W. A. Pantin, *The English Church in the Fourteenth Century* (Cambridge, Eng.: Cambridge Univ. Press, 1955), pp. 256–63; Edmund Colledge, "Margery Kempe," in *Pre-Reformation English Spirituality,* ed. James Walsh (New York: Fordham Univ. Press, 1965), pp. 210–23; and George W. Tuma, *The Fourteenth-Century English Mystics: A Comparative Analysis,* Elizabethan and and Renaissance Studies nos. 61, 62 (Salzburg: Institut für englische Sprache und Literatur, 1977). On the emergence of the affective tradition of devotion to the Sacred Manhood and Passion of Christ, see Dom André Wilmart, *Auteurs spirituels et textes dévots du moyen age latin: Etudes d'histoire littéraire* (Paris: Bloud et Gay, 1932; rpt. Etudes augustiniennes, 1971), pp. 62–63, 127–37, 476–82; and Elizabeth Salter, *Nicholas Love's "Myrrour of the Blessed Lyf of Jesu Christ,"* Analecta Cartusiana no. 10 (Salzburg: IESL, 1974), pp. 119–78.

4. *BMK,* p. 153. In quoting, I have substituted *th* for the 'thorn' letter and *v* and *j* for consonantal *u* and *i,* respectively. For the convenience of those wishing to consult the modernized transcript made by the owner of the unique manuscript, I include correlated page references to W. Butler-Bowdon, *The Book of Margery Kempe: A Modern Version* (New York: The Devin-Adair Co., 1944), p. 140; hereafter cited as B-B.

5. The present state of contextual knowledge does not permit a definitive pronouncement on the extent to which Margery's spirituality manifested itself in a distinctive set of features, although her dual spousal—to God and to John Kempe concurrently—now appears distinctive, the more so in an Englishwoman. The closest analogues, all partial, are continental. For relevant discussion of the increased activity and self-assertion of women in late medieval religious life, see Richard W. Southern, *Western Society and the Church in the Middle Ages* (Harmondsworth: Penguin, 1970), pp. 318–31; Brenda M. Bolton, *"Mulieres Sanctae,"* in Derek Baker, ed., *Sanctity and Society: The Church and the World,* Studies in Church History no. 10 (Oxford: Basil Blackwell, 1973), pp. 77–95; Bolton, "Vitae Matrum: A Further Aspect of the *Frauenfrage,*" in *Medieval Women: Essays Presented to Professor Rosalind M. T. Hill,* ed. Derek Baker, Studies in Church History, Subsidia no. 1 (Oxford: Basil

Blackwell, 1978), pp. 253–74; and Caroline W. Bynum, *Jesus as Mother* (Berkeley and Los Angeles: Univ. of California Press, 1981), pp. 170–262.

6. The identifiably female cast of *The Book of Margery Kempe* has been discussed generally but very suggestively in a four-way comparative study by Mary G. Mason, "The Other Voice: Autobiographies of Women Writers," in *Autobiography: Essays Theoretical and Critical*, ed. James Olney (Princeton: Princeton Univ. Press, 1980), pp. 207–35; esp. pp. 211, 217–21, 231. Mason's other texts are Julian of Norwich's *Showings of Divine Love* (ca. 1393); *A True Relation of My Birth, Breeding, and Life* (1656) by Margaret Cavendish, Duchess of Newcastle; and Anne Bradstreet's "To My Dear Children" (1657).

7. In an unpublished essay on the spirituality of Julian of Norwich and Margery Kempe, Susan Dickman sensitively explores the experiential logic of the "perceived incompatibility between sexuality and spirituality" (pp. 30–32), as this issue is focused at the outset of Margery's *Book*. For a less sympathetic view of Margery's spirituality as a means of resisting and evading the conditions of marriage, see Anthony Goodman, "The Piety of John Brunham's Daughter, of Lynn," in *Medieval Women*, ed. Baker, pp. 252–53.

8. See Elise Boulding, *The Underside of History: A View of Women through Time* (Boulder, Colo.: Westview Press, 1976), pp. 32–33, 146–47, 170, on the persistence of "women's tendency not to specialize" but, instead, to play a wide gamut of roles in culture.

9. Valuable sidelights on clothing as an adjunct of sexual identity are offered in Sandra M. Gilbert's "Costumes of the Mind: Transvestism as Metaphor in Modern Literature," *Critical Inquiry* 7 (Winter 1980), 391–417.

10. See, for example, the specifications regarding apparel in *A Booke of Precedence of all Estates and playcinge to ther Degrees*, ed. Frederick J. Furnivall, EETS ext. ser. 8 (London: N. Trübner and Co., 1862). Relevant period studies include Frances E. Baldwin, *Sumptuary Legislation and Personal Regulation in England* (Baltimore: Johns Hopkins Univ. Press, 1926), esp. pp. 73–95 on Lancastrian England; and Françoise Piponnier, *Costume et vie sociale: la cour d'Anjou (XIVe–XVe siècle)* (The Hague and Paris: Mouton, 1970), esp. pp. 261–88 on the class nuances of female dress.

11. Susan Dickman (p. 43) further proposes to treat the thematic prominence of the world's spite in Margery's *Book* as reflecting the characterization *sint minores et subditit omnibus* that continued to inform Franciscan *imitatio Christi* in the later Middle Ages.

12. As an appreciable body of theory and criticism dealing with first-person writing continues to make clear, there is never an equation to be drawn between an author as an actual historical person and the "I" of that author's text, even—or especially—when the text insists on just such an equation. Relevant bibliographical references are too numerous to compile; suggestive leads in interpreting texts like Margery's *Book* can be found in Joan Webber's *The Eloquent 'I': Style and Self in Seventeenth-Century Prose* (Madison: Univ. of Wisconsin Press, 1968) and in the essays in Olney's collection, cited n. 6 above.

13. E.g., I.68, 69, 74 (*BMK*, pp. 165, 166, 177; B-B, pp. 152, 153, 162). For other listings of wordpairs and discussion of this stylistic staple, see Stone, *Middle English Prose Style*, pp. 121–33.

14. See I.31, 36, 86 (*BMK*, pp. 79, 90–91, 210; B-B, pp. 67, 77, 192). Cf. Dickman (p. 37): "Where Julian means the phrase to describe a kind of physical intimacy equally manifest in Christ's assumption of humanity in the Incarnation, in the suffering of the Passion, and in his willing to 'show' himself to a 'creature living in sinful flesh,' in Margery's *Book* the homeliness of divine love is most often manifest in a kind of domestic intimacy."

15. See, in this connection, I.29, 30, 35, 39, 57, 60, 72, 78, 82, and 83.

16. See, in this regard, the beginnings of chapters 21 and 25 in Book I and the endings of chapters 36, 67, and 85 in Book I. Mason, "The Other Voice," pp. 210–12, notes that a flexible, highly psychologized handling of temporal sequence recurs in female autobiography.

*✒*

# To Restore Honor and Fortune: "The Autobiography of Leonor López de Córdoba"

## *Amy Katz Kaminsky*
## *Elaine Dorough Johnson*

In the aftermath of the fourteenth-century fratricidal war in which Enrique de Trastámara killed and replaced his half-brother Pedro I as King of Castile, eight-year-old Leonor López de Córdoba, daughter of one of Don Pedro's most loyal knights, was imprisoned along with many of her family in the Arsenal of Seville. Doña Leonor narrates the salient events of her nine-year imprisonment and her struggle to recover her station and wealth after Don Enrique's death and her consequent release, in a document that is Spain's first autobiography and that country's first work by a known woman writer. She dictated it sometime after 1412 when she found herself and her family once again out of royal favor.

Reinaldo Ayerbe-Chaux, who published a scholarly edition of the autobiography in 1977, was one of the first to recognize Doña Leonor's narrative as a literary text intended to vindicate the writer and her family, and not merely a useful historical source for sorting out the events of the war between Don Pedro and Don Enrique.[1] It is his version of the autobiography that we have translated, altering punctuation and establishing paragraphs to facilitate reading. Doña Leonor's text in this edition consists of a series of utterances in colloquial language connected by *ands*, commas, and semicolons. The chronology of the narration is broken by frequent shifts into the past, and there are hiatuses of years at a time in the action. However, Doña Leonor's autobiography is structured around three key events—the deaths of her father, her brother, and her son—which are designed to elicit her readers' sympathy and their acknowledgment of the courage, loyalty, honor, and piety she claims for herself and her family. To this end, each of her dying kinsmen is given a final speech. Don Martín, her father, reiterates his fidelity to his king, preferring to die loyal than to live as a traitor;

Don Lope, her thirteen-year-old brother, dying of the plague in the Seville Arsenal, begs to have his chains removed that he might die as a nobleman and not as a slave; and her twelve-year-old son, Juan, also a plague victim, pitifully asks that he not be cast out of his cousin's house as he is dying. Filling the space between these deaths is the elaboration of the two criteria on which the speaking subject builds her claim to honor and exoneration: her noble heritage and her piety. The first half of the text contains an exhaustive catalogue of her lineage, that of her husband's, and of their worldly goods. The second half is an account of her devotion to the Virgin manifested in prayer and charitable acts.

Another underlying structure is the repeated pattern of a warranted rise to greatness, followed by an undeserved fall from favor. Two of these trajectories are expressly charted in the autobiography; a third seems to have precipitated the work's composition. The "I" suggests that her father's station was a result of noble blood and hard work. As the son of a woman who had a brother, Don Martín could not inherit land and titles from the better-connected side of his family; he was, rather, rewarded by King Pedro I for his loyal service. It was a change in monarchs and the treachery of the new sovereign that brought him and his family down. Years later, after she had been freed from prison, Doña Leonor gains the love and support of her aunt and lives in her well-rewarded service for some twenty-one years before her son's death gives her cousins an excuse to drive her away. In the text, this rise and fall is replicated on the religious plane. The Virgin rewards the protagonist's prayers and piety through the generosity of the aunt, but this favor is unexpectedly withdrawn during the plague of 1400–1401 when her son is stricken and dies.

Although Leonor López de Córdoba ends the account with her expulsion from her aunt's house and consequent return to Córdoba, the work was written at least twelve years later, in response to a final fall from grace. During this period she had apparently become the trusted counselor of the Queen Regent of Spain, Catalina de Lancaster, granddaughter of Pedro I, since the *Chronicles of the Kings of Spain* say, rather disapprovingly, that no decision was made at Court without her consent.[2] The royal historian also accuses Doña Leonor of causing discord between the queen and Prince Fernando, Catalina's co-regent and brother-in-law. It is a testament to Doña Leonor's talent for politics, however, that the *Chronicles* record she was saved by this very prince in 1412, when Queen Catalina threatened to burn her alive.[3] As Ayerbe points out, Doña Leonor's falling into disfavor with the queen echoes her estrangement from her aunt.[4] And yet, an equally crucial parallel can be found between Doña Leonor's years at court and her father's career: both knew how to serve a monarch to their own best interests, both risked intrigue, both were highly successful for a time, and both ended badly.

Doña Leonor's autobiography is firmly set within the patriarchal institutions of state, church, and family. During the prison portion of the narrative, she concentrates on her father, brother, and husband and mentions her sisters only in passing, dwelling instead on her brothers-in-law, whose noble blood and great wealth are another testament to her own family's distinction. On the other hand, once she is released from prison, the men in Doña Leonor's family cease to be central to her account. Thus, after her husband loses all his possessions, his importance to her is diminished, and as a consequence, he virtually disappears from the text.[5] It is now her matrifocal family that provides the material support necessary for survival and that ultimately can best serve to establish Doña Leonor's credentials for vindication. Indeed, until she left the queen's service (c. 1412), Leonor López de Córdoba lived in what was essentially a gynocracy. For several years after the release from the Seville Arsenal, according to her autobiography, she resided in the convent founded by her maternal grandparents in which her mother had been raised. More critically, both of her principal protectors were women, as were her principal rivals for their favors. In the case of her aunt, the rivals were female cousins; and according to Ayerbe, it was another lady-in-waiting who ultimately turned Queen Catalina against Doña Leonor.[6] As the role of her aunt's servants in the narrative indicates, even the minor players in these domains ruled by women tended to be women.

The autobiography of Leonor López de Córdoba highlights the considerable autonomy of Spanish noblewomen of the fourteenth century. Doña Leonor herself held title to property and her aunt was free to provide her niece with enough money to buy land and build houses. Although she spoke figuratively when she said she built those houses with her own hands, she did construct, with the substantial material privileges she managed to enlist in her causes, the forceful self and the dramatic life that we know as the autobiography of Doña Leonor López de Córdoba.

## NOTES

1. Reinaldo Ayerbe-Chaux, "Las memorias de doña Leonor López de Córdoba," *Journal of Hispanic Philology*, 2 (1977), 11–33.

2. *Crónicas de los Reyes de Castilla*, Biblioteca de Autores Españoles 68, Cayetano Rosell ed. (Madrid: Real Academia Española, 1953), p. 278.

3. *Crónicas de los Reyes de Castilla*, p. 344.

4. Ayerbe-Chaux, p. 31. It is curious, though not really surprising, that the last we hear of Doña Leonor, in both the *Chronicles of the Kings of Castile* and in her own autobiography, is her retreat to the houses her aunt built for her in Córdoba.

5. As is typical of autobiographical writing, this "omission" has nothing to do with reality, since her husband must have been present long enough to father several children. Although Doña Leonor invokes the name of her brother Alvaro, who was beatified before the chronological account begins, the friar plays no role in the autobiography. Friar Alvaro was

Queen Catalina's confessor, but his sister was apparently considered the more important figure at court, since his dismissal is chronicled as a mere by-product of her banishment. *Crónicas de los Reyes de Castilla*, p. 344.

6. Ayerbe-Chaux, p. 31.

St. Alvaro was born in          King Don Enrique II
Cordoba, year of 1360           died, year 1379
King Don Pedro died year of 1369

## Written Document

In the name of God the Father and of the Son and of the Holy Ghost, three persons, and one single God true in trinity, to which glory be given, to the Father and to the Son and to the Holy Ghost, thus as it was in the beginning, so it is now, and for ever and ever, amen. In the name of which above mentioned Lord and of the Holy Virgin Mary his mother, and lady and advocate of sinners, and to the honor and exaltation of all the angels and saints in the Court of Heaven amen.

Therefore, know all who see this document, how I, Doña Leonor López de Córdoba, daughter of my Lord Grand Master Don Martín López de Córdoba and Doña Sancha Carrillo, to whom God grant glory and heaven, swear by this sign † which I worship, that all that is written here is true for I saw it and it happened to me, and I write it to the honor and glory of my Lord Jesus Christ, and of the Holy Virgin Mary his mother who bore him so that all creatures who suffered might be certain that I believe in her mercy, that if they commend themselves from the heart to the Holy Virgin Mary she will console and succor them as she consoled me. And so that whoever might hear it know the tale of my deeds and miracles that the Holy Virgin Mary showed me, it is my intention that it be left as a record. I ordered it written as you see before you. I am the daughter of the aforesaid Grand Master of Calatrava, in the time of Lord King Don Pedro, who bestowed the honor of giving him the Commandery of Alcantara, which is in the city of Seville. And then he made him Grand Master of Alcantara, and at last of Calatrava, and that Grand Master my father was a descendant of the House of Aguilar and nephew of Don Juan Manuel, son of a niece of his, a daughter with a brother. And he rose to very high rank, as can be found in the *Chronicles of Spain*.

As I have said, I am the daugher of Doña Sancha Carrillo, niece and maid of the most illustriously remembered Lord King Don Alfonso (whom God grant Holy paradise), father of the aforementioned Lord King Don Pedro. My mother died very young, and so my father married me at the age of seven years to Ruy Gutiérrez de Henestrosa, son of Juan Ferrández de Henestrosa, High Chamberlain of Lord King Don Pedro and his High Chancellor of the Secret Seal, and High Steward of Queen Doña Blanca his wife, who married Doña María de Haro, Lady of Haro and los Cameros. My husband inherited many goods from his father and many offices. And his men on horseback numbered three hundred, and forty skeins of pearls as fat as chickpeas, and five hundred Moors, men and women, and two thousand marks of silver in tableware, and the jewels and gems of his household you could not write down on two sheets of paper. And his father and his mother left all this to him because they had no other son or heir. To me, my father gave twenty thousand gold coins upon marriage. And my husband and I resided in Carmona with the daughters of Lord King Don Pedro, and my brothers-in-law, husbands of my sisters, and a brother of mine whose name was Don Lope López de Córdoba Carrillo. My brothers-in-law were named Fernán Rodríguez de Aza, Lord of Aza and Villalobos, and the other Ruy García de Aza, the other Lope Rodríguez de Aza, who were sons of Alvaro Rodríguez de Aza, and of Doña Constanza de Villalobos.

And thus it was, that when Lord King Don Pedro was surrounded in the Castle of Montiel by his brother Lord King Don Enrique, my father went down to Andalusia to bring people to help him, and on the road back discovered that Don Pedro was dead at the hands of his brother. Seeing this misfortune he took the road for Carmona where the lady princesses, daughters of Lord King Don Pedro were, and very close relatives of my husband and mine by my mother. And Lord King Don Enrique seeing himself King of Castile came to Seville and put a blockade around Carmona, and as it was such a strong town, it was blockaded for many months. My father having chanced to leave there, and the people of Real del Rey learning that he had left that town and that there would no longer be such good protection there, twelve knights offered to climb into the town but were captured after scaling the wall. And then my father, advised of that deed, came and ordered their heads cut off for their effrontery. And Lord King Don Enrique, seeing that he could not enter there to get satisfaction for this act by force of arms, sent the High Constable of Castile to negotiate with my father. My father discussed two terms, the first that the lady princesses had to be set free in England with their treasures before he gave the town over to the king. And so it was done, for which reason he sent some illustrious gentlemen, kinsmen of his, born in Córdoba, to accompany them and the other people he deemed necessary. The other term was that he and his children and defenders, and those who had been present in that town by his order be pardoned by the King, and that they and their estates be considered loyal. Thus, it was granted him, signed by the above mentioned High Constable in the name of the King. And by this agreement he gave the town over to the Constable in the King's name. And from there he, his family, and the rest of his people went to kiss the hand of the King. But the Lord King Don Enrique ordered them taken prisoner and put in the Arsenal of Seville. And the previously mentioned Constable, seeing that Lord King Don Enrique had not kept his word, which he had given in his name to the aforementioned Grand Master, left his court and never again returned. The Lord King ordered that they cut off my father's head in the Plaza de San Francisco in Seville, and that his property be confiscated, and that of his son-in-law, defenders, and servants. Going there to be beheaded, he met Mosén Beltrán de Clequin, the French knight trusted by King Don Pedro whom the King set free during the siege of Montiel; and not keeping his promise, Clequin handed him over to King Don Enrique instead so that he could kill him. And when he encountered the Grand Master he said to him: "Lord Grand Master did I not tell you that your exploits would end this way?" And my father answered him: "It is better to die loyal, as I have done, than to live as you have lived, a traitor."

The rest of us were kept prisoner for nine years until Lord King Enrique died. Our husbands had sixty pounds of iron each on their feet, and my brother Don Lope López had a chain on top of the irons, in which there were seventy links. He was a child of thirteen years, the most beautiful creature there was in the world. And they singled out my husband to be put in the hunger tank, where they held him for six or seven days without food or drink because he was a cousin of the lady princesses, daughters of Lord King Don Pedro. At this juncture a plague came, and my two brothers, my brother-in-law, and thirteen knights of the house of my father all died. And Sancho Míñez de Villendra, his high Chamberlain, said to me and to my brothers and sisters: "My lord's children: Pray God that I live, for if I do, you will never die poor." But it pleased God that he died three days later without speaking. And they took them all out to the ironsmith's like slaves to remove their irons. After they were dead my sad little brother Don Lope López asked the jailer who held us to tell Gonzalo Ruiz Bolante to do us a great kindness and a great honor for the love of God: "Sir jailer be so kind as to strike these irons from me before my soul departs, and do not let them take me out to the ironsmith's." He answered him as if he were speaking to a slave: "If it were up to me I would do it," and at that moment his soul departed in my hands. He was but one year older than I, and they took him out on a plank to the ironsmith's like a slave, and they buried him with my brothers and with my sisters, and with my brothers-in-law in San Francisco of Seville. My five brothers-in-law each wore chains of gold on their necks, for they had put on those necklaces at Santa María de Guadalupe and promised not to take them off, until all five might remove them at Santa María. But for their sins one died in Seville, another in Lisbon, another in England, and so they scattered, having willed they should be buried with their gold necklaces. But the friars greedily took his necklace off him after he was buried.* And no one from my lord the Grand Master's house remained in the Seville Arsenal but my husband and me.

Then the very eminent and very honorable, most illustriously and saintedly remembered Lord King Don Enrique died, and he ordered in his will that they let us out of prison and return to us all that was ours. And I stayed at the home of my lady aunt María García Carrillo, and my husband went to reclaim his property and those who held it esteemed him little, because he had no rank nor means to claim it, and you well know how rights depend on the station you have on which to base a claim. And thus was my husband lost, and he wandered seven years through the world, a wretched man, and never did he find a relative or friend who did him a good turn or had pity on him. And at the end of seven years, they told my husband, who was in Badajoz with his uncle Lope Fernández de Padilla in the War of Portugal, that I was doing very well in the house of my lady and aunt Doña María García Carrillo, that my relatives had done me much kindness. He rode on his mule, which was worth very little money, and what he wore was not worth thirty *maravedís*. And he came through the doorway of my lady and aunt.

As I had known that my husband was wandering lost through the world, I consulted with my lady and aunt, sister of my lady and mother, whose name was Doña Teresa Fernández Carrillo (she was in the Order of Guadalajara, which my great grandparents founded and endowed with the money for forty rich females of their lineage to come into that order). I asked her to request that I please be admitted into that order, since, for my sins, my husband and I were undone. And she and the entire order were happy to do it, because my lady mother had been raised in those monasteries, and King Don

---

*This sentence reads "their necklaces" in other editions, but it seems likely that Doña Leonor is referring here to the one brother-in-law who died in Seville.

Pedro had taken her from there. And he had given her to my father to marry, because she was the sister of Gonzalo Díaz Carrillo, and of Diego Carrillo, sons of Don Juan Fernández Carrillo, and of Doña Sancha de Roxas. These uncles of mine were afraid of the aforementioned Lord Don Pedro, for he had killed and exiled many of this family, and he had brought down my grandfather's house and given what he had to another; so these uncles of mine went off to serve King Don Enrique (when he was count) because of this affront. And I was born in Calatayud in the house of the Lord King. His daughters, the lady princesses, were my godmothers, and they brought me with them to the castle in Segovia with my lady mother who died there, and I was of such an age that I never knew her.

After my husband came, as I have said, he went to the house of my lady aunt, which was in Córdoba next to San Hipólito, and she took me in with my husband there in some houses adjacent to hers. And seeing that we had so little peace, for thirty days I said a prayer to the Holy Virgin Mary of Bethlehem, praying every night on my knees three hundred Hail Marys, that she might put it into my lady aunt's mind to consent and open a doorway into her dwellings. And two days before I finished the prayer, I asked my aunt if she would allow me to open that passageway so that we would not have to walk through the street, among all the knights who were in Córdoba, to come and eat at her table. And her grace responded that she would be happy to do so, and I was greatly consoled. When on the following day I tried to open the passageway, maids of hers had turned her against me, so that she would not do it, and I was so disconsolate I lost my patience, and the one who had most set my lady aunt against me died in my hands, swallowing her tongue. And the next day, Saturday, only one day remaining of my thirty days of prayer, I dreamed that in passing by San Hipólito with the dawn bells ringing, I saw on the courtyard walls a very large and very high arch, and that I entered there and picked flowers from the mountainside, and I saw the vast Heavens. At this point I woke up and placed my hope in the Holy Virgin Mary that she would give me a house.

Then there was a raid on the Jewish quarter, and I took an orphan child who was there and had him baptized so that he might be instructed in the faith. And one day, walking back with my lady aunt from mass at San Hipólito, I saw the clerics of San Hipólito dividing up those courtyards where I dreamt the great arch was, and I begged my lady aunt Doña Mencía Carrillo that she be so kind as to buy that place for me, since I had been in her company for seventeen years. She bought them for me and gave them with the condition that a chaplaincy be laid upon the stipulated houses for the soul of

Lord King Don Alfonso, who built that church in the name of San Hipólito, because he was born on that day. These chaplains have another six or seven chaplaincies belonging to Don Gonzalo Fernández, husband of the said lady my aunt, and to their sons, the Marshall and Don Alfonso Fernández, Lord of Aguilar. This favor done, I raised my eyes to God and to the Virgin Mary, giving her thanks. And then there came a servant of the Grand Master, my lord and father, who lives with Martín Fernández, Castellan of los Donceles, who was there hearing mass; and I sent him a request with that servant that as a kinsman he give thanks to my lady aunt for the favor she had done for me. And he was very happy to do so, and did it graciously, saying to her that he received this favor as if it had been done for him personally.

The title having been given me, I cut open a door on the very site where I had seen the arch the Virgin showed me. And it disturbed the abbots that they should hand the lot over to me because I was of grand lineage and my sons would be great, and they were abbots and had no need of great knights near them. But I took it for a good sign, and told them I hoped in God it would be thus, and I came to an agreement with them so that I placed the door where I wanted it. I believe that for the charitable act I performed in raising that orphan in the faith of Jesus Christ, God helped me in giving me the beginning of a house. Before this time, I had gone barefoot in the wind and rain for thirty days to morning prayer to [the shrine of] María el Amortecida, which is in the order of San Pablo de Córdoba, and I prayed to her sixty-three times this prayer which is followed by sixty-six Hail Marys, in homage to the sixty-six years that she lived with bitterness in this world, that she might give me a house; and she gave me a house, and because of her mercy, houses better than I deserved. And the prayer begins: "Holy Mother Mary, great pain did you feel because of your son—you saw him tormented with his great suffering, and your heart came close to death. After his agony he gave you comfort, so intercede with my lady, for you know my pain." At this time, it pleased God that with the help of my lady aunt and of the labor of my hands I built in that courtyard two palaces and a garden and another two or three houses for the servants.

Then there came a very cruel pestilence, and my lady did not want to leave the city. I begged her for mercy to flee with my little children so that they would not die, and this did not please her, but she gave me permission, and I departed from Córdoba, and I went to Santaella with my children. The orphan I brought up lived in Santaella, and he gave me lodging in his house, and all the residents of the town were very happy with my going there, and received me very warmly because they had been servants of my lord and father. And thus they gave me the best house that there was in the place, which belonged to Fernando Alonso Mediabarba. My lady aunt arrived unexpectedly with her daughters, and I removed myself to a small apartment. And her daughters, my cousins, were never favorably disposed toward me because of the kindness their mother did me, and from then on I suffered so much bitterness that it cannot all be written down. And a pestilence came, and my lady departed with her people for Aguilar, and she took me with her, although her daughters thought that was doing too much, because she loved me greatly and had a high opinion of me. And I sent the orphan whom I had raised to Ecija.

The night we arrived in Aguilar the young man came in from Ecija with two tumors on his throat and three dark blotches on his face and a very high fever. Don Alfonso Fernandez, my cousin, was there, and his wife and all his household, and although all of them were my nieces and my friends, they came to me when they found out that my servant had come in that state. They said to me: "Your servant Alonso has come with pestilence, and if Don Alfonso Fernandez sees him, he will wreak havoc being in the presence of such an illness." You who hear this story can well understand the pain that came to my heart for I was angered and bitter. Thinking that such great suffering had entered the house on my account, I had a servant of the lord my father, the Grand Master, called, whose name was Miguel de Santaella, and I begged him to take that young man to his house, and the poor man became afraid and said: "My lady, how shall I take him sick with the pestilence, for it may kill me?" And I said to him: "Son, God shall not will it so." And he took him out of shame. And because of my sins, thirteen people, who kept vigil over him during the night, all died. And I offered a prayer that I had heard a nun say before a crucifix. It seems she was very devoted to Jesus Christ, and it is said that after she heard morning prayer, she came before the crucifix and prayed on her knees seven thousand times: "Merciful son of the Virgin, take pity." And one night the nun heard that the crucifix answered her and said: "You called me merciful and merciful I shall be." I placed great faith in these words and prayed this prayer every night, entreating God that he should want to free me and my children, and if any of them had to be taken away, it should be the older one for he was in great pain. And it was God's will that one night I could not find anyone to watch over that suffering young man, because all those who had watched over him up to then had died. And that son of mine whose name was Juan Fernández de Henestrosa, after his grandfather, and who was twelve years and four months of age, came to me and said: "My lady, is there no one who will watch over Alonso tonight?" And I said to him: "You watch over him for the love of God." And he answered me: "My lady, now that the others have died, do you want it to kill me?" And I said to him: "For the charitable act I am performing, God will take pity on me." And my son, so as not to disobey me, went to watch over him, and because of my sins, that night he came down with the plague and the next day I buried him. And the sick one survived, but all those stated above died. And Doña Teresa, wife of Don Alfonso Fernández my cousin, became very angry that my son was dying for that reason in her house, and with death in his mouth, she ordered him to be taken out. And I was so wrought with anguish that I could not speak for the shame that those noble people made me bear. And my sad little son said: "Tell my lady Doña Teresa that she not have me cast out, for my soul will soon depart for Heaven." And that night he died, and he was buried in Santa María la Coronada, which is in the town. But Doña Teresa had designs against me, and I did not know why. And she had ordered that he not be buried within the town, and thus, when they took him to be buried I went with him. And when I was going down the street with my son, the people, offended for me, came out shouting: "Come out good people and you will see the most unfortunate, forsaken and condemned woman in the world," with cries that rent the Heavens. Since the residents of that place were all liege and subject to my lord father, and although they knew it troubled their masters, they made great display of the grief they shared with me, as if I were their lady.

That night, as I came back from burying my son, they told me that I should go to Córdoba, and I approached my lady aunt to see if she would order me to do it. But she said to me: "Lady niece, I cannot fail to do so, as I have promised my daughter-in-law and my daughters who are of one mind; since they have pressed me to remove you from my presence, I have granted it to them. I do not know what vexation you have caused my daughter-in-law, Doña Teresa, that she feels such ill will toward you." And I said to her with many tears: "My lady, may God not save me if I deserved this." And thus I came to my houses in Córdoba.

# Artemisia Gentileschi: The Artist's Autograph in Letters and Paintings

## Mary D. Garrard

"And I will show Your Most Illustrious Lordship what a woman can do."
With these words, Artemisia Gentileschi ended a letter to her patron Don
Antonio Ruffo, in Sicily. She was writing on August 7, 1649, from Naples, the city that had been her home for nearly twenty years, to assure her
patron that a painting he had commissioned from her was nearly finished.
Ruffo's patronage, and that of other princes, both Italian and foreign,
sustained Gentileschi's professional identity as a painter on a level that
would be deemed successful for any artist, male or female. Yet, as the
passage quoted above may suggest, the fact that she was a woman working
in a man's world was never very far from her thoughts.

Artemisia Gentileschi is today widely regarded as the most creative and
most significant woman artist of the premodern era. Art historians have
long recognized her important position as one of the major Italian followers
of Caravaggio and his innovative dramatic realism. Yet it is only in the wake
of feminist scholarship that Gentileschi's art has begun to be examined from
the viewpoint of its singularly female expression.[1] Her letters, an important
supplement to her biography, tell us something about her exceptional experience as a woman artist and help to illuminate her art.

In many respects Gentileschi's life (1593-ca.1652) followed a typical pattern for a woman artist of the Renaissance-Baroque period. She was the
daughter of an artist, Orazio Gentileschi, who taught her painting. (Since
women were not permitted to obtain academic art training or to draw
from the nude male model, they often found informal access to the profession through a father or another family member.) In the seventeenth century women artists were fairly rare, and thus Gentileschi's reputation was
both enhanced and restricted by her curiosity value. Although she did not

enjoy the phenomenal international success of such sixteenth-century female painters as Sofonisba Anguissola or Lavinia Fontana—phenomenal largely because they were looked upon as phenomena—Artemisia did experience, and occasionally cultivated, an esteem based upon the slyly sexual *double-entendre* of "beauty" associated with both art and femininity. A French artist, for example, who made a drawing of Artemisia's own hand described it on the back of the sheet as a thousand times more beautiful than the hands of Aurora, a hand "that ravished the eyes of the most judicious connoisseur."[2]

In this spirit, collectors often valued portraits of women, and especially women artists, as objects of double beauty—of the picture and of the sitter. One of her patrons and correspondents, the learned Roman scholar Cassiano dal Pozzo, sought to obtain a self-portrait from her—a request he also made of other women artists—to add to his portrait collection of famous personalities.[3] Artemisia's *Self-Portrait as the Allegory of Painting* (Figure 6), probably painted in 1630, is likely to be identical with the work that she promised Cassiano in three letters written to him in 1630. The work appears not to have been delivered, however, since in 1637 (Letter 3, following), she again offered him her self-portrait. A decade later, Artemisia promised another self-portrait to Don Antonio Ruffo to put in his picture gallery in Messina "as all the other Princes do" (Letter 4).

Had Cassiano obtained the *Self-Portrait,* he would have owned a greater rarity than he might have expected. In this painting—which effectively introduces the artist's conception of herself at mid-career—she shrewdly fuses, as only a woman artist could do, two separate artistic traditions, the artist's self-portrait (usually male) and the personification of the art of painting (always female). Artemisia presents herself as deeply engaged in the act of painting, staring with intense concentration into the light that is her source of inspiration, oblivious of the medallion on a golden chain that hangs around her neck. This medallion, a traditional attribute of the allegory of painting, is one of the pictorial details that inform us that the artist and the allegory are one and the same. Yet unlike many male artists, among them Titian and Van Dyck, who proudly display as status symbols in their self-portraits the golden chains given them by their princely patrons, Artemisia appears to discount the material and worldly concerns associated with her medallion (which for the woman artist is a birthright, if we take the allegorical convention literally). Instead, she focuses her attention, seen in an intelligent and unidealized face, on the execution of her picture, as if to suggest that the worth of the art of painting comes not from association with princely favors, but from the simple business of the artist doing her work. It is a commentary on the inherent dignity of the art of painting, presented in terms of uncompromising naturalism.

The *Self-Portrait* bespeaks both intellectual sophistication and serene

6. Artemisia Gentileschi, *Self-Portrait as the Allegory of Painting*. London, Kensington Palace, Copyright Her Majesty, Queen Elizabeth II.

self-confidence, conveying the artist's proud and special participation in the masculine artistic world, and carrying that private statement to a level of allegorical truth. From the beginning, Artemisia's art displayed her ability to give a universal expression to a specifically female experience. Her earliest preserved painting, *Susanna and the Elders,* of 1610 (Figure 7), offers an unusual—and virtually unique—version of this theme of sexual coercion, which emphasizes the victim's anguished discomfort instead of the seducers' lascivious delight. Artemisia's interpretation may be related

7. Artemisia Gentileschi, *Susanna and the Elders*. Pommersfelden, Schloss Weissenstein, Collection of Dr. Karl von Schönborn (photo: owner).

to autobiographical facts. When she was eighteen years old, she was raped, or perhaps forcibly seduced, by one of her father's friends, the painter Agostino Tassi, whom Orazio had asked to teach Artemisia perspective, and who was a frequent visitor to the Gentileschi household in 1610. A trial ensued in 1612, instigated by Orazio, who was, under patriarchal law, the damaged party. Tassi was convicted and served a short jail term; Artemisia was married off hastily to a respectable Florentine. On the surface, the matter ends there: we hear no more about it and not a word on the subject appears in her correspondence. But in the 1610s and 1620s, Artemisia turned several times to a biblical theme that provided an avenue for the expression of psychic vindication: Judith slaying Holofernes. The Uffizi version of this theme (Figure 8) is the most violent of the lot—some call it gory—presenting the Israelite heroine and her maidservant in the act of sawing off the head of the drunken Assyrian general, as blood spurts everywhere. Even today, this picture, with its obvious castration metaphor, shocks viewers, male viewers in particular.

The latest of the existing *Judiths,* a work of the mid-1620s (Figure 9), is more restrained in expression and more heroic in conception. Judith looms large as the protagonist, larger almost than the claustrophobic tent in which the deed is executed. This heavy, powerful heroine, arrested by a sound in the darkness, her face thrown into dramatic irregular relief by the candlelight, is as grand and complex a female character as can be found in art. Nearly as forceful a participant in the event is the maidservant. In this and other versions of the Judith theme, Gentileschi distributes heroic identity—and in a sense, her own participation—equally between the two female characters, underlining the collaborative nature of the enterprise to convey a sense of solidarity and unity between women. This may have been an ideal fantasy on the artist's part, for such relationships are not a conspicuous part of her biography as we can reconstruct it. The only girl in a family of four sons (her mother died when she was twelve), Artemisia was the victim not only of the abuses of Agostino Tassi and his comrade Cosimo Quorli, but also of her own nurse, Tuzia, who is alleged to have betrayed Artemisia to Tassi (and who was described as Tassi's "procuress" by Artemisia during the trial). For most of her working life, the artist seems to have been both independent and alone.

The letters written by Artemisia Gentileschi that have been preserved,[4] scarcely more than two dozen in number, date from the latter part of her life (all but four were written after 1635), a period when her painting style was tamer and more conservative. Addressed for the most part to her patrons, the letters reveal the artist's growing self-confidence and steadily emerging business sense. In her first known letter (No. 1, following), the twenty-seven-year-old employee of the Florentine Grand Duke Cosimo II somewhat timidly informs him of a forthcoming trip to Rome. This pa-

8. Artemisia Gentileschi, *Judith Slaying Holofernes*. Florence, Galleria degli Uffizi (photo: Soprintendenza).

tron's heirs had to be reminded to pay her for the *Judith* she had painted for him (Figure 8), and Artemisia appealed for help in this matter to Galileo, who had lived in Florence under the grand duke's protection from 1609 until he was brought before the Inquisition after Cosimo's death in 1621. In a letter (No. 2) written in 1635 to the famous scientist, by then under house arrest in Arcetri, Artemisia reminds him of his earlier favor, and asks his help again in getting paid for two paintings she had sent to Cosimo's successor, Ferdinando II. Her claim to Galileo, that she had been lavishly patronized by the great rulers of Europe, is probably no

9. Artemisia Gentileschi, *Judith and Her Maidservant*. Detroit, Institute of Arts (photo: Museum).

exaggeration. King Charles I of England owned several of her works (including the *Self-Portrait*, Figure 6), and it was at his invitation that she went to England to work, joining her father there in 1639. Another of her paintings of the mid-1630s was commissioned by King Philip IV of Spain.

In striking contrast with the uncertainty of her early professional situation, the mature Artemisia's established business practice and assured handling of her patrons is conveyed in the letters to Don Antonio Ruffo, a correspondence that was initiated in 1648, when the artist was fifty-five years old. She insists upon getting the price she has set, and asks for a deposit as well. She has learned not to quote a price before a painting is finished, and she does not send drawings in advance. She manages her patrons skillfully, using and sometimes deflating the language of deference and flattery that was characteristic of the age. "Your Most Serene Highness calls a gift of generosity what is actually a tribute of my vassalage"; she wrote to Francesco I d'Este, another patron, in 1635, "you consider to be a gesture of affection and an act of courtesy that which is due Your Grandeur as a sign of obedience."

The glimpse of seventeenth-century artistic practice afforded by Artemisia's letters may seem surprisingly matter-of-fact to the modern reader. One wonders about the role of esthetic values in an artistic practice in which the price of a painting was based on the number of figures depicted (Letter No. 4). And yet this pragmatic fact reveals the continuation of the Italian Renaissance priority of the human figure and anatomical drawing over landscape, still life or other nonhuman elements. (Artemisia's introduction of landscape into her later pictures was in accord with the Baroque expansion of artistic genres.) Indeed, pictures produced under that figure-oriented system confirm indirectly how strongly pure esthetic considerations did count, since at 100 scudi per figure, it would be tempting to crowd the canvas. Artemisia's statement to Ruffo that she will produce a painting that will conform to "my taste and yours" (Letter No. 5) implies a sense of personal style, an awareness of stylistic choices, and a need to satisfy her own artistic standard as well as, or even before, pleasing the patron. Her insistence on standards runs through the letters. In another letter to Ruffo (July 24, 1649), she explains that a picture will not be ready as soon as he wants it: "I work as uninterruptedly and as fast as I can, but not to jeopardize the perfection of the painting."

Artemisia's letters tell us far more about a professional career than about a personal life. We find not a word of sentiment about her immediate family members; her two daughters—at least the expenses of their marriages—are mentioned only as professional hindrances. As for her husband, from whom she must have parted ways sometime before 1624, when she is listed in a Roman census as head of a household, Artemisia asks Cassiano dal Pozzo casually in a postscript if he can tell her whether he is alive or dead (Letter No. 3). On the other hand, she speaks more positively of friends in Rome, whom she plans or would like to visit. The personality that emerges from the letters is that of an independent woman, who never defined herself as wife and mother, but instead thought of herself as a professional artist whose orbit was the world of princes and dukes.

However, Artemisia Gentileschi's letters also contain signs of an ambivalent attitude toward herself as a woman artist in a masculine art world. She proceeds from an assumption that women are taken less seriously than men: "If I were a man, I cannot imagine it would turn out this way" (Letter No. 6). And yet, in a letter to Ruffo (March 13, 1649) she attempts to disarm her patron with playful self-deprecation, even as she asserts pride in her work, to remind him that, as an artist, she is an exception to her sex: "I shall not bore you any longer with such womanly. nonsense. But the works will speak for themselves." *I* am a mere woman, she seems to say, but my *works* partake of sex-blind universality. Moreover, since professional limitations have made it difficult for a woman to compete successfully with men, the handicap of being female becomes a spur to achievement and an ultimate source of self-esteem. "You will find the spirit of Caesar in this soul of a woman," Artemisia proclaims (Letter No. 5), her play on the words *animo* and *anima* underlining the gender difference that makes her claim distinctive.

But while the letters underline individual triumph over gender handicap, the paintings tell us something more. Within a vigorous painting style that is not susceptible to gender stereotyping, Artemisia conveys a generic identification with women, whose subterranean struggles against men's oppression are given lucid visual form. In Gentileschi's paintings, women are convincing protagonists and courageous heroes, perhaps for the first time in art. From the viewpoint of history, the creation of such characters showed "what a woman can do" in a spectacular manner—and in more ways than one.

## NOTES

1. Interpretations of Gentileschi's paintings presented here are drawn from my own articles ("Artemisia Gentileschi's Self-Portrait as the Allegory of Painting," *Art Bulletin*, LXII, 1 (March 1980), pp. 97–112; "Artemisia and Susanna," in M. D. Garrard and Norma Broude, eds., *Feminism and Art History: Questioning the Litany* (New York, 1982), pp. 147–72), and from the working manuscript of a book I have recently completed on the paintings of Artemisia Gentileschi. See also Eleanor Tufts, *Our Hidden Heritage: Five Centuries of Women Artists* (New York, 1974), Chapter 5; Ann Sutherland Harris, in A. S. Harris and Linda Nochlin, *Women Artists: 1550–1950* (Los Angeles and New York, 1976), pp. 118–24; and Germaine Greer, *The Obstacle Race: The Fortunes of Women Painters and Their Work* (New York, 1979), Chapter 10. Fundamental to Gentileschi studies also are Roberto Longhi, "Gentileschi padre e figlia," *L'Arte*, 1916, pp. 245–314; and R. Ward Bissell, "Artemisia Gentileschi, A New Documented Chronology," *Art Bulletin*, L, 2 (June 1968), pp. 153–67.

2. Pierre Rosenberg, "La main d'Artémise," *Paragone*, 261 (November 1971), pp. 69–70.

3. Cassiano's art collections, among the richest in Italy, included works by major international artists, of whom Nicholas Poussin is perhaps the most renowned.

4. For Italian texts of Artemisia Gentileschi's letters, see: Eva Menzio, ed., *Artemisia*

*Gentileschi/Agostino Tassi: Atti di un processo per stupro,* Milan, 1981, pp. 161–73 (Letters 1, 3–6); Giovanni Bottari and Stefano Ticozzi, *Raccolta di lettere sulla pittura, scultura ed architettura* (Milan, 1822), I, pp. 348ff. (Letters 1 and 3); Alessandro Vesme, "Nuovi Documenti," *Archivio Storico dell'Arte,* 2 (1889), pp. 423–25; Vincenzo Ruffo, "Galleria Ruffo nel secolo XVII in Messina con lettere di pittori ed altri documenti inediti," *Bollettino d'arte,* 1916, pp. 21ff. (Letters 4 through 6); *Le Opere di Galileo Galilei* (Florence, 1936), XVI, 318–19 (Letter 2); A. M. Crinò, "Due lettere autografe inedite di Orazio e Artemisia Gentileschi de' Lomi," *Rivista d'arte* 29 (1954), pp. 202–06; and A. M. Crinò, "More Letters from Orazio and Artemisia Gentileschi," *The Burlington Magazine,* 1960, pp. 264–65.

1. Letter to the Grand Duke Cosimo II de Medici, in Florence. Written in Florence, February 10, 1619 [1620].[1]

Most Serene Lord and My Most Honorable Master,

With this letter I wish to inform Your Most Serene Highness about the short trip to Rome that I have decided to take, so that it will not disturb you. The many minor illnesses that I have suffered as well as the many worries I have had with my home and family have prompted me to take this decision. So I shall spend a few months there with my friends to recover from my troubles. During that time and within two months at the most, I assure Your Most Serene Highness that you shall have what you ordered and for which I received an advance of fifty scudi.

While I pray to God for the happiness and good health of your Most Serene Highness, I bow to you most humbly, and I entrust myself to your benevolence with all my heart.

Your Most Serene Highness's most humble and obedient servant Artemisia Lomi[2]

2. Letter to Galileo Galilei, in Arcetri. From Naples, October 9, 1635.

My Most Illustrious Sir and Most Respected Master,

I know that Your Lordship will say that if I had not had the occasion to avail myself of your assistance, I would never have thought of writing to you; and, indeed, because of the infinite obligations I have toward you, you could draw that logical conclusion, not knowing how often I tried to have news of you, without being able to obtain reliable information from anyone. But now that I know you are there in good health, thank God, I want to disregard other possible avenues and appeal to you, whom I can depend on for favorable assistance, without relying on any other Lord. And I do it without hesitation as another case has occurred similar to the one concerning the painting of that Judith which I gave His Serene Highness the Grand Duke Cosimo of glorious memory,[3] and which would have been forgotten if it had not been for Your Lordship's assistance. Because of your assistance, I obtained an excellent remuneration. Therefore, I beg you to do the same now, because I see that no one has mentioned the two large paintings which I sent recently to His Serene Highness[4] with one of my brothers. I don't know whether he liked them; I only know, through a third party, that the Grand Duke has received them, and nothing else. This mortifies me considerably, for I have seen myself honored by all the kings and potentates of Europe to whom I have sent my works, not only with great gifts but also with most favored letters, which I keep with me. Most recently, the Lord Duke of Ghisa[5] gave my brother 200 piasters in payment for a painting of mine, which my brother had brought him; but I never received them because my brother went elsewhere. From His Most Serene Highness, my natural prince [i.e., Ferdinando II], I have received no favor. I assure Your Lordship that I would have valued the smallest favors from him more than the many I have received from the king of France, the king of Spain, the king of England, and all the other princes of Europe, given my desire to serve him and to return to my homeland,[6] and in consideration of the services I rendered His Serene Highness, his father, for many years.

His Most Serene Highness's generosity, to which all skilled and learned persons resort, is well known. It is no wonder, then, that I, having placed myself among them, should have resolved to dedicate some fruits of my labor to him— indeed it is I, more than any other,

who ought to pay him this debt on account of both vassalage and servitude. So I cannot believe that I have not satisfied His Highness, since I have fulfilled my obligation. Therefore, I wish to know the truth from you, if you will give me the details in this matter with regard to the Prince.

This will mitigate the sorrow that I feel because this most devout demonstration of mine was passed over in such deep silence. You will be doing me a great favor, which I will value above any other I have received from Your Lordship. I kiss your hands a thousand times and shall live as your usual grateful servant. And here I pay my deep respects.

Your Most Illustrious Lordship's
Most Humble and Obedient Servant
Artimitia [sic] Gentileschi

If Your Lordship will be so kind as to answer me, please write to me in care of Sir Francesco Maria Maringhi.[7]

3. Letter to Cassiano dal Pozzo, in Rome. From Naples, October 24, 1637.

The confidence I have always had in Your Lordship's kindness, and now the urgent matter of settling my daughter in marriage, induces me to appeal to your generosity and ask you for assistance and advice, which I trust I will obtain as I did other times. My Lord, I need a small amount of money to bring this marriage to conclusion.

Since I do not have any funds or means, I have kept for this purpose some paintings measuring eleven and twelve palms each. It is my intention to offer them to Cardinals Francesco Padrone and D[on] Antonio; however, I do not want to go through with these plans without having Your Lordship's excellent advice, as I want to act only under your auspices and not otherwise. With greatest affection, I thus beg you to honor me with your reply, giving me your opinion on the matter so that, if necessary, I can dispatch someone with the above-mentioned paintings immediately. Among the paintings there is one for Monsignor Filomarino[8] and another for Your Lordship, in addition to my portrait which you once requested for inclusion among [your] other renowned painters.

I assure you that as soon as I have freed myself from the burden of this girl, I want to come there immediately to enjoy my native home and to serve my friends and masters.

To end, I kiss Your Lordship's hands with affection and pray for all good things from Heaven.

Please send me news whether my husband is alive or dead.
[unsigned]

4. Letter to Don Antonio Ruffo, in Messina. From Naples, January 30, 1649.

Most Illustrious Sir and My Master,
By God's will, Your Most Illustrious Lordship has received the painting and I think that by now you must have seen it. I fear that before you saw the painting you must have thought that I was arrogant and presumptuous. But I hope to God that after seeing it you will agree that I was not totally wrong. In fact, were it not for Your Most Illustrious Lordship, of whom I am so affectionate a servant, I would not have given it for one hundred and sixty, because in every other place where I have been, I was paid one hundred scudi per figure. And this was in Florence as well as in Venice, and in Rome and even in Naples when there was more money. Whether this is due to merit or luck, Your Most Illustrious Lordship, a discriminating nobleman with all of the wordly virtues, will judge what I am.

I sympathize greatly with Your Lordship, because a woman's name causes doubt until her work is seen. Please forgive me, for God's sake, if I gave you reason to think me greedy. As for the rest I will not trouble you any longer. I will only say that on other occasions I will serve you with greater perfection, and if Your Lordship likes my work, I will send you also my portrait so that you can keep it in your gallery as all the other Princes do.

And thus I end this letter and I most humbly bow to Your Most Illustrious Lordship with the assurance that as long as I live I will be ready for any orders from you. To end, I kiss your hands.

Your Most Illustrious Lordship's most humble servant Artemisia Gentileschi

5. Letter to Don Antonio Ruffo. Naples, November 13, 1649.

My Most Illustrious Sir,

I prefer not to discuss our business in this letter in case that gentleman [the bearer] will read it. With regard to your request that I reduce the price of the paintings, I will tell Your Most Illustrious Lordship that I can take a little from the amount that I asked, but the price must not be less than four hundred ducats, and you must send me a deposit as all other gentlemen do. However, I can tell you for certain that the higher the price, the harder I will strive to make a painting that will please Your Most Illustrious Lordship and that will conform to my taste and yours. With regard to the painting which I have already finished for Your Most Illustrious Lordship, I cannot give it to you for less than I asked, as I have already overextended myself to give the lowest price. I swear, as your servant, that I would not have given it even to my father for the price that I gave you. Don Antonio, my Lord, I beg you, for God's sake, not to reduce the price because I am sure that when you see it, you will say that I was not presumptuous. Your nephew, the Duke, thinks that I must have great affection for you to charge you such a price. I only wish to remind you that there are eight [figures], two dogs and landscape and water. Your Most Illustrious Lordship will understand that the expense for models is staggering.

I am going to say no more except what I have in my mind, that I think Your Most Illustrious Lordship will not suffer any loss with me and that you will find the spirit of Caesar in this soul of a woman.

And thus I most humbly bow to you.

Your Most Illustrious Lordship's most humble servant Artemisia Gentileschi.

6. Letter to Don Antonio Ruffo. From Naples, November 13, 1649.

My Most Illustrious Sir,

I received a letter of 26th October which I greatly appreciated, particularly noting how my Master always concerns himself with favoring me despite my unworthiness. In it, you tell me about that gentleman who wishes to have some paintings by me, that he would like a Galatea and a Judgment of Paris, and that Galatea should be different from the one that Your Most Illustrious Lordship owns. There was no need for you to suggest this to me, since by the grace of God and of the Most Holy Virgin, it would occur to a woman with my kind of talent to vary the subjects in my paintings; never has anyone found in my pictures any repetition of invention, not even of one hand.

As for the fact that this gentleman wishes to know the price before the work is done, believe me, as I am your servant, that I do it most unwillingly since it is very important to me not to err and thus burden my conscience, which I value more than all the gold in the world. I know that by erring I will offend my Lord God and I thus fear that God will not bestow his grace on me. Therefore, I never quote a price for my works until they are done. However, since Your Most Illustrious Lordship would like me to do it, I will do what you command. Tell this gentleman that I want five hundred ducats for both; he can show them to the whole world and, should he find anyone who does not think that the paintings are worth two hundred scudi more, I do not want him to pay me the agreed price. I assure Your Most Illustrious Lordship that these are paintings with nude figures requiring very expensive female models, which is a big headache. When I find good ones they fleece me and at other times, one must suffer their trivialities with the patience of Job.

As for my doing a drawing and sending it, I have made a solemn vow never to send my drawings because people swindled me. In particular I just today found out that, in order to spend less, the Bishop of St. Gata, for whom I did a drawing of souls in Purgatory, commissioned another painter to do the painting using my work. If I were a man I cannot imagine it would turn out this way, because when the concept [*inventione*] has been realized and defined with lights and darks, and established by means of planes, the rest is a trifle. I think that this gentleman is wrong to ask for drawings since he can see the design and the composition of the Galatea.

I don't know what else to say except that I kiss Your Most Illustrious Lordship's hands and most humbly bow to you, praying for the greatest happiness from Heaven.

Your Most Illustrious Lordship's most humble servant Artemisia Gentileschi

I advise Your Most Illustrious Lordship that when I ask a price I don't do as they do in Naples, where they ask thirty and then give it to you for four. I am Roman and thus I shall always act in the Roman manner.

## NOTES

The selection of letters presented here was translated by Efrem G. Calingaert. Punctuation and paragraphs have been inserted in the interest of clarity. In my forthcoming book, these translations, edited by Calingaert and myself, are slightly different in form but not in substance.

1. This letter is dated in the Florentine style; the actual year is 1620.

2. Lomi was Orazio Gentileschi's paternal name, used by Artemisia during her Florentine period, presumably to stress the family's Florentine origins.

3. Cosimo II de' Medici (1590–1621), Grand Duke of Tuscany, was Artemisia's principal Florentine patron; see Letter 1.

4. Ferdinando II de' Medici (1610–70), the son of Cosimo II and, in 1635, the ruling grand duke.

5. Charles of Lorraine (1571–1640), Duke of Guise and Joyeuse, who, after an active political and military career in France, retired to Florence following some differences with Richelieu in 1622.

6. That is, Florence. Artemisia liked to stress her Tuscan ancestry to Tuscans, as is also seen in her habitual Florentine signature. She was in fact born in Rome, which she emphasized to Cassiano dal Pozzo (Letter 3) and to Don Antonio Ruffo (Letter 6).

7. One of several persons mentioned in Artemisia's letters who at present remains unidentified.

8. Ascanio Filomarino, an active art patron, was archbishop of Naples in the 1640s. Francesco and Antonio Barberini were nephews of Pope Urban VIII, who shared in the Barberini family's noted art-collecting activities.

# Giving Weight to Words:
# Madame de Sévigné's Letters
# to Her Daughter

*Elizabeth C. Goldsmith*

"In our age [she] would probably have been one of the great novelists," Virginia Woolf remarked in her essay on Madame de Sévigné.[1] Written at a time when the familiar letter was accorded the status of a literary genre, Sévigné's vast body of letters was much admired by her contemporaries and, while not published during her lifetime, had a readership far surpassing the actual number of her correspondents.[2] For Woolf, Sévigné's skill lay in her ability to capture the spoken voice in the written word: "It is natural to use the present tense, because we live in her presence. We are very little conscious of a disturbing medium between us—that she is living, after all, by means of written words. But now and then with the sound of her voice in our ears and its rhythm rising and falling within us, we become aware . . . that we are, of course, being addressed by one of the great mistresses of the art of speech" (p. 54).

Alleviating the reader's awareness of this "disturbing medium" has long been a principal goal of the epistolary writer. Seventeenth-century authors of epistolary manuals regularly tell their readers that in writing a letter they must imagine they are speaking.[3] In his introduction to a collection of model letters published in 1689, Pierre Richelet insists that "when one wants to write a letter, one must convince oneself that writing and speaking to an absent person, amounts to the same thing." Like other authors of epistolary manuals, however, Richelet recognizes that letters and speech are also different, since we have recourse to the written medium when our interlocutor is absent and speech is precluded. Because of this, he continues, "It is necessary to imagine that words in speech are lost in the air, and that they remain in writing on paper, so that one must be more careful about what comes from the pen than from the mouth, because the person who reads has all the time s/he wants to notice mistakes, while they easily escape the ear of the listener."[4]

A more permanent form of expression, epistolary discourse is also more challenging than speech, even when the spoken word achieves the level of conversational art. For as seventeenth- and eighteenth-century theoreticians of epistolary style emphasize, conversational speech lacks the integrity of written discourse because it owes its effects in part to nonverbal forms of expression. "A spoken conversation may be pleasing in part because of the advantages accompanying pronunciation, while a written discourse can only please by its essential graces," writes Vaumorière, in his 1689 letter manual.[5] Unlike letter readers who have a palpable object to examine at will, listeners find that words addressed to them escape their grasp: "What we see on paper remains exposed to our critical eye, and most things that are said to us slip away from our thoughts" (p. 4). Notwithstanding the more complex nature of letters, the writer should consider conversation as the model for epistolary rhetoric and strive to create an ongoing, reciprocal commitment to dialogue with the interlocutor.

The differing dynamics of conversational exchange and letter writing are a central preoccupation in Madame de Sévigné's letters, the most renowned of private correspondences of the seventeenth century. In this epistolary corpus, the metaphor of correspondence as conversation is repeatedly examined and ceaselessly manipulated in the author's commentary on the act of letter writing.[6] This is especially true of the letters to her daughter, for which Sévigné is best known today, although with the loss of Madame de Grignan's half of the correspondence, these are, ironically, the letters whose replies are no longer extant. And yet, it is precisely in this now one-sided mother-daughter dialogue that the reader observes Sévigné's strongest, most passionate preoccupation with the principles of reciprocity and exchange.

Madame de Sévigné's intense love for her daughter provoked much commentary in Sévigné's own lifetime, and it continues to preoccupy her readers today. One reader has recently argued that Sévigné's devotion to Madame de Grignan was an attempt to re-create her attachment to her own mother, who had died when she was a young girl.[7] More typically, since Saint-Simon the daughter has been viewed as an undeserving idol who aroused in her mother, as Woolf put it, "a passion that was twisted and morbid," and that "caused her many humiliations (p. 52). In this vein, other readers have seen in Sévigné's attachment to her daughter a Proustian obsession with the person who loved her the least.[8] The question of whether the daughter "deserved" the adoration expressed in the letters is impossible to resolve and ultimately irrelevant to the letters as text. More important, perhaps, is the inscribed feeling of conflict between the mother's love for her daughter and her love of writing: "I find, in writing this, that nothing is less tender than what I am saying: What? I love to write you! Then that is a sign that I love your absence, my daughter; and that is what is horrible."[9] This conflict can never be totally resolved in Sévigné's written representations of her daughter. But her letters bespeak a persistent effort to efface the distance between language and love, absence and presence, by recreating the conditions of speech in written conversation.

Chief among the thematic structures that highlight Sévigné's desire to transform the letter into a spoken dialogue is her obsessive attention to the mechanics of receiving messages.[10] The schedule of mail delivery, the arrival of a courier, the physical appearance of a letter, the sound of opening an envelope, these material features of letter writing are all noted with apparent fascination. From the beginning of her correspondence with Madame de Grignan she ritualizes postal routines and insists on a regular rhythm of exchange. Careful to arrange the continued delivery of her daughter's letters during her travels, she views their arrival at a pre-established location as a personal accomplishment, the successful test of a system she has created: "I arrive here, where I find a letter from you, so well have I managed to give order to our exchanges" (I, 259). She often determines her itinerary by the places where she will receive a letter, or where mail is frequently delivered: "The mail arrives here three times a week, I feel like staying here. . . . It's a shame to leave such a beautiful and charming place, where one finds this consolation." (I, 265). When she moves from Paris for her prolonged visits to her country estate, her system is reordered to assure a regular rhythm of exchange, and if the routine is disrupted she theorizes over its effect on the quality of her writing.

Through the repeated disruptions and rearrangements of the postal schedule, Sévigné gradually recognizes that her missives fall into two types of discourse: the letter of response to a recently received message, on the one hand, and on the other, the "provisional" letter (*la lettre de provision*), which is often apologetic in tone and articulates a stronger sense of isolation from the addressee: "I think that you see that I am responding Wednesday to your two letters," she writes her daughter, "and Friday I . . . depend on my own resources, which sometimes makes for a poor letter" (II, 376). The letters with no mention of a recently received response are written, she says, "on the point of a needle" (II, 176), for her anxiety puts her at a loss for words: "I am unhappy, I am poor company. When I have received your letters, my words will come to me again" (I, 272). But the loss is never total, since it is still with a verbal message that she announces her verbal powers have been reduced by her daughter's silence. More often, Sévigné draws attention to the excessively self-absorbed quality of her "provisional" letters, which, lacking the referential context of her daughter's message, turn inward from interlocution to monologue. She deems them self-indulgent, written only out of personal needs: "I write provisionally . . . it's that I'm very worried about you, and I love to converse with you all the time; and this is my only consolation right now" (I, 173). Without her daughter's letter to anchor her own message, Sévigné sees her text as superfluous, transgressing the limits of their epistolary system and violating their agreed-upon code of restraint: "I'm taking advantage of you, my dear girl, today I wanted to allow myself this letter in advance; my heart needed it. I won't make a habit of it" (I, 175). In fact, these letters *are* habitual, products of her daughter's prolonged silences, which generate a feeling of dissociation and despair: "I look for you everywhere and all the places where I saw you hurt me. You see, my daughter, that the smallest things having to do with you make an impression on my poor brain. I wouldn't tell you of these weaknesses, which I'm sure you laugh at, except that today's letter is somewhat up in the air, since I have not yet received news from you" (II, 265). Cut off from the reassurance of interlocution, Sévigné perceives a vast realm of probability, which gives shape to vague and undefined fears: "Those are the horrors of separation. One is at the mercy of all these thoughts. One can think, without being mad, that all that is possible can happen. All unhappy moods are forebodings, all dreams are omens, all forethought is warning" (I, 246). At the same time, a letter written without reference to a previous reply gives her a special power over her addressee. "I have an advantage over you when I write you; you don't answer at all, and I push my words as far as I want to" (II, 464). By that token, her unhappiness, caused by her daughter's silence, is transformed through the act of letter writing into a pleasure that *requires* solitude and silence to be properly enjoyed. Sévigné discovers, then, that written dialogue allows her pleasurable freedoms that she does not experience in conversation. At a distance, the daughter is always listening.

In Sévigné's letters, epistolary dialogue with her daughter assumes a privileged status with respect to speech, all the more so when compared with the conversation of less worthy listeners. From her earliest letters to Grignan, the world of speech and the epistolary world are described as two economic systems governed by different codes of trade and exchange, which grant different values to her own verbal resources. She is, by her own admission, a thoroughly gregarious individual, dependent for affirmation on verbal interchange and social visibility. She declares herself extremely impressionable and easily swayed by the current of linguistic exchange: "I always share the opinion of the person I last hear speak." However she sometimes regards social conversation as wasteful, requiring words to be spent prodigiously, an excess that dissipates instead of nourishing the participants. The language of society at Rennes, for instance, is consumed as immoderately as the food, thus preventing the possibility of gaining true sustenance from either of these activities. In the same letter describing this linguistic excess she suggests that it results in a kind of madness: "Coming, going, complimenting, exhausting oneself, becoming totally mad, like a lady-in-waiting; that is what we did yesterday, my dear" (II, 1040). Sévigné contrasts the feasting and verbalizing at Rennes with the silence and moderation of her own country estate, to which she would like to escape: "I am extremely hungry for fasting and silence. I don't have much wit, but it seems that I'm spending what I do have in loose change, which I throw away and dissipate in silliness . . ." (II, 1040). A week later she writes from her country home that she is finally enjoying "silence and abstinence," the sign of a retreat into an exclusive system of written communication where the value of words that had begun to escape her control is reinstated. By withholding verbal investments from the world of speech she is able to give more to her letter correspondent: "What I save on the public, it seems to me that I give it back to you" (II, 314).

Sévigné's willful flights from speech to writing are most dramatic when they coincide with her physical moves from Paris to Les Rochers. The rural environment promotes an intensified self-consciousness, through a paring down of social ties, while moving back to Paris allows her, as she writes, "to empty my head of myself a bit," but it also means a dissipation of the self. In Paris, "the diversity of objects dissipates too much, and distracts and diminishes passion" (II, 871). Leaving a crowded salon represents an attempt to "collect" herself: "I needed this moment of rest to put my head back on a bit, and to regain a kind of composure" (I, 717). At Les Rochers, where she is isolated, her verbal energy is channeled into her preferred correspondence with her daughter, and acquires special linguistic traits: less focused on the referential function and third person narration, it is markedly structured around the first- and second-person axis of dialogue.[11]

In this epistolary dialogue, Grignan's language can provide the most affirming reflection of her mother. In an early letter written from her country estate, for instance, Sévigné weighs her daughter's approval against the flattery of a provincial neighbor:

> You say too many kind things about my letters, my dear. I count absolutely on all of your endearments. I have said for a long time that you are true. . . . The divine Plessis is simply and precisely false; I do her too much honor to even deign to speak ill of her. She plays the capable lady, the fearful one, the best girl in the world, but above all she counterfeits *me,* so that she also gives me the sort of pleasure I would get if I saw myself in a mirror that made me ridiculous, and if I spoke to an echo that answered me with nonsense (I, 300).

As the favored interlocutor, the daughter is the "true" counterpart to her mother, in contrast with the annoying mimicry of the provincial Mademoiselle du Plessis. Both Grignan, in her letters, and Plessis, in her conversation, attempt to offer a gratifying reflection of their interlocutor, and present her with a complimentary exchange of words. But the daughter's epistolary echo is deemed the "true" one, while the irritating neighbor simply debases her partner through an unconvincing imitation of her voice. For flattery, as a mode of communication, poses a serious threat to the stability of verbal exchange. La Rochefoucauld, like Madame de Sévigné, terms it "a false coin," which is given currency only by our vanity, a counterfeit language disrupting the image of perfect reciprocity essential to the ideal of sociability.[12] As Jean Starobinski has written in studying the impact of flattery on the aristocratic elite to which Madame de Sévigné belonged, "when the granting of favors is solicited by artful speaking, imbalance is established, equality disappears, and the law of 'interest' is substituted for or is added to the law of pleasure."[13] For Sévigné, the correspondence with her daughter is an ongoing trade between purportedly equal partners in which the "value" or meaning of words is both immediately comprehensible and durable over time. This idealized vision of communication sustains her claim that her daughter's words are rare, durable truths in a world of false, insubstantial "paroles": ". . . they have that character of truth which, I always maintain, imposes itself with authority, while falsehood remains weighed down under a load of words without having the power of persuasion" (I, 154–55). She draws attention to this special value which she ascribes to her daughter's written expressions of sentiment: "Cruel girl! why do you sometimes hide from me such precious treasures? . . . let me enjoy this wealth without which my life is hard and unpleasant; these are not words, they are truths" (I, 160).

These precious "treasures" are revealed more often in writing than in speech, however, for according to Sévigné's letters both women feel they cannot always display their "true" selves in each other's presence, and both cite an inequality in their relationship as the cause. "I don't want you to say that I was a curtain that hid you," Sévigné writes, protesting her daughter's accusation that her presence could be stifling (I, 155). Through the distance and absence that the letter signifies, however, the most passionately loving self can emerge. Waiting for a letter to appear, Sévigné writes: "The thought of that moment when I will have the yes or no of having letters from you, fills me with an emotion I cannot control. . . . It is the same feeling that makes me fear my own shadow every time your affection is hidden under your temperament; it's the mail that hasn't arrived" (II, 1007).

Ultimately, of course, it is only by appropriating her daughter's written words in her own discourse that Sévigné can claim a privileged sincerity for epistolary expression. The authority of Grignan's words is established only in her mother's reply; the interpretive and repossessive function of a response is necessary to determine the value of the letter's message. Sévigné fully exploits the privilege of the letter *reader* who has, as Richelet remarks, "all the time s/he wants" (p. 4). The power of the interlocutor's words can be enhanced or diminished by the reader, as they are woven into the other's epistolary text. "If you think that these words pass superficially into my heart, you are wrong" writes Sévigné; "I feel them sharply, they establish themselves there, I say them and repeat them to myself, and I even take pleasure in repeating them to you, so as to renew your vows and your promises. Sincere people like you give a great weight to their words" (III, 868). The "weight" of these words is measured by the extended play of repetition and leisurely meditation, acts that are not possible in spoken dialogue and that, for Madame de Sévigné, "renew" and strengthen the reciprocal commitment that is the basis of all communication.

## NOTES

1. Virginia Woolf, "Madame de Sévigné," in *Death of the Moth and Other Essays* (New York: Harcourt Brace Jovanovich, 1970), p. 51.

2. On the epistolary genre in seventeenth-century France see Roger Duchêne, *Madame de Sévigné et la lettre d'amour* (Paris: Bordas, 1970), pp. 67–114.

3. The influence of seventeenth-century theories of conversation on the development of norms for epistolary style has been studied in a recent article by Mireille Gérard, "Art épistolaire et art de la conversation: les vertus de la familiarité," *Revue d'Histoire Littéraire de la France*, 78 (1978), pp. 958–74.

4. Pierre Richelet, *Les Plus belles Lettres des meilleurs auteurs français* (Lyon: Benoit Bailly, 1689), p. 4. All English translations in this article are my own.

5. Paul de Vaumorière, *Lettres sur toutes sortes de sujets,* . . . (Paris, 1689), pp. 3–4.

6. The interpretation of this metaphor is, in my view, at the heart of the debate between proponents of biographical and textual readings of Sévigné. Roger Duchêne maintains that her letters function primarily as private conversations and thus cannot be approached as a closed text; they must be understood as fragmentary reflections of a lived reality. Bernard Bray and Bernard Beugnot argue that the transfer of spoken conversation to written correspondence shifts personal communication to a new, literary mode. See Roger Duchêne, "Du Destinataire au public, ou les métamorphoses d'une correspondance privée," *Revue d'Histoire Littéraire de la France,* 76 (1976), p. 39; Bernard Bray, "L'Epistolier et son public en France au 17e siècle," *Travaux de linguistique et de littérature,* II (1973), p. 17; and Bernard Beugnot, "Style ou styles épistolaires?" *Revue d'Histoire Littéraire de la France,* 78 (1978), p. 949. For a more complete summary of this ongoing discussion see Louise K. Horowtiz, "The Correspondence of Madame de Sévigné: Letters or Belles-Lettres?" *French Forum,* 6 (1981), pp. 13–27.

7. Harriet Ray Allentuch, "My Daughter/Myself: Emotional Roots of Madame de Sévigné's Art," *Modern Language Quarterly,* 43 (1982), pp. 121–37.

8. See, for example, Jean Cordelier, *Madame de Sévigné par elle-même* (Paris: Editions des Seuil, 1967), p. 33; and Roger Duchêne, *Madame de Sévigné ou la chance d' être femme* (Paris: Fayard, 1982), pp. 173–74.

9. Madame de Sévigné, *Correspondance*, ed. Roger Duchêne (Paris: Gallimard, 1974–78), II, 579. All quotations from Madame de Sévigné's letters will be drawn from this edition.

10. This obsession has often struck Sévigné's readers, including Proust's Marcel (*A La Recherche du temps perdu* [Paris: Gallimard, 1954], I, 653). See also Elizabeth C. Goldsmith, "Proust on Madame de Sévigné's Letters: Some Aspects of Epistolary Writing," *Papers on French Seventeenth Century Literature*, VIII (1981), pp. 117–27.

11. For a discussion of Sévigné's use of literary conventions opposing court and country see Elizabeth C. Goldsmith, "Madame de Sévigné's Epistolary Retreat," *Esprit Créateur*, 23, No. 2 (1983), pp. 70–79.

12. La Rochefoucauld, *Maximes* (Paris: Garnier, 1967), p. 41.

13. Jean Starobinski, "Sur la flatterie," *Nouvelle revue de la psychanalyse*, 4 (1971), p. 138. For an analysis of the art of conversation as produced by the idiolect of the *honnête homme*, see Domna C. Stanton, *The Aristocrat as Art* (New York: Columbia Univ. Press, 1980), pp. 139–46.

✒

## CHAPTER EIGHT

# "My Childhood Years": A Memoir by the Czarist Cavalry Officer, Nadezhda Durova

## Mary Fleming Zirin

In late 1807 Alexander I ordered a young soldier brought from the western frontier of Russia to St. Petersburg for an interview. The soldier's diary describes their meeting:

> "I have heard," said the Emperor, "that you are not a man. Is that true?" I could not muster the courage to reply at once: "Yes, Your Majesty! It's true!"[1] I stood for a minute with downcast eyes and remained silent; my heart was throbbing, and my hand trembled in the czar's grasp. The Emperor waited. At last I raised my eyes to him, and as I uttered my response I saw that the Emperor was blushing. Instantly I began to blush, too; I lowered my eyes and did not raise them again until the moment when an involuntary motion of sorrow brought me to the Emperor's feet. Questioning me in detail about the reasons that had led me to join the army, the Emperor greatly praised my fearlessness, saying that this was an example to Russia; that all my commanders praised me highly, calling my courage exceptional; that he was pleased to confirm it; and that, therefore, he wished to reward me and return me with honor to my father's home, giving. . . .
>
> The Emperor had no time to finish; at the phrase "to return home," I cried out in horror and threw myself at once to the Emperor's feet.[2]

The interview ended happily. Nadezhda Durova (1783–1866) convinced Alexander I to permit her to continue masquerading as an adolescent soldier; he granted her a commission in the Mariupol' Hussars, a government subvention, and the pseudonym "Alexandrov" derived from his own name. Devoted to her czar-liberator, Durova served with distinction throughout the Napoleonic wars and was the only woman ever to receive the St. George Cross for heroism.

Durova may be a unique figure in the tradition of the woman warrior, which antedates even the Greek tales of the Amazons. Although women have fought as men throughout the history of human warfare, by and large their stories are lost to history. In Durova's instance, however, a military life based on a fierce sense of vocation was followed by a brief, productive literary career twenty years later. She published two volumes of polished excerpts from the irregularly kept diaries of her army days, *The Cavalry-Maid: It Happened in Russia* [Kavalerist-devitsa: Proisshestvie v Rossii], 1836, and *The Notes of Aleksandrov (Durova): An Addendum to* The Cavalry-Maid [Zapiski Aleksandrova (Durovoj): Dobavlenie k *Devitse-kavalerist*], 1839, as well as a number of works of prose fiction drawn mainly from materials gathered during her military travels.[3] Nineteenth-century critics became increasingly impatient with what they regarded as rambling, over-dramatic fictional tales, but the Russian public was fascinated by her story. Over the years Durova's life has been the subject of biography, novels, and even an opera, replete with fanciful additions, but never with the conviction of her own narrative.[4]

Durova's diaries have a pioneering place in the tradition of auto-biographical works by Russian women.[5] Despite or perhaps because of her anomalous position, she expressed specifically female, even feminist perspectives and attitudes. Her pages abound with sympathetic vignettes of women she met on her travels and at provincial army posts. Durova saw her successful military career as evidence of the untapped capabilities of women in general. During the headlong Russian retreat before the Napoleonic invaders in 1812, she worried about falling ill: "it will be ascribed not to the excesses of these exertions, but to the weakness of my sex."[6] Her own sex was her intended audience. Offering her diaries to Alexander Pushkin for his journal *The Contemporary,* Durova recommended them as of particular interest "for our female compatriots."[7] In *The Cavalry-Maid,* while describing her early days in the cavalry, Durova addressed those who could best comprehend the joy she took in her newfound freedom—girls of her own age:

> Only you can understand how much this happiness means to me, you who have to account for every step, who are eternally sheltered and eternally guarded, God knows from whom or what, from the cradle to the grave.—Only you, I repeat, can understand the joyous emotions that overwhelm me when I see deep forests, vast fields, mountains, valleys, and streams and realize that I can roam them all with no one to answer to and with no fear of anyone's prohibition.[8]

Combined with this sense of freedom, however, Durova views her double masquerade (as a male and as a perpetual adolescent) with wry, self-deprecating humor throughout the diaries. As a woman and an outsider, she can also laugh at the manifestations of masculine ambition and the gamecock ways of Russian officers. Such phrases as "I found this all very funny" and "I could hardly keep from laughing" occur often in her accounts of peacetime quarters, training, duty, and excursions. Her flippancy, her frank descriptions of foul-ups on the battlefield and corruption in the army, and her feisty confrontations with superior officers may all contribute to the fact that Durova's diaries have never been republished in full in the Soviet Union.[9]

"My Childhood Years," Durova's short introductory memoir to *The Cavalry-Maid*, is remarkable for the way in which it confronts the female condition. In a mixture of romantic rhetoric about nature, freedom and fate, psychological analysis, and autobiographical detail, Durova explains the factors that led her to rebel against the expected behavior and prescribed destiny of women. Some elements may seem all too familiar to twentieth-century readers: rejection from birth by a mother who desired a son—this scene finds its novelistic counterpart in *Madame Bovary*, published twenty years later—and identification with a beloved father to the point of emulating his career.[10]

Like all autobiographical texts, "My Childhood Years" conceals as much as it reveals and mingles fact with fiction. Although Durova portrays herself as a sixteen-year-old virgin when she joined the army, the historical record suggests that she was twenty-three and had returned to her father's house from a failed marriage and the birth of a son. Leaving aside the esthetic appeal of this picaresque fiction, it is clear that censorship during the reign of Nicholas I would not have permitted the publication of the memoirs of a runaway wife, nor would the Russian public of the 1830s have received them with sympathy. Indeed, Durova's long story, "Fate's Toy," in which a wife is first corrupted by her husband and then condemned by her community, shows how well the author understood the limits of social tolerance.[11] Insofar as we know, Durova nowhere described her unhappy experiences as wife and abandoning mother. In "My Childhood Years," however, these experiences are very much present as subtext; the passages devoted to her mother's sufferings and relentless cruelty to her daughter are far more ambiguous in sentiment than we might expect from one who represented herself merely as innocent victim. Despite the "fictions" of the memoir, Durova's basic dilemma rings true: she either had to reject the strong affinities she clearly felt for happy and secure women (like the aunts she describes in the memoir and many of the women encountered during her army life) or risk ending up as miserable and unfulfilled as her mother had been. The diaries testify that she did not regret her radical decision to seek a freer life in a male world.

Ultimately, Durova's beloved father was no less cruel than her mother. In 1816 he demanded that she leave the army to become the "staff of his old age," and as a dutiful "son" she obeyed. Except for her foray into the literary world in the 1830s, Durova spent the rest of her long life in obscurity in her native Kama river region west of the Urals. She was described by those who knew her in her hometown of Sarapul, and later in Elabuga, as a kindly eccentric who retained the masculine dress and speech that guaranteed her independence and who lavished her pension and affection on a "family" of stray dogs.[12] At her death in 1866 Nadezhda Durova was buried with military honors.

## NOTES

The Center for Russian and East European Studies and the Slavic Reference Service of the University of Illinois, Champaign-Urbana, as well as the patient Interlibrary Loan staff of the California Institute of Technology, Pasadena, furnished invaluable support for this work.

1. Gender-marked adjectives and participial past-tense verb endings remind the Russian reader that it is a woman who narrates the story. There is no way to reproduce this effect in English.

2. Nadezhda Durova, *Kavalerist-devitsa* (St. Petersburg: 1836), part 1, pp. 161–63.

3. Between 1837 and 1840 Durova published two novels, *Gudishki* (the name of twelve villages in Lithuania) and *The Corner* [*Ugol*], and the following works (stories or novellas) that the Russians designate *povest'* (tale): *Count Mavritsy* [*Graf Mavritsij*], *Nurmeka* (the Tatar heroine's name), *Fate's Toy, or Illicit Love* [*Igra sud'by, ili Protivuzakonnaja ljubov'*], *The Pavilion* [*Pavil'on*], *The Sulphur Spring* [*Sernyj kljuch*], *Buried Treasure* [*Klad*], and *Yarchuk, The Dog Who Saw Ghosts* [*Jarchuk, Sobaka-dukhovidets*]. The titles suggest a range from the "society tale" (svetskaja povest') to the historical romance and Gothic fiction. A third autobiographical work, Durova's bitter memoir on her literary celebrity, appeared in 1838: *A Year of Life in Petersburg, or The Disadvantages of the Third Visit* [*God zhizni v Peterburge, ili Nevygody tret'ego poseshchenija*]. For a resume of Durova's literary career, see my article, "Nadezhda Durova," *Modern Encyclopedia of Russian and Soviet Literatures*, Harry B. Weber, ed., Vol. 6, 1982, pp. 96–98. Detailed bibliographies of works by and about Durova can be found in: N. N. Golitsyn, *Bibliograficheskij slovar' russkikh pisatel'nits*, SPb., 1889 (rpt., Leipzig, 1974), pp. 88–89, and K. D. Muratova, ed., *Istorija russkoj literatury XIX veka: Bibliograficheskij ukazatel'*, Moscow, 1962, pp. 320–21.

4. Golitsyn, cited above, lists critics' articles about Durova's works as they appeared. Vissarion Belinsky's series of reviews is representative of the enthusiastic reception given Durova's *The Cavalry-Maid* and the progressive disillusionment with her fiction; see the Soviet edition of Belinsky's complete works (*Polnoe sobranie sochinenij*), Vols. 3, 1953, 148–57 and 4, 1954, 308–09, 315–18, 382–83). Biographical literature about Durova includes: A. Saks, *Kavalerist-devitsa: Shtabs-rotmistr A. A. Aleksandrov (Nadezhda Andreevna Durova)*, SPb, 1912; E. S. Nekrasova's excellent article, "Nadezhda Andreevna Durova," *Istoricheskij vestnik*, 1890, 9, 585–612; and Barbara Heldt's popular article, "Nadezhda Durova: Russia's Cavalry

Maid," *History Today*, February 1983, pp. 24–27. Three novels inspired by Durova's life are: D. L. Mordovtsev's *1812* [*Dvenadtsatyj god*], published in 1885; *A Daring Life* [*Smelaja zhizn'*], 1908, by the children's writer Lidia Churilova-"Charskaja"; and Ja. Rykachev's 1942 *Nadezhda Durova*. Alexander Gladkov's 1941 verse play *Long, Long Ago* [*Davnym-davno*] and his 1962 film scenario *A Hussar Ballad* [*Gusarskaja ballada*] are listed in Soviet sources as works based on Durova's experiences—see the articles on Gladkov and Durova in the *Short Literary Encyclopedia* (*Kratkaja literaturnaja entsiklopedija*, Vol. 2, 1964, cols. 192 and 822–23)—but Gladkov has denied that his heroine, who in Hussar disguise burns to fight a duel but faints at the sight of a mouse, was inspired to any extent by Durova (A. Gladkov, *Teatr: Vospominanija i razmyshlenija*, M., 1980, 329–30). The eponymous opera, by A. Bogatyrev, appeared in 1957.

5. Durova's diaries were among the first autobiographical works by Russian women to find their way into print. Only a few short personal reminiscences from family archives had appeared earlier, most notably, *The Memoirs of Princess Natal'ja Borisovna Dolgorukaja* (1714–1771); see Charles E. Townsend's edition and translation, Columbus, Ohio: Slavica, 1977. Barbara Heldt, in a book *Terrible Perfection. Women and Russian Literature* (Indiana University Press, 1987), argues that because of the domination of prose fiction by male writers, Russian women developed their own authentic voices primarily in poetry and autobiography. The poetic achievements of Anna Akhmatova, Marina Tsvetaeva, and Bella Akhmadulina and recent memoirs by Eugenia Ginzburg and Nadezhda Mandelstam support her contention. Heldt's discussion of the memoirs of Anna Labzina (1758–1828; *Reminiscences* [*Vospominanija*], SPb., 1914; rpt, Cambridge, Mass.: Oriental Research Partners, 1974) and Elizaveta Vodovozova (1844–1923; *At the Dawn of Life* [*Na zare zhizni*], SPb., 1922) focuses on the authors' relationship with their mothers.

6. *Kavalerist-devitsa*, 1836, part 2, p. 54.

7. Durova's letter of August 5, 1835; see the Academy of Sciences edition of Pushkin's complete works (*Polnoe sobranie sochinenij*, Vol. 16, 1949, p. 43). The great poet was only too happy to publish Durova's account of the Russian campaign of 1812–14 (*Sovremennik*, 1836, 2, 52–132). "Lively, original, fine style. Their success is without question," Pushkin wrote her on March 27 (*PSS* 16, 99).

8. Nadezhda Durova, *Zapiski kavalerist-devitsy*, Kazan', 1960, p. 37.

9. The Soviets, in a text that apparently has become canonical (*Zapiski kavalerist-devitsy*, Kazan' 1960, Moscow 1962, and Kazan' 1976 and 1979), omit without explanation over half of the 1836 *Kavalerist-devitsa*. This version includes "My Childhood Years" in full but, of the ten years Durova spent in the cavalry, covers only the periods from September 1806 to December 1807 and from September 1812 to the spring of 1813. The 1839 *Zapiski* (Notes), which seem to be made up of materials left over from the more unified 1836 memoirs, have not been reprinted in the U.S.S.R.. They are available through University Microfilms in the United States.

10. Fifty years later, the mathematician Sofia Kovalevskaja (1850–1891) suggested in *her* memoirs of childhood (1889) that her distinguished career was at least partially a result of her mother's lack of love for her, the middle child. By Kovalevskaja's account, she learned to use her precocious intellect to get from masculine relatives and teachers the affection her mother denied her (Sofya Kovalevskaya, *A Russian Childhood*, tr. and intro. by Beatrice Stillman, N. Y.: Springer-Verlag, 1978).

11. First published in a journal as "Elena, The Beauty of T." ("Elena, T-skaja krasavitsa," *Biblioteka dlja chtenija*, 1837, Vol. 23, part 1), it appeared in Durova's edition of four of her works, *Povesti i rasskazy* [Tales and Stories], SPb., 1839, as *Igra sud'by* . . . [Fate's Toy . . . ].

12. N. I. Kutshe, "Durova-Aleksandrov (Biograficheskaja zametka)," *Istoricheskij vestnik*, 1894, 3, 788–93, and F. F. Lashmanov, "Nadezhda Andreevna Durova (Materialy k biografii)," *Russkaja starina*, 1890, 9, 657–64.

MY CHILDHOOD YEARS:
A Memoir by the Czarist Cavalry Officer Nadezhda Durova

My mother, born Alexandrovicheva, was one of the most beautiful girls in the Ukraine.[1] As her sixteenth birthday approached, throngs of suitors appeared to seek her hand. From this multitude my mother's heart preferred Hussar Captain Durov; unfortunately, this choice was not that of her father, a proud, ambitious Ukrainian gentleman. He ordered my mother to put out of her head the fanciful notion of marrying a damned Russian, especially a soldier. My grandfather was a great despot in his family: all of his decrees were to be blindly obeyed, and there was no way to placate him or change any of his once-announced intentions. The consequence of this immoderate strictness was that one blustery autumn night my mother, who slept in the same room as her elder sister, got out of bed without a sound, took her cloak and hood, and in stocking feet, with bated breath, crept past her sister's bed, quietly opened the door into the drawing room, quietly closed it, dashed nimbly across, and opening the outside door, flew like an arrow down the long chestnut-lined drive that led to the wicket-gate. My mother hurriedly unlocked this little door and threw herself in the captain's embrace. He was waiting for her with a coach hitched to four strong horses which, like the wind then raging, raced them down the Kiev road.

In the first village they were married and then drove on directly to Kiev, where Durov's regiment was quartered. Although my mother's conduct could be excused by her youth, love, and the virtues of my father, a very handsome man of gentle character and captivating ways, it was so contrary to the patriarchal mores of the Ukrainian land that my grandfather in an initial fit of rage cursed his daughter.

For two years my mother continued to write to her father and to beg his forgiveness, but in vain: he would hear none of it, and his rage grew in proportion to their attempts to mollify it. My parents had almost given up hope of propitiating a man who considered obstinacy a mark of character and would have resigned themselves to their lot with no more letters to her implacable father, when my mother's pregnancy revived her fading courage. She began to hope that the birth of her child would restore her to parental grace.

My mother desperately wanted a son and spent her entire pregnancy in the most seductive daydreams. "I will have a son as handsome as a cupid," she would say. "I'll call him Modest. I'll nurse him myself, raise him myself, and educate him, and my son, my darling Modest, will be the joy of my life. . . ." So my mother imagined, but her time arrived, and the pangs preceding my birth came as a most unpleasant surprise to her. They had played no role in Mama's dreams and produced her first unfavorable impression of me. They had to send for an *accoucheur,*[2] who insisted on bloodletting. This terrified my mother, but there was nothing else to do; she could only yield to necessity. Soon after the blood was let, I came into the world, the poor creature whose appearance destroyed all my mother's dreams and dashed all her hopes.

"Give me my child!" said my mother, as soon as she had somewhat recovered from her pain and terror. The child was brought and placed on her lap. But alas! this was no son as handsome as cupid. This was a daughter—and an *epic-warrior* daughter! I was unusually large, had thick black hair, and was bawling loudly. Mother pushed me off her lap and turned to the wall.

Mama was well in a few days and, yielding to the advice of her friends, regimental ladies, decided to nurse me herself. They told her that a mother who nurses her child will find that the act itself makes her begin to love it. I was brought in; my mother took me from the woman's arms, put me to her breast, and gave me to suck. But I evidently felt the lack of maternal love in that nourishment and, therefore, refused all attempts to force me to take her breast. Mama decided that she would overcome my stubbornness with patience and continued to hold me against her breast, but bored that I kept refusing, she stopped watching me and began to talk to a lady visitor. At that point, apparently directed by the fate that intended me for a soldier's uniform, I suddenly gripped my mother's breast and squeezed it with all the strength of my gums. My mother gave a piercing shriek, jerked me from her breast, and dropping me back into the servant's arms, fell face down onto her pillow. "Take her away; get that good-for-nothing child out of my sight, and never show her again," said Mama, waving her hand and burying her head in the pillow.

When I was four months old, my father's regiment received orders to march to Kherson. Since these were domestic maneuvers, Papa took his family along. I was entrusted to the supervision and care of my mother's maid, a girl of her own age. During the day the maid sat with Mama in the carriage, holding me on her lap. She fed me cow's milk from a bottle and kept me so tightly swaddled that my face grew livid and my eyes suffused with blood. I rested at each overnight halt because I was given to a peasant woman brought in from the village who unswaddled me, put me to her breast, and slept all night with me. Thus after each day's march, I had a new wet nurse.

Neither the changing wet nurses nor the painful swaddling impaired my health. I was very strong and vigorous, but incredibly vociferous as well. One day my mother was totally out of sorts; I had kept her awake all night. The march began at daybreak. Mama settled down to sleep in the carriage, but I started crying again and, in spite of all my nurse's effort to soothe me, bawled louder by the hour. My mother's endurance snapped. She lost her temper and, snatching me from the maid's arms, threw me out of the window! The Hussars cried out in horror, jumped off their horses, and picked me up covered with blood and showing no signs of life. They would have returned me to the carriage, but Papa galloped up, took me from their arms, and in tears, placed me on his saddle. Trembling and crying, as white as a corpse, he rode on without saying a word or turning his head in my mother's direction. To everyone's astonishment I came back to life and, against all hopes, was not lastingly injured. I just bled from the mouth and nose from the violent collision. Papa raised his eyes to heaven in joyful gratitude, clutched me to his breast, and approaching the carriage, said to my mother, "Thank God you are no murderess! Our daughter is alive, but I'll never place her in your power again; I'll care for her myself." With this he rode off and carried me with him until that night's halt without a word or glance toward my mother.

From that memorable day in my life, my father entrusted me to God's Providence and the care of Flank Hussar Astakhov, who was always at Papa's side in quarters and on maneuvers. I spent only nights in my mother's room; as soon as Papa got up and left, I was taken away, too. My guardian Astakhov carried me around all day long, taking me into the squadron stables, setting me on the horses, giving me a pistol to play with, and brandishing his saber while I clapped my hands and laughed out loud at the sight of flying sparks and glittering steel. In the evening he would take me to hear the musicians who played various pieces at dusk; I would listen until I fell asleep. Only sleeping could I be returned to our quarters. Awake, I went numb with terror and clung wailing to Astakhov's neck at the mere sight of my mother's room. From the time of my aerial voyage out the carriage window, Mama never entered into anything that concerned me. She had another daughter to console her, this one really as handsome as a cupid, on whom, as they say, the sun rose and set.

Soon after my birth my grandfather forgave my mother and did it in the most solemn way: he went to Kiev, asked the bishop to absolve him of his impetuous oath never to pardon his daughter, and only after obtaining pastoral absolution, wrote to my mother to forgive her and bless her marriage and the child born of it. He asked her to come and see him to receive both the paternal blessing and marriage settlement in person.[3] My mother found it impossible to accept this invitation until my father was forced to retire. I was four and a half when he realized that he would have to leave the military. There were two cradles in his quarters beside my cot; with such a family campaign life had become impossible. He went to Moscow to seek a position in the civil service, and my mother took me and the two other children to live with her father until her husband's return. Once she had taken me from Astakhov's arms, my mother could no longer be calm or cheerful for a single moment. Each day my strange sallies and chevalresque spirit angered her. I knew all the words of command by heart, was wild about horses, and when Mama tried to make me knit laces, I begged her in tears to give me a pistol, as I said, "to make it click." In short, I was making the best possible use of Astakhov's upbringing! Each day my martial inclinations grew, and each day mother liked me less. I did not forget anything that I had learned in the constant company of the Hussars; I ran and galloped around the room in all directions, shouting at the top of my lungs: "Squadron! To the right, face! From your place march, MARCH!" My aunts laughed out loud, and Mama, vexed and despairing beyond measure, took me to her room, stood me the corner, and drove me to bitter tears with threats and abuse.

My father obtained the post of governor in a district capital and moved his entire family there. My mother, who had come to dislike me wholeheartedly, seemed bent on doing everything possible to intensify and confirm my already invincible passion for freedom and the military life. She never allowed me to stroll in the garden; she never allowed me to leave her side for even half an hour. I was forced to sit all day in her room and weave lace. She herself taught me to sew and knit, and when she saw I had neither inclination nor skill for these pursuits, that everything ripped and broke in my hands, she lost her temper and whipped those hands painfully.

I turned ten. My mother was careless enough to tell my father in my presence that she could no longer cope with Astakhov's pupil; that the Hussar upbringing was deep-rooted; that the fire in my eyes frightened her; and that she would rather see me dead than with such inclinations. Papa answered that I was still a child, and she should pay me no attention. With the years I would take on new inclinations, and all this would pass. "Don't take these childish ways so much to heart, my dear," said Papa. But fate decreed that my mother would not believe or follow her husband's good advice. She continued to keep me under lock and key, denying me every youthful pleasure. I submitted in silence, but repression matured my intelligence. I resolved firmly to shake off her heavy yoke and, like an adult, began laying plans to do so. I decided to take every opportunity to learn to ride horseback, to fire a gun, and to leave my father's house in disguise. In order to begin realizing this intended revolution in my life, I never missed a chance to slip away from mother's supervision. Such chances came whenever visitors arrived to see Mama. They kept her occupied, and I—beside myself with joy—ran out to the garden to my arsenal, that is, the dark corner behind the shrubbery where I stored my bow and arrows, a saber, and a broken musket. Busy with my weapons, I was oblivious to everything on earth, and only the shrill cries of the maids looking for me brought me running in alarm to meet them. They led me back to the room where punishment was always ready and waiting.

Thus passed two years until I turned twelve. That year Papa bought himself a riding horse, a Circassian stallion, almost untameable. Since he was a superb horseman, my father broke this handsome animal himself and named him Alcides. Now all my plans, intentions, and desires were concentrated on this steed. I decided to take every opportunity to make friends with him—and I succeeded. I gave him bread, sugar, and salt; I took oats from the coachman on the sly and spread them in his manger; I stroked and cajoled him, speaking to him as if he could understand me, until at last I had the unapproachable steed following me like a gentle lamb.

Nearly every day I got up at dawn, quietly left my room, and ran to the stable. Alcides greeted me with a whinny; I gave him bread and sugar and led him out into the yard. Then I brought him up to the porch and mounted him from the steps. His quick movements, frisks, and snorts never frightened me. I held onto his mane and let him canter all around our spacious yard with no fear of being carried outside the gates, because they were still locked. On one occasion this sport was interrupted by the arrival of the groom who, with a shriek of fear and astonishment, rushed to stop Alcides, who was cantering around with me. But the steed averted his head, reared, and broke into a gallop around the yard, frisking and kicking. It was fortunate for me that Efim was so numb with fear that he lost his voice; otherwise his shout would have aroused the household and drawn me harsh punishment. I quieted Alcides easily, cajoling him with my voice and patting and stroking his shoulder. He slowed to a walk, and when I hugged his neck and pressed my face to it, he stopped at once, because this was the way I always dismounted or, more accurately, slipped off him. Now Efim approached to take him, muttering through his teeth that he would tell my mother, but I promised to give him all my pocket money if he would say nothing and allow me to lead Alcides back into the stable by myself. Efim's face lighted up at this promise; he smiled, stroked his beard, and said, "Well, so be it , if the rogue obeys you better than me!" I led Alcides triumphantly into the stable, and to Efim's surprise, the un-tamed steed followed me meekly, bending his neck and bringing his head down to nibble my hair or shoulders.

With each passing day I grew more daring and enterprising, afraid of nothing on earth but my mother's wrath. It seemed very strange to me that girls of my age were afraid to be alone in the dark; on the contrary, I was prepared in the dead of night to go into a cemetery, a forest, an empty house, a cave, or a subterranean vault. In brief, there was nowhere I would not go as boldly at night as during the day. Although I, like other children, had been told tales of ghosts, corpses, wood goblins, brigands, and drowned maidens who tickled people to death, and although I believed this nonsense wholeheartedly, it had no power to frighten me. On the contrary, I thirsted for dangers and longed to be surrounded by them; I would have gone seeking them, had I had the least freedom, but my mother kept her ever-vigilant eye on my every step and every movement.

One day my mother took an excursion with other ladies to a dense pine forest on the far side of the Kama and took me with her in order, as she said, to keep me from breaking my head at home alone. This was the first time in my life I had been taken out into the open where I could see dense forest and vast fields and the wide river! I could not catch my breath for joy, and as soon as we entered the forest, out of my mind with bliss, I ran away at once and kept run-ning until the voices of the company were no longer audible. Then my joy was complete and perfect: I ran, skipped, picked flowers, and climbed to the crown of tall trees to see farther. I clambered up slender birches and, holding tight to the crown, leaped off; the sap-ling set me down gently onto the ground! Two hours flew like two minutes! Meanwhile they were searching for me and calling me in chorus. I heard them, but how could I part with such captivating freedom! At last, completely worn out, I returned to the company. I had no trouble locating them, since the calling voices had never ceased. I found my mother and all the ladies in a terrible state of anxiety. They cried out in joy when they caught sight of me, but Mama, guessing from my content expression that I had gone off on my own rather than strayed, flew into a violent rage. She poked my back and called me a damned pest of a girl, sworn to anger her al-ways and everywhere! We returned home. Mama dragged me by the ear from the drawing room directly to her bedroom and ordered me to get to work on a lace pillow with no straightening up or looking around. "Just you wait, you wretch, I'll tie you to a leash and feed you nothing but bread." With these words she went to tell Papa about what she called my monstrous behavior, while I remained to sort bobbins, set pins, and think about the lovely world of nature that I had just seen for the first time in all its majesty and beauty! From that day, although my mother's supervision and severity became even more relentless, they could no longer either intimidate me or hold me back.

From morning to night I sat over work which, I must confess, was the vilest imaginable because, unlike other girls, I could not, would not, and did not want to learn it, but ripped, ruined, and tangled it until a canvas sphere lay before me with a strip of repulsive, snarled mess stretched across it—my bobbin lace. I sat patiently over it all day long, patiently because my plan was complete, and my intentions firm. As soon as night fell, when the house quieted down, the doors were locked, and the light went out in Mama's room, I got up, dressed noiselessly, sneaked out across the back porch, and ran straight to the stables; I took out Alcides and led him across the garden to the cattle yard. Here I mounted him and rode down a narrow lane straight to the riverbank and to Startsev Mountain, where I dismounted again and, holding onto his halter, led him uphill. I had not learned to bridle him and had no way of getting him voluntarily to climb the mountain, which had such a precipitous pitch at that spot that I took him by the halter. When we reached a level place, I sought out a stump or hillock from which to remount. Then I slapped Alcides on the neck and clucked my tongue until my trusty steed broke into a canter, a gallop, and even a breakneck dash. At the first hint of dawn I returned home, put the horse in the stable, and went to sleep without undressing. It was this that led finally to the discovery of my nightly excursions. The maid who tended me kept finding me fully clothed in bed each morning and told my mother, who decided to find out how and why this was happening. She saw me go out in the dead of night fully clothed and, to her inexpressible horror, lead the wicked stallion out of the stables! Deciding that I was sleepwalking, she did not dare stop me or call out for fear of startling me. She ordered a manservant and Efim to watch me, went to Papa's room, woke him up, and told him all about it. Astonished, my father hastily got out of bed to see this singular occurrence for himself. But it had all ended sooner than they expected, and Alcides and I had been returned in triumph, each to his proper place. The servant whom Mother had ordered to follow me saw me trying to mount the horse and, unlike Mama, convinced

10. Nadezhda Durova in the uniform of the Mariupol Hussars in 1810.

that I was no sleepwalker, came out of ambush and asked me, "And where are you off to, miss?"

After this affair, my mother definitely wanted to rid herself of my company and decided to take me to my old grandmother Alex-androvicheva in the Ukraine. I was fourteen by then, tall, slim, shapely. But my martial spirit was stamped on my features, and al-though I had pale skin, bright rosy cheeks, sparkling eyes, and black brows, each day my mirror and Mama told me that I was ugly. My face was pitted from smallpox, my features irregular, and mother's constant repression of my freedom, her strictness and occasional cruelty had marked an expression of fear and sorrow on my physiognomy. Perhaps I would have at last forgotten all my Hussar habits and become an ordinary girl like the rest, if my mother had not always depicted woman's lot in the most dismal way. In my presence she would describe the fate of that sex in the most prejudicial terms: woman, in her opinion, must be born, live, and die in slavery; eternal bondage, painful dependence, and repression of every sort were her destiny from the cradle to the grave; she was full of weaknesses, devoid of accomplishments, and capable of nothing; in short, woman was the most unfortunate, insignificant, and contemptible being on earth! This description left me reeling. I swore, even if it cost me my life, to part company with the sex I supposed to be under God's curse. Papa, too, often said, "If I had a son instead of Nadezhda, I wouldn't have to worry about my old age; he would be my staff in the evening of my days." I would be ready to cry at these words from my father, whom I loved extravagantly. These two so contradictory emotions—love for my father and aversion to my own sex—troubled my young soul equally, and I passed my days working out plans to escape the sphere allotted by nature and custom to the female sex with a resolve and constancy rare in one so young.

This was my frame of mind and will when my mother delivered me at barely fourteen to my grandmother in the Ukraine and left me there. My grandfather was no longer alive. Our entire family consisted of my eighty-year-old grandmother, an intelligent and pious woman who had once been a beauty and was noted for her unusually gentle character; her son, my uncle, a middle-aged man, handsome, kind, sensitive, and insufferably capricious, who was married to a young woman of rare beauty from the Lizogub family of Chernigov; and, finally, my aunt, a spinster of about forty-five. I liked my uncle's young and beautiful wife best, but I never remained willingly in the company of my relations; they were so grand, so devout, such implacable enemies of military inclinations in a girl that I was afraid even to think about my cherished intentions in their presence. Although they in no way restricted my freedom and I could roam wherever I wished all day long without fear of scolding, if I had dared even to hint at horseback riding, I think they would have condemned me to ecclesiastic penance, so genuine was their horror at the mere thought of such illicit and, in their opinion, unnatural practices for women, especially for girls!

Under the clear sky of the Ukraine my health improved perceptibly, although at the same time I became black with the sun and even uglier than before. Here no one corseted me or drove me to death with bobbin lace. With my passion for nature and freedom, I spent all my days either running through the summer parks of my uncle's estate or boating on the Uday in the large boat the Ukrainians call a "doob." Perhaps had they known about this latter pastime, they might not have permitted it, but I was careful to undertake my navigation after dinner when my young aunt's vigilant eyes were closed in sleep. Uncle went off on errands about the estate or read the newspapers, to which my spinster aunt listened with great interest. There remained only grandmother who might have seen me, but her sight was no longer sharp and I rowed about under her windows in complete security.

In the spring another aunt, Znachko-Yavorskaya, who lived near the city of Lubny, came to visit. She became attached to me and asked grandmother's permission to take me to stay with her for the summer.

Here my occupations and pleasures were both entirely different. My aunt was a strict woman who maintained assiduous order and propriety in everything. She was hospitable and on good terms with the best society among the landowners of the district, had a good cook, and gave frequent dances. I found myself in a new sphere. Since I never heard abuse or reproach of the female sex, I began to make my peace with woman's lot, especially as I saw the polite and obliging attentions of men. Aunt dressed me very well and tried to rid my face of sunburn. My military dreams began to fade by degrees from my mind. Woman's role no longer seemed so terrible to me, and at last I grew to like my new way of life. Acquiring a friend completed the pacification of my turbulent resolve; another niece, Ostrogradskaya, a year younger than I, was also living with my aunt. We two were inseparable. We spent our mornings in Aunt's room, reading, drawing, or playing; after dinner we were free to roam until teatime and went off immediately to the *levada* (that is what they called the parcel of land usually adjoining the garden and separated from it only by a ditch). I would bound the ditch with the agility of a wild goat, my cousin followed suit, and we spent our allotted excursion flying far and wide through all the neighbors' *levadas*.

My aunt, like all Ukrainian women, was very devout and observed every ritual prescribed by religion. Every holiday she attended mass, vespers, and matins, and my cousin and I had to do the same. At first I was very reluctant to get up before dawn to go to church, but among our neighbors lived a gentry woman named Kiriakova and her son, who always came to church also. While we waited for the services to begin, Kiriakova would talk to my aunt, and her son, a young man of twenty-five, would join us, or rather me, because he spoke only to me. He was quite handsome, with beautiful black eyes, black hair and brows, and a youthful, fresh face. I began to enjoy the divine service and rose for matins even earlier than my aunt. At last my aunt noticed my conversations with young Kiriak. She began to observe us and questioned my cousin, who told her at once that Kiriak had taken my hand and asked me to give him my ring, saying that then he would consider himself sanctioned to speak to my aunt. After this explanation from my cousin, my aunt sent for me: "What does our neighbor's son say to you whenever you are together?" I had no gift for dissembling and told her immediately everything that had passed between us. Aunt shook her head, greatly displeased. "No," she said, "that's not the way to seek a girl's hand! Why on earth speak to you? He should have come directly to your family." After that I was sent back to my grandmother. I pined for young Kiriak long afterward. This was my first attachment, and I think that if I had been permitted to marry him, I would have relinquished my martial plans forever. But the fate that intended me for a battlefield career decreed otherwise. The elder Kiriakova asked Auntie to inquire whether I had any dowry and, when she heard that it consisted of nothing more than a few yards of ribbon, linen, and muslin, forbade her son to think of me.

I had turned fifteen when one day my uncle received a letter that plunged us all into grief and perplexity. The letter was from Papa; he was writing to my mother, begging her to forgive him and come home, and swearing to give it all up. No one could make head or tails of it. Where was my mother? Why was a letter to her addressed to the Ukraine? Had she left my father, and why? My uncle and grandmother were lost in conjecture.

Some two weeks after the letter arrived, I was out boating on the Uday when I suddenly heard the shrill voice of Grandmother's chambermaid: "Missy! Missy! you're to go to Grandmother!"[4] Hearing this summons frightened me; I turned the boat and mentally bade farewell to my obliging "doob," supposing that now they would order it chained to the pilings and that my excursions on the river were finished forever. "How did Grandmother happen to see me?" I asked, pulling up to the shore.

"Grandmother didn't see you," answered Agafya, "but Stepan has come for you. Your mother sent him."

Mama! For me! Was it possible? Oh, beautiful land, did I really have to leave you? . . . I hurried home. There I saw our old servant who had accompanied my father on all his campaigns. Gray-haired

Stepan respectfully handed me a letter. My father wrote that he and
my mother wished me to come home right away, that they missed
having me with them.

This I could not understand. I knew that my mother disliked me;
therefore, it was Papa who wanted me home, but why on earth had
my mother agreed? Whatever my conjectures, and however much I
regretted the necessity of leaving the Ukraine, the constraints on my
freedom that awaited me, and the unpleasant exchange of a fine climate for a cold and harsh one, I could only obey. For two days they
cooked, baked, and roasted; they gave me a huge basket of delicacies
and packed all my belongings. On the third day my venerable grandmother hugged me to her breast and, kissing me, said: "Go, my
child! The Lord's blessing on your journey! And his blessing on your
journey through life as well!" She placed her hand on my head and
quietly called down God's protection on me. The prayer of this
righteous woman was heard: throughout my turbulent military life I
have often had occasion to witness the evident intercession of the
Almighty.

There is nothing to say about my journey under the care of old
Stepan, in company with his twelve-year-old daughter Annushka. It
began and ended the way all such voyages begin and end; we traveled by slow stages over a long time and at last arrived. As I opened
the door to the drawing room of my father's house, I heard my little
sister Cleopatra saying, "Mama, come here. A young lady's arrived!"
Against my expectations, Mama received me affectionately. She was
pleased to see that I had taken on the modest and steadfast appearance so becoming to a young girl. Although I had grown a good
deal in a year and a half and was almost a head taller than my mother,
I no longer had the martial air that made me look like Achilles in
woman's dress, nor the Hussar ways that had driven her to despair.

After a few days at home I learned why they had been forced to
send for me. My father, never indifferent to beauty, had betrayed my
mother in her absence. He had taken a pretty girl, the daughter of a
local citizen, as his mistress. Mama knew nothing about it for a long
time after her return, until one of her acquaintances decided to oblige
her by disclosing the fateful secret and poisoned her life with the
strongest venom of all—jealousy! My unhappy mother listened
numbly to the tale her recklessly obliging friend had to tell and, having
heard her out, left without a word and took to her bed. When Papa
came home, she tried to speak gently and calmly to him, but how
could that be within her power! With her first words the torment in
her heart overcame her. Sobs stopped her voice. She beat her breast,
wrung her hands, and cursed the day of her birth and the moment she

first knew love. She begged my father to kill her and thus spare her the unbearable agony of living with his neglect. Papa was horrified to find my mother in such a state. He tried to placate her, begging her to disregard absurd tales, but when he saw how well informed she was of the whole affair, he swore by God and his conscience to quit his illicit alliance. Mother believed him, calmed down, and forgave him. Papa kept his word for a time. He left his mistress and even arranged a marriage for her, but then he took her back again. Mother, in despair, decided to part forever from her unfaithful husband; she set out for her mother's house in the Ukraine but stopped in Kazan. Unaware of this, Papa wrote to the Ukraine to persuade her to forgive him and return home. Meanwhile, he received a letter from my mother. She wrote that she was not strong enough to leave him, that she could not bear the thought of parting for good from a husband whom she still loved beyond measure, even though he had so cruelly abused her. She implored him to think twice and assume his responsibilities. Papa was touched; he repented and asked Mama to return. It was then that she sent for me, in the belief that the presence of his beloved daughter would force him to forget entirely the unworthy object of his affections.

Unhappy woman! She was fated to be deceived in all her hopes and to drink the bitter cup to the end! Papa went from one attachment to the next and never returned to my mother. She languished, faded, fell ill, went to Perm to be treated by the famous Gral, and died at thirty-five, more a victim of unhappiness than disease! . . . Alas, in vain I wash these lines with my tears. Woe to me, the first cause of my mother's misfortunes! My birth, sex, looks, inclinations—none of them were what my mother wanted. My existence poisoned her life; constant vexation ruined her already naturally irritable character and made her cruel. Even her exceptional beauty could not save her then. Father stopped loving her, and an untimely grave brought an end to her love, hatred, suffering, and unhappiness.

Mother, taking no more pleasure in society, began to lead a reclusive life. I took advantage of this circumstance to ask Papa's permission to ride horseback. Papa ordered a Cossack coat tailored for me and gave me his Alcides. From that time I was my father's constant companion on his excursions outside town. He enjoyed teaching me to ride well, to keep a firm seat in the saddle, and to manage the horse with skill. I was a quick student. Papa admired my agility, ease, and fearlessness. He told me that I was the living image of him as a youth and that, had I been born a boy, I would have been the staff of his old age and an honor to his name! This set my head awhirl—and this time for good! The entrancing pleasures of society, life in the Ukraine, and Kiriak's black eyes faded like a dream from my memory, and my imagination danced with brightly colored pictures of my childhood in camp among the Hussars. It all came back to me. I could not understand why I had not thought about my plan for nearly two years. My mother, depressed by grief, now described woman's lot in even more horrific colors. Martial ardor flared in my soul with invincible strength, my mind swarmed with dreams, and I began actively to search for ways to realize my previous intention: to become a soldier, to be a son to my father, and to part forever from the sex whose lot and eternal dependence had begun to terrify me.

Mother had not yet left for Perm for treatment when a Cossack regiment came to our city to quell the Tatars' constant thievery and murder.[5] Papa frequently invited the colonel and officers to dinner and rode horseback with them outside town, but I took the precaution to forego these excursions. I wanted to make sure that they never saw me in my Cossack coat and got an impression of my appearance in man's dress. I had had a brainstorm when the Cossacks arrived. Now I saw a foolproof way to carry out my long-cherished plan; I saw the possibility of waiting for the Cossacks' departure to accompany them to the regions where regular troops were stationed.

Finally the decisive time came to carry out the plan as I had sketched it. The Cossacks received orders to move out; they departed on September 15, 1806. Their first full day's rest would be some thirty miles from town. The seventeenth was my name day,[6] and the day on which, either through fate, coincidence of circumstance, or unconquerable predilection, it was fixed for me to leave my father's house and take up an entirely new way of life. On September 17 I awoke before dawn and sat by my window to await its coming. Perhaps this would be the last that I would ever see in my native land! What lay in store for me in the turbulent world? Would my mother's curse and my father's grief not pursue me? Would they survive? Could they endure until my colossal plan succeeded? How terrible it would be if their deaths took from me the goal of my actions! These thoughts swarmed all at once or passed one by one through my mind. My heart constricted and tears glistened on my eyelashes. Now the dawn was breaking. Its scarlet glow soon flooded the sky, and the beautiful light, spreading into my room, lit the objects there. My father's saber, which hung on the wall directly opposite the window, seemed to catch fire. My spirits revived. I took the saber from the wall, unsheathed it, and looked at it, lost in thought. This saber had been my toy when I was still in swaddling clothes, the consolation and exercise of my adolescent years. Why should it not now be my defense and glory in a military career as well? "I will wear you with honor," I said, kissing the blade and returning it to the sheath. The sun rose. That day Mama presented me with a gold chain, and Papa, three hundred rubles and a Hussar saddle with a scarlet saddlecloth; my little brother even gave me his gold watch. As I received my parents' gifts, I thought sadly that they had no idea that they were outfitting me for a long and dangerous road.

I spent the day with my friends. At eleven o'clock in the evening I came in to bid Mama goodnight as I usually did before bedtime. Unable to suppress my emotions, I kissed her hands several times and pressed them to my heart, something that I had never done before, nor dared to do. In spite of her dislike for me, Mama was touched by these unusual effusions of childlike affection and submission; kissing me on the head, she said: *"Go with God!"* These words held great significance for me, who had never heard a single affectionate word from my mother. I took them as a blessing, kissed her hand once more, and went out.

My rooms were in the garden. I occupied the lower floor of our garden cottage, and Papa lived upstairs. He was in the habit of dropping in on me for half an hour every evening. He enjoyed hearing me tell him where I had been and what I had done or read. Now, expecting my father's customary visit, I laid my Cossack uniform out on the bed behind the curtain, set an armchair near the stove, and stood beside it to wait for Papa to come back to his rooms. Soon I heard leaves rustle under someone's footsteps on the drive. My heart leaped! The door opened, and Papa entered. "Why are you so pale?" he asked, sitting down in the armchair. "Aren't you well?" With an effort I suppressed the sigh that threatened to rend my breast. It was the last time that my father would come into my room with the assurance of finding his daughter there. Tomorrow he would pass it by in grief, with a shudder. In it would be a sepulchral void and silence! Papa looked fixedly at me. "What's wrong? Perhaps you're ill?" I said that I was just tired and and chilled. "Why don't you have them heat your room? It's getting cold and damp." After a short silence Papa asked, "Why won't you order Efim to run Alcides on a lunge? There's no getting near him. You haven't ridden him for a long time yourself and you won't let anyone else ride him. He's so restless that he rears up even in his stall; you really should give him exercise." I said that I would order it done and fell silent again. "You seem so sad, my dear. Goodnight; go to bed," said Papa, getting up and kissing my forehead. He put one arm around me and hugged me tight. I kissed both his hands, trying to restrain the tears threatening to stream from my eyes. My body was trembling, betraying the emotions in my heart. Alas! Papa ascribed it to the cold. "You see, you're chilled through," he said. Once more I kissed his hands. "My good daughter!" said Papa fondly. He patted my cheek and left the room. I knelt beside the armchair in which he had been sitting and bowed to the ground before it, kissing and washing with my tears the spot on the floor where his foot had rested. Half an hour later, when my sorrow had somewhat abated, I got up in order to take off my feminine clothes. I went to the mirror, cut off my curls, and put them away in a drawer; I removed my black satin wrapper and put on the Cossack uniform. After tying the black silk sash tight around my waist and donning the high cap with a crimson crown, I spent a quarter of an hour studying the transformation in my appearance. My cropped hair gave me a totally new physiognomy. I was certain that no one would dream of doubting my sex. The loud rustle of leaves and the snort of a horse told me that Efim was leading Alcides into the outer yard. For the last time I stretched my arms to the image of the Mother of God that had received my prayers for so many years and went out. The door of my father's house closed behind me at last, and—who could tell?—perhaps might never open for me again!

Ordering Efim to take Alcides by the direct route to Startsev Mountain and to wait for me at the edge of the forest, I hurried to the banks of the Kama and dropped my wrapper there, laying it on the bank with all the trappings of woman's dress. I was not so barbarous as to intend for my father to think that I had drowned, and I was convinced that he would not. I just wanted to make it easier for him to answer without confusion any embarrassing questions from our short-witted acquaintances. Having left my clothing on the bank, I took a goat track leading directly uphill. The night was cold and clear; a full moon shone. I stopped to cast one last glance at the beautiful and majestic view that opened out from the heights: beyond the Kama, Perm and Orenberg provinces could be seen for boundless distances. Wide dark forests and mirror lakes were displayed as if in a painting. The city at the foot of the precipitous mountain slumbered in the midnight quiet. The moon's rays sparkled and were reflected on the gilded domes of the cathedral and lit the roof of the house in which I grew up. . . . What was my father thinking now? Did his heart tell him that tomorrow his beloved daughter would no longer come to wish him good morning?

In the night silence I could hear distinctly Efim's shout and a great snort from Alcides. I ran to meet them, and just in time: Efim was shivering with cold and cursing Alcides, whom he could not manage, and me for my delay. I took my horse from his hands, mounted, gave him the fifty rubles I had promised him, begged him not to say anything to Papa, and releasing Alcides' reins, disappeared in a flash from the dumbfounded Efim's sight.

Alcides galloped without letup for over two miles. But I had to cover thirty miles that night to the village which I knew to be the day's halt designated for the Cossack regiment, and so, reining in my steed's quick pace, I slowed to a walk. Soon I came into a dark pine forest twenty miles across. Since I wanted to conserve Alcides' strength, I continued the walking pace, surrounded by the dead silence of the forest and the dark of the autumn night, deep in reflection: "And so I'm on my own! Free! Independent! I have taken what is mine by right: my freedom. Freedom! A precious gift from heaven, everyone's inalienable birthright. I have found a way to take it, to protect it from all future claims against it; from now on it will be my portion and my reward to the grave!"

Clouds covered the sky. The forest became so dark that I could not see twenty feet ahead. At last a cold wind rising from the north forced me to go faster. Alcides broke into a full trot, and at dawn I came into the village where the Cossack regiment had stopped for the day.

## NOTES

I have used the text published by Durova in her lifetime in *Kavalerist-devitsa,* SPb., 1836. It differs little from Soviet editions.

1. Durova uses the term "Malorossija" (Little Russia) which applied technically to the part of the Ukraine that fell under Russian suzerainty in 1654. I have substituted the more familiar term *Ukraine* throughout. In general, in this translation I have tried to avoid "local color" except in cases like Durova's descriptions of the Ukraine, where she finds life somewhat exotic and strives to share that perception with her Russian contemporaries.

2. "Akusher," the French word in Russian transliteration. It was used for a male midwife, usually one who had some formal medical education.

3. In the Russian empire, women were entitled to at least a small share of the family property (including serfs).

4. The maid's hail is in Ukrainian, but it would be readily understood by a Russian speaker.

5. The phrase "to quell . . . murder" does not appear in Soviet editions.

6. Russians bore the name of a saint and celebrated that day on the church calendar whether it coincided with their birthday or not.

# Neither Auction Block nor Pedestal: "The Life and Religious Experience of Jarena Lee, A Coloured Lady"

*Frances Smith Foster*

In the past twenty years, scholars of early black American literature have made strides in unearthing and analyzing the work of nineteenth-century women. Henry Louis Gates, Jr., has revealed information concerning Harriet E. Wilson's *Our Nig; or, Sketches from the Life of a Free Black* that alters by some thirty-five years the earliest date for the first novel published by a black woman writer in the United States.[1] Jean Fagan Yellin has published evidence verifying the authenticity of Harriet Jacobs's narrative, *Incidents in the Life of a Slave Girl*.[2] Jacobs's autobiographical work is one of many narratives now known to have been written by black women of the last century.[3] And the poems of Phillis Wheatley and Frances Harper, the fiction of Harper and Pauline Hopkins, the essays of Anna Cooper and Maria Stewart—all have become familiar in black studies. While many more such works existed and will likely be brought to light in coming years, those extant span the nineteenth century and were written by women sufficiently varied in rank and region to allow scholars to challenge popular notions of nineteenth-century literature, particularly in the areas of black autobiography and women's literature.

*The Life and Religious Experience of Jarena Lee, a Coloured Lady* was published in 1836 and republished in an expanded version in 1849.[4] Although it is in itself a fascinating story of a free black woman who became the first female minister in the African Methodist Episcopal Church, Lee's narrative is especially important because it controverts the tendency to consider nineteenth-century black autobiography as synonymous with the slave narrative and the black autobiographer as synonymous with the male slave.

Since slavery was the condition of the majority of the black people in antebellum America, it is not surprising that the majority of autobiographical texts by blacks in the nineteenth century are the testimonies of exslaves concerning their lives in bondage and their struggles to be free. As Houston Baker has written, "the initial state of the black narrative is usually one of bondage, imprisonment, or circumscription—either physical or mental, or both together—and the pattern of action involves an attempt to break out of this narrow arena."[5] Typically, such a text attests to the horrors of slavery and the necessity to free those in bondage, climaxing with the hero's dangerous but successful escape and his rebirth as a new man, a moment symbolized by his choosing a new name. The slave narrative's aim was to argue that slaves were men who could function as members of a free society and that their industry, piety, and intellect needed only free soil in which to blossom. Any inclination to confess struggles against sin, temptation, or existing social norms could not be indulged. Moreover, slave narratives did not encourage complex or individualized characters. The protagonist is usually male. Female characters are generally depicted as mothers unable to nurture their offspring or women unable to preserve their virtue and graces. With the notable exception of the handful of slave narratives written by women, female characters are objects of pity; the male protagonist laments his inability to protect their virtue and to provide them with hearth and home.

By contrast, Jarena Lee, like other female protagonists such as Nancy Prince and Zilpha Elaw,[6] is a free, northern urban woman with no personal knowledge of southern rural life or slavery. Although she was not unaware or unconcerned with the problems of slavery, her interests are at once broader and more personal. She identifies racial prejudice as more pervasive than slavery and sexism as inextricably bound with racism in oppressing her and her kind. Unlike slave narrators who emphasize their ignorance of basic personal referents such as birthdate or parentage, in order to reveal simultaneously the dehumanizing aspects of slavery, Lee's opening sentence claims a definite origin from which she begins her travels and experiences: "I was born February 11th, 1783, at Cape May, state of New Jersey. At the age of seven years I was parted from my parents, and went to live as a servant maid, with a Mr. Sharp, at the distance of about sixty miles from my place of birth."[7] Lee's second sentence stresses her precocious independence by the role she assumes in going to work as a maid for an impersonally identified "Mr. Sharp," and by her willingness to travel far from her parental home. The image that Lee conveys is not that of a fugitive breaking away from the imprisoning community, but a pioneer breaking into the community and developing a sense of selfhood, one, in fact, that has more in common with the characterizations of women in seventeenth- and eighteenth-century literature as "forthright, earthy and capable,"[8] rather than the frail, dependent, emotional nineteenth-century creatures who must be protected by men from the rigors of the out-side world.

This "Cult of True Womanhood," as the nineteenth-century ideal of femininity has been called, promoted the virtues of "piety, purity, sub-missiveness and domesticity,"[9] and made the home and the private-sphere woman's natural habitat. As Nina Baym has observed: "laws aiming to keep her there were for her own benefit as well as the public good; women who felt legally or culturally restrained were unnatural; women who for whatever reason, *had* to leave the home were pitiable and of no account."[10] That this Cult of True Womanhood strongly influenced black literature is confirmed by the tragic mulatto figure that dominates nineteenth-century black fiction and by the values expressed in the private writings of many free black women.[11] From the opening lines of her narrative, however, Jarena Lee establishes herself as an independent woman who decided to work outside the home not only to support herself but also because it was the right thing to do. She refutes the notion that the ultra-feminine lady by the hearth is the only one deserving respect, since she identifies herself as a "coloured lady." Although her characterization does not indicate a revolt against the established virtues of womanhood, she essentially argues for a more liberal interpretation by demonstrating that even when her activities appeared unseemly to others, she did not abandon domesticity, submission, purity and piety.

Jarena Lee's narrative is a spiritual autobiography written, she says, "for the satisfaction of such as may follow after me, when I am no *more*, . . ." (p. 24). In the manner of the Puritan and Quaker conversion narratives, it contains a confession of sin, a testimony of conversion, and demonstra-tions of subsequent commitment to God's work. The text, however, is shaped by the factors of race and sex. In her quest for religious fulfillment, she apparently investigated doctrines ranging from Roman Catholicism to those of independent fundamentalist evangelists, eventually embracing Methodism and regularly worshipping with the English Church in Phila-delphia. She insists, though, that she always felt "a wall between me and a communion with that people, which was higher than I could possibly see over, and seemed to make this impression upon my mind, *this is not the people for you*" (p. 5). She encountered Richard Allen and, upon joining that congregation,[12] had her long-sought conversion experience within three weeks. Lee thus makes it clear that she needed the community of blacks, even though she did not limit her ministry to any race. And yet, within that community, she experienced further difficulties because of sex-ual prejudices. For although her congregation accepted her sanctification, the Methodist Church did not allow women ministers. Lee details this setback and her subsequent six-year marriage to a minister, whose work she was convinced to support by a dream, as further trials of her faith.

Clearly, however, this protagonist's reluctance to acknowledge her call to ministry is based largely on the awareness that it is not considered proper for women to preach. She adheres to the definition of proper female conduct until convinced that God sometimes demands greater demonstrations of submission and piety. Only after a voice urges her to " 'Preach the Gospel; I will put words in your mouth, and will turn your enemies to become your friends'" (p. 12), does she approach Richard Allen with her intentions. To her readers she justifies her actions by declaring that "as unseemly as it may appear now-a-days for a woman to preach, it should be remembered that nothing is impossible with God" (p. 14). And yet, when she begins her own ministry, she confines her activities to visiting the sick, holding prayer meetings, and exhorting only in private homes "as I found liberty" (p. 18). When "an altogether supernatural impulse" (p. 21) forces her to interrupt a sermon to testify and the bishop accepts this as divine sanction, her apprehension is replaced with "a sweet serenity, a holy joy of a peculiar kind" (p. 21), and she begins to speak publicly. Ultimately, believing that God did not want her to be diverted from her calling, Lee broke up her household, found friends to care for her two surviving children, and forsook "all to preach the everlasting Gospel" (p. 22).

Jarena Lee is to be counted among a significant number of nineteenth-century black female evangelists who forsook the hearth to travel and spread the Gospel. These women went to the West Indies, the rural South, or simply into the ghettos of their own cities to teach and to create institutions for the protection and betterment of women, children, and men. Aware that their lives deviated from the conventions for both blacks and women, they did not, however, present themselves as models for either group. Instead, they asserted the right and the necessity for self-definition according to their understanding of divine intentions for them as individuals. Although the autobiographical details may vary, these narratives present female protagonists who can enrich our concepts of history and literature and thus of our notions of selfhood.

## NOTES

1. Harriet E. Wilson, *Our Nig; or, Sketches from the Life of a Free Black* (1856; reprinted, New York: Vintage Books, 1983). Prior to Gates' information, the first novel by an Afro-American woman was thought to be Emma Kelly's *Megda*, published in 1891.

2. [Harriet Jacobs], *Incidents in the Life of a Slave Girl. Written By Herself*. Ed. L. Maria Child (1861; reprinted, New York: Harcourt Brace Jovanovich, 1973). Jean Fagan Yellin, "Written By Herself: Harriet Jacobs' Slave Narrative," *American Literature* 53 (November 1981): 479–86. Until Yellin's discoveries, many had proclaimed the narrative as having been substantially created by Lydia Maria Child.

3. See Bert James Lowenberg and Ruth Bogin, eds., *Black Women in Nineteenth Century American Life* (University Park: Pennsylvania State Univ. Press, 1976).

4. Jarena Lee, *Religious Experience and Journal of Mrs. Jarena Lee, Giving an Account of Her Call to Preach the Gospel* (Philadelphia: printed for the author, 1849). The 1849 version was four times as long as the first publication.

5. Houston A. Baker, Jr., *Singers of Daybreak: Studies in Black American Literature* (Washington, D.C.: Howard Univ. Press, 1974), p. 9.

6. See for example Zilpha Elaw, *Memoirs* (London: printed for the author, 1846); Nancy Prince, *A Narrative of the Life and Travels of Mrs. Nancy Prince* (Boston: printed for the author, 1853); or Maria W. Stewart, *Productions of Mrs. Maria W. Stewart* (Boston: printed for the author, 1835).

7. *The Life and Religious Experience of Jarena Lee, A Coloured Lady, Giving An Account of Her Call to Preach the Gospel* (Philadelphia, printed for the author, 1836), p. 3. Subsequent references to Lee's narrative are from this edition and appear in the text.

8. See Ann Stanford, "Images of Women in Early American Literature," in *What Manner of Woman*, ed. Marlene Springer (New York: New York Univ. Press, 1977), p. 187.

9. Barbara Welter, "The Cult of True Womanhood: 1820–1860," *American Quarterly* 28 (Summer 1966), p. 152.

10. Nina Baym, "Women in American Literature, 1796–1870," in *What Manner of Woman*, p. 212.

11. Martin Delany's rebuke to those whose survival did not necessitate their continuing in domestic service reveals an acceptance of the notion that women's place is in the home:

"We do not say too much, when we say, as an evidence of the deep degradation of our race, in the United States, that there are those among us, the wives and daughters, some of the *first ladies*, . . . whose husbands are industrious, able and willing to support them, who voluntarily leave home, and become chambermaids, and stewardesses, . . . in all probability, to enable them to obtain some more fine or costly article of dress or furniture.

"We have nothing to say against those whom *necessity* compels to do these things, those who can do no better; we have only to do with those who can, and will not, or do not do better."

Martin Robison Delany, *The Condition, Elevation, Emigration and Destiny of the Colored People of the United States* (1852; reprinted, New York: Arno Press, 1969), pp. 198–99.

12. Richard Allen, one of the first two black men ordained in the American Methodist Church, was preaching at St. George's in Philadelphia. As the number of black members increased, the white members began to impress increasingly greater limitations upon their participation. Shortly after Lee's membership, Allen led the black members in protests that culminated in their creation of a separate church, the African Methodist Episcopal Church. In 1816 Allen was elected Bishop of the AME Church. By 1818 there were sixteen churches and a membership of 6,748, about one-half of that number in the Philadelphia church. The AME Church was the first black Protestant denomination in the United States and continues to this day as a major force in the black religious world.

The
LIFE
and
RELIGIOUS EXPERIENCE
of
JARENA LEE,
A Coloured Lady,
Giving an account of her call to preach the gospel.

Revised and corrected from the original manuscript,
Written by herself.

Philadelphia:
Printed and published for the author.
1836.


And it shall come to pass . . . that I will pour out my
Spirit upon all flesh; and your sons, and your
*daughters* shall prophecy.

Joel ii. 28.


I was born February 11th, 1783, at Cape May, state of New Jersey.
At the age of seven years I was parted from my parents, and went to
live as a servant maid, with a Mr. Sharp, at the distance of about
sixty miles from the place of my birth.

My parents being wholly ignorant of the knowledge of God, had
not therefore instructed me in any degree in this great matter. Not
long after the commencement of my attendance on this lady, she had
bid me to do something respecting my work, which in a little while
after, she asked me if I had done, when I replied, yes—but this was
not true.

At this awful point, in my early history, the spirit of God moved
in power through my conscience, and told me I was a wretched sinner. On this account so great was the impression, and so strong were
the feelings of guilt, that I promised in my heart that I would not tell
another lie.

But notwithstanding this promise my heart grew harder after a
while; yet the spirit of the Lord never entirely forsook me, but continued mercifully striving with me, until his gracious power converted my soul.

The manner of this great accomplishment, was as follows: In the
year 1804, it so happened that I went with others to hear a mission-

ary of the Presbyterian order preach. It was an afternoon meeting, but few were there, the place was a school room; but the preacher was solemn, and in his countenance the earnestness of his master's business appeared equally strong, as though he were about to speak to a multitude.

At the reading of Psalms, a ray of renewed conviction darted into my soul. These were the words, composing the first verse of the Psalms for the service:

Lord, I am vile, conceived in sin,
Born unholy and unclean.
Sprung from man, whose guilty fall
Corrupts the race, and taints us all.

This description of my condition struck me to the heart, and made me to feel in some measure, the weight of my sins, and sinful nature. But not knowing how to run immediately to the Lord for help, I was driven of Satan, in the course of a few days, and tempted to destroy myself.

There was a brook about a quarter of a mile from the house, in which there was a deep hole, where the water whirled about among the rocks; to this place it was suggested, I must go and drown myself.

At the time I had a book in my hand; it was on a Sabbath morning, about ten o'clock; to this place I resorted, where on coming to the water I sat down on the bank, and on my looking into it; it was suggested, that drowning would be an easy death. It seemed as if some one was speaking to me, saying put your head under, it will not distress you. But by some means, of which I can give no account, my thoughts were taken entirely from this purpose, when I went from the place to the house again. It was the unseen arm of God which saved me from self murder.

But notwithstanding this escape from death, my mind was not at rest—but so great was the labour of my spirit and the fearful oppressions of a judgment to come, that I was reduced as one extremely ill. On which account a physician was called to attend me, from which illness I recovered in about three months.

But as yet I had not found him of whom Moses and the prophets did write, being extremely ignorant: there being no one to instruct me in the way of life and salvation as yet. After my recovery, I left the lady, who during my sickness, was exceedingly kind, and went to Philadelphia. From this place I soon went a few miles into the country, where I resided in the family of a Roman Catholic. But my anxiety still continued respecting my poor soul, on which account I used to watch my opportunity to read in the Bible; and this lady observing this, took the Bible from me and hid it, giving me a novel in its stead—which when I perceived, I refused to read.

Soon after this I again went to the city of Philadelphia; and commenced going to the English Church, the pastor of which was an Englishman, by the name of Pilmore,[1] one of the number, who at first preached Methodism in America, in the city of New York.

But while sitting under the ministration of this man, which was about three months, and at the last time, it appeared that there was a wall between me and a communion with that people, which was higher than I could possibly see over, and seemed to make this impression upon my mind, *this is not the people for you.*

But on returning home at noon I inquired of the head cook of the house respecting the rules of the Methodists,—as I knew she belonged to that society—who told me what they were; on which account I replied that I should not be able to abide by such strict rules not even one year. However, I told her that I would go with her and hear what they had to say.

The man who was to speak in the afternoon of that day, was the Rev. Richard Allen, since Bishop of the African Episcopal Methodists in America. During the labors of this man that afternoon, I had come to the conclusion, that this is the people to which my heart unites, and it so happened, that as soon as the service closed he invited such as felt a desire to flee the wrath to come, to unite on trial with them—I embraced the opportunity. Three weeks from that day, my soul was gloriously converted to God, under preaching, at the very outset of the sermon. The text was barely pronounced, which was: "I perceive thy heart is not right in the sight of God," when there appeared to *my* view, in the centre of the heart *one* sin; and this was *malice,* against one particular individual, who had strove deeply to injure me, which I resented. At this discovery I said, *Lord* I forgive *every* creature. That instant it appeared to me as if a garment, which had entirely enveloped my whole person, even to my fingers' ends, split at the crown of my head, and was stripped away from me, passing like a shadow from my sight; when the glory of God seemed to cover me in its stead.

That moment, though hundreds were present, I did leap to my feet, and declare that God, for Christ's sake, had pardoned the sins of my soul. Great was the ecstasy of my mind, for I felt that not only the sin of *malice* was pardoned, but all other sins were swept away together. That day was the first when my heart had believed, and my tongue had made confession unto salvation. The first words uttered, a part of that song, which shall fill eternity with its sound, was *glory to God*. For a few moments I had power to exhort sinners, and to tell of the wonders and of the goodness of him who had clothed me with *his* salvation. During this, the minister was silent, until my soul felt its duty had been performed, when he declared another witness of the power of Christ to forgive sins on earth was manifest in my conversion.

From the day on which I first went to the Methodist church, until the hour of my deliverance, I was strangely buffetted by that enemy of all righteousness—the devil.

I was naturally of a lively turn of disposition; and during the space of time from my first awakening until I knew my peace was made with God, I rejoiced in the vanities of this life, and then again sunk back into sorrow.

For four years I had continued in this way, frequently labouring under the awful apprehension that I could never be happy in this life. This persuasion was greatly strengthened, during the three weeks which was the last of Satan's power over me, in this peculiar manner: on which account, I had come to the conclusion that I had better be dead than alive. Here I was again tempted to destroy my life by drowning; but suddenly this mode was changed, and while in the dusk of the evening, as I was walking to and fro in the yard of the house, I was beset to hang myself with a cord suspended from the wall enclosing the secluded spot.

But no sooner was the intention resolved on in my mind than an awful dread came over me, when I ran into the house; still the tempter pursued me. There was standing a vessel of water; into this I was strongly impressed to plunge my head, so as to extinguish the life which God had given me. Had I have done this, I have been always of the opinion that I should have been unable to have released myself; although the vessel was scarcely large enough to hold a gallon of water. Of me may it not be said, as written by Isaiah, (chap. 65, verses 1, 2) "I am sought of them that asked not for me; I am found of them that sought me not." Glory be to God for his redeeming power, which saved me from the violence of my own hands, from the malice of Satan, and from eternal death; for had I have killed myself, a great ransom could not have delivered me; for it is written, "No murderer hath eternal life abiding in him." How appropriately can I sing

Jesus sought me, when a stranger,
  Wandering from the fold of God;
He to rescue me from danger,
  Interposed his precious blood.

But notwithstanding the terror which seized upon me, when about to end my life, I had no view of the precipice on the edge of which I was tottering, until it was over, and my eyes were opened. Then the awful gulf of hell seemed to be open beneath me, covered only, as it were, by a spider's web, on which I stood. I seemed to hear the howling of the damned, to see the smoke of the bottomless pit, and to hear the rattling of those chains which hold the impenitent under clouds of darkness to the judgment of the great day.

I trembled like Belshazzar, and cried out in the horror of my spirit, "God be merciful to me a sinner." That night I formed a resolution to pray; which, when resolved upon, there appeared, sitting in one corner of the room, Satan, in the form of a monstrous dog, and in a rage, as if in pursuit, his tongue protruding from his mouth to a great length, and his eyes looked like two balls of fire; it soon, however, vanished out of my sight. From this state of terror and dismay I was happily delivered under the preaching of the Gospel as before related.

This view which I was permitted to have of Satan in the form of a dog is evidence, which corroborates in my estimation, the Bible account of a hell of fire, which burneth with brimstone, called in the Scripture the bottomless pit, the place where all liars, who repent not, shall have their portion; as also the Sabbath breaker, the adulterer, the fornicator, with the fearful, the abominable, and the unbelieving, this shall be the portion of their cup.

This language is too strong and expressive to be applied to any state of suffering in *time*. Were it to be thus applied, the reality could nowhere be found in human life; the consequence would be, that *this* scripture would be found a false testimony. But when made to apply to an endless state of perdition, in eternity, beyond the bounds of human life, then this language is found not to exceed our views of a state of eternal damnation.

During the latter part of my state of conviction, I can now apply to my case, as it then was, the beautiful words of the poet:

The more I strove against its power,
I felt its weight and guilt the more;
Till late I hear'd my Saviour say,
Come hither soul, I am the way.

This I found to be true, to the joy of my disconsolate and despairing heart, in the hour of my conversion to God.

During this state of mind, while sitting near the fire one evening, after I had heard Rev. Richard Allen, as before related, a view of my distressed condition so affected my heart, that I could not refrain from weeping and crying aloud; which caused the lady with whom I then lived to inquire with surprise, what ailed me; to which I answered that I knew not what ailed me. She replied that I ought to pray. I arose from where I was sitting, being in an agony, and weeping convulsively, requested her to pray for me; but at the very moment when she would have done so, some person rapped heavily at the door for admittance; it was but a person of the house, but this occurrence was sufficient to interrupt us in our intentions; and I believe to this day, I should then have found salvation to my soul. This interruption was doubtless also the work of Satan.

Although at this time, when my conviction was so great, yet I knew not that Jesus Christ was the Son of God, the second person in the adorable trinity. I knew him not in the pardon of my sins, yet I felt a consciousness that if I died without pardon, that my lot must inevitably be damnation. If I would pray—I knew not how. I could form no connexion of ideas into words; but I knew the Lord's prayer; this I uttered with a loud voice, and with all my might and strength. I was the most ignorant creature in the world; I did not even know that Christ had died for the sins of the world, and to save sinners. Every circumstance, however, was so directed as still to continue and increase the sorrows of my heart, which I now know to have been a godly sorrow which wrought repentance, which is not to be repented of. Even the falling of the dead leaves from the forests, and the dried spires of the mown grass, showed me that I too must die in like manner. But my case was awfully different from that of the grass of the field, or the widespread decay of a thousand forests, as I felt within me a living principle, an immortal spirit, which cannot die, and must forever either enjoy the smiles of its Creator, or feel the pangs of ceaseless damnation.

But the Lord led me on. Being gracious, he took pity on my ignorance; he heard my wailings, which had entered into the ear of the Lord of Sabaoth. Circumstances so transpired that I soon came to a knowledge of the being and character of the Son of God, of whom I knew nothing.

My strength had left me. I had become feverish and sickly through the violence of my feelings, on which account I left my place of service to spend a week with a coloured physician, who was a member of the Methodist society, and also to spend this week in going to places where prayer and supplication was statedly [regularly] made for such as me.

Through this means I had learned much, so as to be able in some degree to comprehend the spiritual meaning of the text, which the minister took on the Sabbath morning, as before related, which was,

"I perceive thy heart is not right in the sight of God." Acts, chap. 8, verse 21.

This text, as already related, became the power of God unto salvation to me, because I believed. I was baptized according to the direction of our Lord, who said, as he was about to ascend from the mount, to his disciples, "Go ye into all the world and preach my gospel to every creature, he that believeth and is baptized shall be saved."

I have now passed through the account of my conviction, and also of my conversion to God; and shall next speak of the blessing of sanctification.

A time after I had received forgiveness flowed sweetly on; day and night my joy was full, no temptation was permitted to molest me. I could say continually with the psalmist, that "God had separated my sins from me, as far as the east is from the west." I was ready continually to cry

Come all the world, come sinner thou,
All things in Christ are ready now.

I continued in this happy state of mind for almost three months, when a certain coloured man, by name William Scott, came to pay me a religious visit. He had been for many years a faithful follower of the Lamb; and he had also taken much time in visiting the sick and distressed of our colour, and understood well the great things belonging to a man of full stature in Christ Jesus.

In the course of our conversation, he inquired if the Lord had justified my soul. I answered, yes. He then asked me if he had sanctified me. I answered, no; and that I did not know what that was. He then undertook to instruct me further in the knowledge of the Lord respecting this blessing.

He told me the progress of the soul from a state of darkness, or of nature, was threefold; or consisted in three degrees, as follows: First, conviction for sin. Second, justification from sin. Third, the entire sanctification of the soul to God. I thought this description was beautiful, and immediately believed in it. He then inquired if I would promise to pray for this in my secret devotions. I told him, yes. Very soon I began to call upon the Lord to show me all that was in my heart, which was not according to his will. Now there appeared to be a new struggle commencing in my soul, not accompanied with fear, guilt, and bitter distress, as while under my first conviction for sin; but a labouring of the mind to know more of the right way of the Lord. I began now to feel that my heart was not clean in his sight; that there yet remained the roots of bitterness, which if not destroyed, would ere long sprout up from these roots, and overwhelm me in a new growth of the brambles and brushwood of sin.

By the increasing light of the Spirit, I had found there yet remained the root of pride, anger, self-will, with many evils, the result of fallen nature. I now became alarmed at this discovery, and began to fear that I had been deceived in my experience. I was now greatly alarmed lest I should fall away from what I knew I had enjoyed; and to guard against this I prayed almost incessantly, without acting faith on the power and promises of God to keep me from falling. I had not yet learned how to war against temptation of this kind. Satan well knew that if he could succeed in making me disbelieve my conversion, that he would catch me either on the ground of complete despair, or on the ground of infidelity. For if all I had passed through was to go for nothing, and was but a fiction, the mere ravings of a disordered mind, then I would naturally be led to believe that there is nothing in religion at all.

From this snare I was mercifully preserved, and led to believe that there was yet a greater work than that of pardon to be wrought in me. I retired to a secret place (after having sought this blessing, as well as I could, for nearly three months, from the time brother Scott had instructed me respecting it) for prayer, about four o'clock in the afternoon. I had struggled long and hard, but found not the desire of my heart. When I rose from my knees, there seemed a voice speaking to me, as I yet stood in a leaning posture—"Ask for sanctification." When to my surprise, I recollected that I had not even thought of it in my whole prayer. It would seem Satan had hidden the very object from my mind, for which I had purposely kneeled to pray. But when this voice whispered in my heart, saying, "Pray for sanctification," I again bowed in the same place, at the same time, and said, "Lord *sanctify* my soul for Christ's sake?" That very instant, as if lightning had darted through me, I sprang to my feet, and cried, "The Lord has sanctified my soul!" There was none to hear this but the angels who stood around to witness my joy—and Satan, whose malice raged the more. That Satan was there, I knew; for no sooner had I cried out "The Lord has sanctified my soul," than there seemed another voice behind me saying, "No, it is too great a work to be done." But another spirit said, "Bow down for the witness—I received it—*thou art sanctified!*" The first I knew of myself after that, I was standing in the yard with my hands spread out, and looking with my face toward heaven.

I now ran into the house and told them what had happened to

me, when, as it were, a new rush of the same ecstasy came upon me, and caused me to feel as if I were in an ocean of light and bliss.

During this, I stood perfectly still, the tears rolling in a flood from my eyes. So great was the joy that it is past description. There is no language that can describe it, except that which was heard by St. Paul, when he was caught up to the third heaven, and heard words which it was not lawful to utter.

## MY CALL TO PREACH THE GOSPEL

Between four and five years after my sanctification, on a certain time, an impressive silence fell upon me, and I stood as if some one was about to speak to me, yet I had no such thought in my heart. But to my utter surprise there seemed to sound a voice which I thought I distinctly heard, and most certainly understood, which said to me, "Go preach the Gospel!" I immediately replied aloud, "No one will believe me." Again I listened, and again the same voice seemed to say, "Preach the Gospel; I will put words in your mouth, and will turn your enemies to become your friends."

At first I supposed that Satan had spoken to me, for I had read that he could transform himself into an angel of light, for the purpose of deception. Immediately I went into a secret place, and called upon the Lord to know if he had called me to preach, and whether I was deceived or not; when there appeared to my view the form and figure of a pulpit, with a Bible lying thereon, the back of which was presented to me as plainly as if it had been a literal fact.

In consequence of this, my mind became so exercised that during the night following, I took a text and preached in my sleep. I thought there stood before me a great multitude, while I expounded to them the things of religion. So violent were my exertions, and so loud were my exclamations, that I awoke from the sound of my own voice, which also awoke the family of the house where I resided. Two days after, I went to see the preacher in charge of the African Society,[2] who was the Rev. Richard Allen (the same before named in these pages) to tell him that I felt it my duty to preach the gospel. But as I drew near the street in which his house was, which was in the city of Philadelphia, my courage began to fail me; so terrible did the cross appear, it seemed that I should not be able to bear it. Previous to my setting out to go to see him, so agitated was my mind that my appetite for my daily food failed me entirely. Several times on my way there, I turned back again; but as often I felt my strength again renewed, and I soon found that the nearer I approached to the house of the minister, the less was my fear. Accordingly, as soon as I came to the door, my fears subsided, the cross was removed, all things appeared pleasant—I was tranquil.

I now told him that the Lord had revealed it to me that I must preach the gospel. He replied by asking, in what sphere I wished to move in? I said, among the Methodists. He then replied, that a Mrs. Cook, a Methodist lady, had also some time before requested the same privilege; who it was believed, had done much good in the way of exhortation, and holding prayer meetings; and who had been permitted to do so by the verbal license of the preacher in charge at the time.[3] But as to women preaching, he said that our Discipline knew nothing at all about it—that it did not call for women preachers. This I was glad to hear, because it removed the fear of the cross—but not no sooner did this feeling cross my mind, than I found that a love of souls had in a measure departed from me; that holy energy which burned within me as a fire, began to be smothered. This I soon perceived.

O how careful ought we to be, lest through our bylaws of church government and discipline, we bring into disrepute even the word of life. For as unseemly as it may appear nowadays for a woman to preach, it should be remembered that nothing is impossible with God. And why should it be thought impossible, heterodox, or improper for a woman to preach, seeing the Saviour died for the woman as well as the man?

If the man may preach, because the Saviour died for him, why not the woman, seeing he died for her also? Is he not a whole Saviour, instead of a half one, as those who hold it wrong for a woman to preach, would seem to make it appear?

Did not Mary *first* preach the risen Saviour, and is not the doctrine of the resurrection the very climax of Christianity—hangs not all our hope on this, as argued by St. Paul? Then did not Mary, a woman, preach the gospel? For she preached the resurrection of the crucified Son of God.

But some will say that Mary did not expound the Scripture, therefore she did not preach, in the proper sense of the term. To this I reply, it may be that the term *preach,* in those primitive times, did not mean exactly what it is now *made* to mean; perhaps it was a great deal more simple then, than it is now: if it were not, the unlearned fishermen could not have preached the gospel at all, as they had no learning.

To this it may be replied by those who are determined not to believe that it is right for a woman to preach, that the disciples, though they were fishermen, and ignorant of letters too, were inspired to do so. To which I would reply, that though they were inspired, yet that inspiration did not save them from showing their ignorance of letters, and of man's wisdom; this the multitude soon found out, by listening to the remarks of the envious Jewish priests. If then, to preach the gospel, by the gift of heaven, comes by inspiration solely, is God straitened; must he take the man exclusively? May he not, did he not, and can he not inspire a female to preach the simple story of the birth, life, death, and resurrection of our Lord, and accompany it too, with power to the sinner's heart. As for me, I am fully persuaded that the Lord called me to labour according to what I have received, in his vineyard. If he has not, how could he consistently bear testimony in favour of my poor labours, in awakening and converting sinners?

In my wanderings up and down among men, preaching according to my ability, I have frequently found families who told me that they had not for several years been to a meeting, and yet, while listening to hear what God would say by his poor coloured female instrument, have believed with trembling, tears rolling down their cheeks—the signs of contrition and repentance towards God. I firmly believe that I have sown seed in the name of the Lord, which shall appear with its increase at the great day of its accounts, when Christ shall come to make up his jewels.

At a certain time I was beset with the idea that soon or late I should fall from grace, and lose my soul at last. I was frequently called to the throne of grace about this matter, but found no relief; the temptation pursued me still. Being more and more afflicted with it, till at a certain time when the spirit strongly impressed it on my mind to enter into my closet, and carry my case once more to the Lord; the Lord enabled me to draw nigh to him, and to his mercy seat, at this time, in an extraordinary manner; for while I wrestled with him for the victory over this disposition to doubt whether I should persevere, there appeared a form of fire, about the size of a man's hand, as I was on my knees; at the same moment, there appeared to the eye of faith a man robed in a white garment, from the shoulders down to the feet; from him a voice proceeded, saying: "Thou shalt never return from the cross." Since that time I have never doubted, but believed that God will keep me until the day of redemption. Now I could adopt the very language of St. Paul, and say that nothing could have separated my soul from the love of God, which is in Christ Jesus. From that time, 1807, until the present, 1833, I have not yet doubted the power and goodness of God to keep me from falling, through sanctification of the spirit and belief of the truth.

### MY MARRIAGE

In the year 1811, I changed my situation in life, having married Mr. Joseph Lee, Pastor of a Coloured Society at Snow Hill, about six miles from the city of Philadelphia. It became necessary therefore for me to remove. This was a great trial at first, as I knew no person at Snow Hill, except my husband; and to leave my associates in the society, and especially those who composed the band of which I was one.[4] Not but those who have been in sweet fellowship with such as really love God, and have together drank bliss and happiness from the same fountain, can tell how dear such company is, and how hard it is to part from them.

At Snow Hill, as was feared, I never found that agreement and closeness in communion and fellowship, that I had in Philadelphia among my young companions, nor ought I to have expected it. The manners and customs at this place were somewhat different, on which account I became discontented in the course of a year, and began to importune my husband to remove to the city. But this plan did not suit him, as he was the Pastor of the Society; he could not bring his mind to leave them. This afflicted me a little. But the Lord soon showed me in a dream what his will was concerning this matter.

I dreamed that as I was walking on the summit of a beautiful hill, that I saw near me a flock of sheep, fair and white, as if newly wash-ed; when there came walking toward me a man of grave and digni-fied countenance, dressed entirely in white, as it were in a robe, and looking at me, said emphatically, "Joseph Lee must take care of these sheep, or the wolf will come and devour them." When I awoke, I was convinced of my error, and immediately, with a glad heart, yielded to the right way of the Lord. This also greatly strengthened my hus-band in his care over them, for fear the wolf should by some means take any of them away. The following verse was beautifully suited to our condition, as well as to all the little flocks of God scattered up and down this land:

> Us into Thy protection take,
>   And gather with Thine arm;
> Unless the fold we first forsake,
>   The wolf can never harm.

After this, I fell into a state of general debility, and in an ill state of health; so much so, that I could not sit up; but a desire to warn sinners to flee the wrath to come burned vehemently in my heart, when the Lord would send sinners into the house to see me. Such opportunities I embraced to press home on their consciences the things of eternity, and so effectual was the word of exhortation made through the Spirit, that I have seen them fall to the floor crying aloud for mercy.

From this sickness I did not expect to recover; and there was but one thing which bound me to earth, and this was, that I had not as yet preached the gospel to the fallen sons and daughters of Adam's race, to the satisfaction of my mind. I wished to go from one end of the earth to the other, crying, Behold, behold the Lamb! To this end I earnestly prayed the Lord to raise me up, if consistent with his will. He condescended to hear my prayer, and to give me a token in a dream, that in due time I should recover my health. The dream was as follows: I thought I saw the sun rise in the morning, and ascend to an altitude of about half an hour high, and then become obscured by a dense black cloud, which continued to hide its rays for about one-third part of the day, and then it burst forth again with renewed splendour.

This dream I interpreted to signify my early life, my conversion to God, and this sickness, which was a great affliction, as it hindered me, and I feared would forever hinder me from preaching the gospel, was signified by the cloud; and the bursting forth of the sun, again, was the recovery of my health, and being permitted to preach.

I went to the throne of grace on this subject, where the Lord made this impressive reply in my heart, while on my knees: "Ye shall be restored to thy health again, and worship God in full purpose of heart."

This manifestation was so impressive that I could but hide my face, as if someone was gazing upon me, to think of the great goodness of the Almighty God to my poor soul and body. From that very time I began to gain strength of body and mind, glory to God in the highest, until my health was fully recovered.

For six years from this time I continued to receive from above such baptisms of the Spirit as mortality could scarcely bear. About that time I was called to suffer in my family by death—five, in the course of about six years, fell by his hand; my husband being one of the number, which was the greatest affliction of all.

I was now left alone in the world, with two infant children, one of the age of about two years, the other six months, with no other dependence than the promise of Him who hath said, "I will be the widow's God, and a father to the fatherless." Accordingly, he raised me up friends, whose liberality comforted and solaced me in my state of widowhood and sorrows. I could sing with the greatest propriety the words of the poet.

> He helps the stranger in distress,
> The widow and the fatherless,
> And grants the prisoner sweet release.

I can say even now, with the Psalmist, "Once I was young, but now I am old, yet I have never seen the righteous forsaken, nor his seed begging bread." I have ever been fed by his bounty, clothed by his mercy, comforted and healed when sick, succoured when tempted, and every where upheld by his hand.

## THE SUBJECT OF MY CALL TO PREACH RENEWED

It was now eight years since I had made application to be permitted to preach the gospel, during which time I had only been allowed to exhort, and even this privilege but seldom. This subject was now renewed afresh in my mind; it was as a fire shut up in my bones. About thirteen months passed on, while under this renewed impression. During this time, I had solicited of the Rev. Bishop Richard Allen, who at this time had become Bishop of the African Episcopal Methodists in America, to be permitted the liberty of holding prayer meetings in my own hired house, and of exhorting as I found liberty, which was granted me. By this means, my mind was relieved, as the house was soon filled when the hour appointed for prayer had arrived.

I cannot but relate in this place, before I proceed further with the above subject, the singular conversion of a very wicked young man. He was a coloured man, who had generally attended our meetings, but not for any good purpose; but rather to disturb and to ridicule our denomination. He openly and uniformly declared that he neither believed in religion, nor wanted anything to do with it. He was of a Gallio disposition, and took the lead among the young people of colour. But after a while he fell sick, and lay about three months in a state of ill health; his disease was a consumption. Toward the close of his days, his sister who was a member of the society, came and desired me to go and see her brother, as she had no hopes of his recovery; perhaps the Lord might break into his mind. I went alone, and found him very low. I soon commenced to inquire respecting his state of feeling, and how he found his mind. His answer was, "O tolerable well," with an air of great indifference. I asked him if I should pray for him. He answered in a sluggish and careless manner, "O yes, if you have time." I then sung a hymn, kneeled down and prayed for him, and then went my way.

Three days after this, I went again to visit the young man. At this time there went with me two of the sisters in Christ. We found the Rev. Mr. Cornish, of our denomination, labouring with him. But he said he received but little satisfaction from him. Pretty soon, however, brother Cornish took his leave; when myself, with the other two sisters, one of which was an elderly woman named Jane Hutt, the other was younger, both coloured, commenced conversing with him, respecting his eternal interest, and of his hopes of a happy eternity, if any he had. He said but little; we then kneeled down together and besought the Lord in his behalf, praying that if mercy were not clear gone forever, to shed a ray of softening grace upon the hardness of his heart. He appeared now to be somewhat more tender, and we thought we could perceive some tokens of conviction, as he wished us to visit him again, in a tone of voice not quite as indifferent as he had hitherto manifested.

But two days had elapsed after this visit, when his sister came for me in haste, saying, that she believed her brother was then dying, and that he had sent for me. I immediately called on Jane Hutt, who was still among us as a mother in Israel, to go with me. When we arrived there, we found him sitting up in his bed, very restless and uneasy, but he soon laid down again. He now wished me to come to him, by the side of his bed. I asked him how he was. He said, "Very ill;" and added, "Pray for me, quick?" We now perceived his time in this world to be short. I took up the hymnbook and opened to a hymn suitable to his case, and commenced to sing. But there seemed to be a horror in the room—a darkness of a mental kind, which was felt by us all; there being five persons, except the sick young man and his nurse. We had sung but one verse, when they all gave over singing, on account of this unearthly sensation, but myself. I continued to sing on alone, but in a dull and heavy manner, though looking up to God all the while for help. Suddenly, I felt a spring of energy awake in my heart, when darkness gave way in some degree. It was but a glimmer from above. When the hymn was finished, we all kneeled down to pray for him. While calling on the name of the Lord, to have mercy on his soul, and to grant him repentance unto life, it came suddenly into my mind never to rise from my knees until God should hear prayer in his behalf, until he should convert and save his soul.

Now, while I thus continued importuning heaven, as I felt I was led, a ray of light, more abundant, broke forth among us. There appeared to my view (though my eyes were closed) the Saviour in full stature, nailed to the cross, just over the head of the young man, against the ceiling of the room. I cried out, brother look up, the Saviour is come, he will pardon you, your sins he will forgive. My sorrow for the soul of the young man was gone; I could no longer pray—joy and rapture made it impossible. We rose up from our knees, when lo, his eyes were gazing with ectasy upward; over his face there was an expression of joy; his lips were clothed in a sweet and holy smile; but no sound came from his tongue; it was heard in its stillness of bliss, full of hope and immortality. Thus, as I held him by the hand his happy and purified soul soared away, without a sigh or a groan, to its eternal rest.

I now closed his eyes, straightened out his limbs, and left him to be dressed for the grave. But as for me, I was filled with the power of the Holy Ghost—the very room seemed filled with glory. His sister and all that were in the room rejoiced, nothing doubting but he had entered into Paradise; and I believe I shall see him at the last and great day, safe on the shores of salvation.

But to return to the subject of my call to preach. Soon after this, as above related, the Rev. Richard Williams was to preach at Bethel Church, where I with others were assembled.[5] He entered the pulpit, gave out the hymn, which was sung, and then addressed the throne of grace; took his text, passed through the exordium, and commenced to expound it. The text he took is in Jonah, 2d chap. 9th verse,—"Salvation is of the Lord." But as he proceeded to explain, he seemed to have lost the spirit; when in the same instant, I sprang, as by an altogether supernatural impulse, to my feet, when I was aided from above to give an exhortation on the very text which my brother Williams had taken.

I told them that I was like Jonah; for it had been then nearly eight years since the Lord had called upon me to preach his gospel to the fallen sons and daughters of Adam's race, but that I had lingered like him, and delayed to go at the bidding of the Lord, and warn those who are as deeply guilty as were the people of Ninevah.

During the exhortation, God made manifest his power in a manner sufficient to show the world that I was called to labour according to my ability, and the grace given unto me, in the vineyard of the good husbandman.

I now sat down, scarcely knowing what I had done, being frightened. I imagined, that for this indecorum, as I feared it might be called, I should be expelled from the church. But instead of this, the Bishop rose up in the assembly, and related that I had called upon him eight years before, asking to be permitted to preach, and that he had put me off; but that he now as much believed that I was called to that work, as any of the preachers present. These remarks greatly strengthened me, so that my fears of having given an offence and made myself liable as an officer subsided, giving place to a sweet serenity, a holy joy of a peculiar kind, untasted in my bosom until then.

The next Sabbath day, while sitting under the word of the gospel, I felt moved to attempt to speak to the people in a public manner, but I could not bring my mind to attempt it in church. I said, Lord, anywhere but here. Accordingly, there was a house not far off which was pointed out to me; to this I went. It was the house of a sister belonging to the same society with myself. Her name was Anderson. I told her I had come to hold a meeting in her house, if she would call in her neighbours. With this request she immediately complied. My congregation consisted of but five persons. I commenced by reading and singing a hymn, when I dropped to my knees by the side of a table to pray. When I arose I found my hand resting on the Bible, which I had not noticed till that moment. It now occurred to me to take a text. I opened the Scripture, as it happened, at the 141st Psalm, fixing my eye on the 3d verse, which reads: "Set a watch, O Lord, before my mouth, keep the door of my lips." My sermon, such as it was, I applied wholly to myself, and added an exhortation. Two of my congregation wept much, as the fruit of my labour this time. In closing I said to the few, that if any one would open a door, I would hold a meeting the next sixth-day evening; when one answered that her house was at my service. Accordingly, I went and God made manifest his power among the people. Some wept, while others shouted for joy. One whole seat of females, by the power of God, as the rushing of a wind, were all bowed to the floor at once, and screamed out. Also a sick man and woman in one house, the Lord convicted them both; one lived, and the other died. God wrought a judgment—some were well at night, and died in the morning. At this place I continued to hold meetings for about six months. During that time I kept house with my little son, who was very sickly. About this time I had a call to preach at a place about thirty miles distant, among the Methodists, with whom I remained one week, and during the whole time not a thought of my little son came into my mind; it was hid from me, lest I should have been diverted from the work I had to do, to look after my son. Here by the instrumentality of a poor coloured woman, the Lord poured forth his spirit among the people. Though, as I was told, there were lawyers, doctors, and magistrates present to hear me speak, yet there was mourning and crying among sinners, for the Lord scattered fire among them of his own kindling. The Lord gave his handmaiden power to speak for his great name, for he arrested the hearts of the people, and caused a shaking amongst the multitude, for God was in the midst.

I now returned home, found all well; no harm had come to my child, although I left it very sick. Friends had taken care of it which was of the Lord. I now began to think seriously of breaking up housekeeping, and forsaking all to preach the everlasting Gospel. I felt a strong desire to return to the place of my nativity, at Cape May, after an absence of about fourteen years. To this place, where the heaviest cross was to be met with, the Lord sent me, as Saul of Tarsus was sent to Jerusalem, to preach the same gospel which he had neglected and despised before his conversion. I went by water, and on my passage was much distressed by sea sickness, so much so that I expected to have died, but such was not the will of the Lord respecting me. After I had disembarked, I proceeded on as opportunities offered, toward where my mother lived. When within ten miles of that place, I appointed an evening meeting. There were a goodly number came out to hear. The Lord was pleased to give me light and liberty among the people. After meeting, there came an elderly lady to me and said she believed the Lord had sent me among them; she then appointed me another meeting there two weeks from that night. The next day I hastened forward to the place of my mother, who was happy to see me, and the happiness was mutual between us. With her I left my poor sickly boy, while I departed to do my Master's will. In this neighborhood I had an uncle who was a Methodist, and who gladly threw open his door for meetings to be held there. At the first meeting which I held at my uncle's house, there was, with others who had come from curiosity to hear the coloured woman preacher, an old man, who was a deist, and who said he did not believe the coloured people had any souls—he was sure they had none. He took a seat very near where I was standing, and boldly tried to look me out of countenance. But as I laboured on in the best manner I was able, looking to God all the while, though it seemed to me I had but little liberty, yet there went an arrow from the bent bow of the gospel, and fastened in his till then obdurate heart. After I had done speaking, he went out, and called the people around him, said that my preaching might seem a small thing, yet he believed I had the worth of souls at heart. This language was different from what it was a little time before, as he now seemed to admit that coloured people had souls, as it was to these I was chiefly speaking;

and unless they had souls, whose good I had in view, his remark must have been without meaning. He now came into the house, and in the most friendly manner shook hands with me, saying he hoped God had spared him to some good purpose. This man was a great slave holder, and had been very cruel; thinking nothing of knocking down a slave with a fence stake, or whatever might come to hand. From this time it was said of him that he became greatly altered in his ways for the better. At that time he was about seventy years old, his head as white as snow; but whether a converted man or not, I never heard.

The week following, I had an invitation to hold a meeting at the Court House of the County, when I spoke from the 53d chap. of Isaiah, 3d verse. It was a solemn time, and the Lord attended the word; I had life and liberty, though there were people there of various denominations. Here again I saw the aged slaveholder, who notwithstanding his age, walked about three miles to hear me. This day I spoke twice, and walked six miles to the place appointed. There was a magistrate present, who showed his friendship by saying in a friendly manner that he had heard of me: he handed me a hymnbook, pointing to a hymn which he had selected. When the meeting was over, he invited me to preach in a schoolhouse in his neighbourhood, about three miles distant from where I then was. During this meeting one backslider was reclaimed. This day I walked six miles, and preached twice to large congregations, both in the morning and evening. The Lord was with me, glory be to his holy name. I next went six miles and held a meeting in a coloured friend's house, at eleven o'clock in the morning, and preached to a well behaved congregation of coloured and white. After service, I again walked back, which was in all twelve miles in the same day. This was on Sabbath, or as I sometimes call it, seventh-day; for after my conversion I preferred the plain language of the Quakers: On fourth day, after this, in compliance with an invitation received by note, from the same magistrate who had heard me at the above place, I preached to a large congregation, where we had a precious time: much weeping was heard among the people. The same gentleman, now at the close of the meeting, gave out another appointment at the same place, that day of the week. Here again I had liberty, there was a move among the people. Ten years from that time, in the neighbourhood of Cape May, I held a prayer meeting in a school house, which was then the regular place of preaching for the Episcopal Methodists; after service, there came a white lady of the first distinction, a member of the Methodist Society, and told me that at the same schoolhouse, ten years before, under my preaching, the Lord first awakened her. She rejoiced much to see me, and invited me home with her, where I staid till the next day. This was bread cast on the waters, seen after many days.

From this place I next went to Dennis Creek meeting house, where at the invitation of an elder, I spoke to a large congregation of various conflicting sentiments, when a wonderful shock of God's power was felt, shown everywhere by groans, by sighs, and loud and happy amens. I felt as if aided from above. My tongue was cut loose, the stammerer spoke freely; the love of God, and of his service, burned with a vehement flame within me; his name was glorified among the people.

But here I feel myself constrained to give over, as from the smallness of this pamphlet I cannot go through with the whole of my journal, as it would probably make a volume of two hundred pages; which, if the Lord be willing, may at some future day be published. But for the satisfaction of such as may follow after me, when I am no more, I have recorded how the Lord called me to his work, and how he has kept me from falling from grace, as I feared I should. In all things he has proved himself a God of truth to me; and in his service I am now as much determined to spend and be spent, as at the very first. My ardour for the progress of his cause abates not a whit, so far as I am able to judge, though I am now something more than fifty years of age.

As to the nature of uncommon impressions, which the reader cannot but have noticed, and possibly sneered at in the course of these pages, they may be accounted for in this way: It is known that the blind have the sense of hearing in a manner much more acute than those who can see: also their sense of feeling is exceedingly fine, and is found to detect any roughness on the smoothest surface, where those who can see can find none. So it may be with such as I am, who has never had more than three months schooling; and wishing to know much of the way and law of God, have therefore watched the more closely the operations of the Spirit, and have in consequence been led thereby. But let it be remarked that I have never found that Spirit to lead me contrary to the Scriptures of truth, as I understand them. "For as many as are led by the *Spirit* of God are the sons of God."—Rom. viii. 14.

I have now only to say, May the blessing of the Father, and of the Son, and of the Holy Ghost, accompany the reading of this poor effort to speak well of his name, wherever it may be read. AMEN.

## Notes

1. Pilmore: Joseph Pilmore (1739–1825) was one of the founders of Philadelphia's St. George's Methodist Church.

2. The Free African Society was founded in 1787 as a nonsectarian benevolent body dedicated to improving the physical and moral conditions of black people.

3. Lee may be referring to Dorothy Ripley, a visitor from Britain, who petitioned Allen to speak at St. George's in 1803. Although Allen denied her petition, Ripley took it upon herself to address the congregation following one of Allen's sermons. Her act sparked a disturbance in the church. See "Letter of Richard Allen to Dorothy Ripley, May 11, 1803," *Journal of Negro History* 1 (1916), 436–38.

4. Although the AME Conference minutes published the names of its ministers, there is no mention of Joseph Lee. The 1818 record does note the death of "Joseph Lea, a man of God, who has labored for many years in the ministry, during which time he supported the character of a Christian and a faithful minister, a kind and loving husband and a tender father." Jarena Lee's husband died about that time. The difference between Philadelphia and Snow Hill, New Jersey, may be inferred from the 1816 AME Conference census, which lists 3,311 members in Philadelphia and 56 in Snow Hill.

5. Richard Williams was an elder in the Baltimore AME Congregation.

# Fanny Mendelssohn Hensel:
# Musician in Her Brother's Shadow

## *Marcia J. Citron*

Fanny Mendelssohn Hensel (1805–1847), four years senior to Felix, her celebrated brother, was the eldest of four children born to the successful banker,
Abraham Mendelssohn, and his cultured wife, Lea Salomon. Granddaughter
of the illustrious philosopher-theologian Moses Mendelssohn (1729–1786),
Fanny was raised in a family that would assume a central position in the
musico-intellectual life of Berlin and count luminaries such as Alexander von
Humboldt and G. W. F. Hegel within its circle.

The musical talent derived from the maternal side of the family. Many
members of Lea's family, including Lea herself, were musicians trained in
the Berlin tradition promulgated by Johann Philipp Kirnberger (1721–
1783), a student of J. S. Bach. It was Lea who gave Fanny and Felix their
first piano lessons. At Fanny's birth, Lea had claimed the child had "Bach
fingers"; and indeed, by the age of twelve, she could play all twenty-four
preludes of one volume of Bach's *The Well-Tempered Clavier* from memory. Soon after, the Berlin pedagogue, Ludwig Berger, became Fanny's
and Felix's piano instructor, and in 1820 they entered the relatively new,
but prestigious Berlin Sing Academy and studied theory and composition
with its leader, Karl Friedrich Zelter (1758–1832).[1] Given this training, it is
not surprising that Fanny's earliest compositions date from this period.

Beginning in 1821, however, the musical paths of the two siblings began
to diverge: Felix was clearly being groomed for the possibility of making a
career in music, and Fanny was not.[2] She continued her activities in composition and piano, but her father made it clear on at least two occasions
that these activities were to be secondary to "your real calling, the *only*
calling of a young woman—I mean the state of a housewife."[3] She married the court painter Wilhelm Hensel (1794–1861) in 1829, bore her only

child, Sebastian, the following summer, and in general seems to have had a happy marriage. Her compositional output became less intense and concentrated after 1830, but starting in 1831, she assumed an increasingly important role in organizing and directing the Sunday musicales that the Mendelssohns had instigated as early as 1823. Here she played host to the major musical artists of the day as they passed through Berlin, and performed on the piano as soloist, chamber music partner, accompanist, and choral director. Traditionally a socially acceptable means of displaying a woman's creative and intellectual prowess, the salon, centered at home, served to introduce both Fanny's and Felix's music.

Fanny composed approximately four hundred and fifty pieces.[4] Most of her *oeuvre* consists of lieder and piano pieces, but she also wrote works with orchestra, including an oratorio, and a few chamber pieces. Fanny's compositions garnered praise from contemporaries, including Goethe, the composer-pianist Ignaz Moscheles, the Berlin theorist-composer Adolph Bernhard Marx, and the Scottish music critic John Thomson. They became familiar with her music through private performances, given by Fanny or Felix, because her scores remained almost entirely in manuscript form, at least until the last year of her life. Her first foray into the professional world of music through publication was hidden—three pieces in each of Felix's lieder collections Opus 8 (1827) and Opus 9 (1830), under his name.[5] The first piece issued under her own authorship was a lied, "Die Schiffende," contributed to an anthology in January 1837.[6] Five months later, Lea wrote to Felix asking him to encourage and assist Fanny in publishing her works,[7] but Felix responded negatively: "Fanny, as I know her, possesses neither the inclination nor calling for authorship. She is too much a woman for that, as is proper, and looks after her house and thinks neither about the public nor the musical world, unless that primary occupation is accomplished. Publishing would only disturb her in these duties, and I cannot reconcile myself to it."[8] Felix's negative views undoubtedly played an influential role in the nonpublication of her music for another decade,[9] for as Fanny herself reveals, she felt the need for his approval of any publishing venture: "On this issue alone it's crucial to have your consent, for without it I might not undertake anything of the kind."[10] Yet, in all other avenues of her musical activities, from composing, to performing, to leading the Sunday musicales, to critiquing his music, Felix was very supportive of his "Fenchel." Unlike these "amateur" activities, however, publishing signified authorship, authority, and professionalism.

To date, Fanny Hensel has been treated almost exclusively as a peripheral figure to Felix,[11] and this includes her writings. Most of her diaries and many of her letters are located in private possession or restricted in public collections, but one large group is accessible: the two hundred seventy-nine extant letters to her brother that are part of Oxford's vast "Green Books" collection of letters addressed to Felix.[12] These letters, almost entirely unpublished, furnish considerable information about Fanny's life and music, disclose her role in shaping Felix's works in progress, and illuminate the contemporary artistic world through the eyes of a fine-tuned critical mind.[13]

Both of the letters here, presented in their entirety, come from the Green Books. The first dates from July 30, 1836, two months after Felix's oratorio *St. Paul* had received its successful premiere. Goethe, whom the family had known personally and whose spirit is near and dear to their hearts, occupies a prominent place in the letter. That both brother and sister happen to be reading Goethe's biography, *Dichtung und Wahrheit,* is interpreted as a sign of spiritual affinity between them. The jocular tone Fanny adopts in reference to a woman Felix may be thinking of marrying sheds light on the warmth of their relationship. While she discusses the repertoire and schedule of her musicales, she expresses a desire to be associated with Felix's activities—to work on the piano arrangement of his oratorio and to keep up with the latest revisions of the piece. Particularly significant are Fanny's statements about the great influence Felix exerts over her and the warning to "treat me with great care."

With the passage of a decade, the span between the first and second letters, Felix gained greater distinction as a composer, pianist, and conductor, and their relationship underwent important changes. Whereas ten years earlier Fanny occupied a prominent place in shaping Felix's oratorio *St. Paul,* now she knows not one note of his second oratorio, *Elijah.* Her resentment over Felix's recent lack of written communication is evidence that she still harbors the wish to enter his world, the professional world of music that has largely been denied her. When Fanny launches into the topic of publishing, the wording she chooses betrays pent-up frustration and even bitterness, in part directed at Felix.[14] Her assurance that he will not be bothered by her publishing hints at sarcasm, and her statement that she has always needed encouragement rings true, though she was never encouraged by her acclaimed brother to publish under her own autograph.

Less than a year later Fanny Hensel is dead. She suffered a swift, fatal stroke on May 14, 1847, while rehearsing Felix's *Die erste Walpurgisnacht* with her choir. One hundred and forty years later her music and writings are still largely shrouded in obscurity. Only when her work is finally published will we be able to assess the significance of her achievements and acquire greater understanding of the problems and challenges facing gifted women in the nineteenth century.

## NOTES

1. It was relatively unusual for a female to receive training in theory and composition. Women's musical education was generally confined to suitable female areas, especially piano and voice.

2. Felix, as a mere twelve-year old, was taken by Zelter to Goethe and touted as a *Wunderkind*. Four years later, Felix went with Abraham on a trip to Paris and was encouraged to make musical contacts and imbibe the French musical atmosphere. Just as important, Abraham took Felix to the well-known composer Luigi Cherubini (1760–1842) to receive an expert's assessment of his son's potential for success as a professional musician.

3. Letter to Fanny of November 14, 1828, in Sebastian Hensel, *The Mendelssohn Family (1729–1847)*, 2nd ed., trans Carl Klingemann, Vol. 1 (New York: Harper & Brothers, 1882); facs. ed. (New York: Greenwood Press, 1968), p. 84.

4. The number is an estimate because relatively few of her works were published, and a significant share of her autographs are in private possession. She Rudolf Elvers, "Verzeichnis der Musik-Autographen von Fanny Hensel in dem Mendelssohn-Arkiv zu Berlin," *Mendelssohn Studien*, I (Berlin: Duncker & Humblot, 1972), 169–74; and *idem.*, "Weitere Quellen zu den Werken von Fanny Hensel," *Mendelssohn Studien*, II (1975), pp. 215–20.

5. "Das Heimweh," "Italien," and the duet "Suleika" are No. 2, No. 3, and No. 12 of Opus 8. "Sehnsucht," "Verlust," and "Die Nonne" are No. 7, No. 10, and No. 12 of Opus 9.

6. Published by the Berlin firm of Schlesinger.

7. Unpublished letter of June 7, 1837, in the "Green Books" collection of letters addressed to Felix, the Bodleian Library, Oxford.

8. My translation. Letter of June 24, 1837, which is incorrectly dated June 2, 1837, as published in Felix Mendelssohn-Bartholdy, *Briefe aus den Jahren 1830 bis 1847*, ed. Paul Mendelssohn Bartholdy and Carl Mendelssohn Bartholdy, 3rd ed., 2 vols. (Leipzig: Hermann Mendelssohn, 1875), II, pp. 88–89. The autograph is located in the New York Public Library.

9. With the exception of the lied "Schloss Liebeneck," published in an anthology in 1839.

10. Letter to Felix, November 22, 1836, from the Green Books.

11. Recent exceptions are an article by the present author, "The Lieder of Fanny Mendelssohn Hensel," *The Musical Quarterly*, LXIX (1983), 570–94; and two unpublished doctoral dissertations by Victoria Sirota (Boston, 1981) and Carol Quin (Kentucky, 1981). See also my study, "Felix Mendelssohn's Influence on Fanny Hensel as a Professional Composer," *Current Musicology* 37/38 (1984), 9–18.

12. For an index to the more than 5,000 items, see Margaret Crum, *Catalogue of the Mendelssohn Papers in the Bodleian Library,* Vol. 1 (Tutzing: Hans Schneider, 1980).

13. The author has prepared an edition of Fanny's letters to Felix in English translation and the original German for Pendragon Press (1987).

14. In only one previous letter to Felix, of June 2, 1837 (Green Books), does Fanny's bitterness toward her brother approach the level in this letter. The impetus for the anger in the earlier letter, however, centers on the fact that the family has not met Felix's wife and Fanny senses that Felix is alienating himself from her and the family. I suspect that Felix's lack of support for her publishing plans also played a role.

Berlin, July 30, 1836

It doesn't occur to me to be angry or request a few personal letters, dear Felix. I certainly would have already replied to your previous letter,[1] but when I sat down earlier, took out some paper, picked up the quill, and considered what I should write, I didn't know anything, just like Humboldt's monkeys, who can't speak because they have nothing to say. But the manifold delights in your most recent letter[2] provide me with things to write about even though there's nothing to report here. Among other things, one of the most enjoyable turned out to be one of those little coincidences that occur more often as we get older and which I don't care to ascribe to chance. You are reading Goethe's biography for the first time since childhood, and I've been engaged in the same activity for several weeks. Eckermann's book[3] no doubt prompted this reading, but there may be several thousand people reading that book but not Goethe's biography afterward. I was also thinking that if I ever return to Frankfurt, I must become acquainted with that city in connection with his life.[4] I'm reading the 4th volume to Hensel now, just as I did with the Eckermann.

Furthermore, your lovely young lady from Frankfurt arouses my interest not inconsiderably.[5] You would not believe how I wish for your marriage; I sincerely feel that it would be best for you. If I were Sancho[6] I would cite a whole list of maxims to hasten a favorable decision: "nothing ventured, nothing gained;" "fortune favors the brave;" "grab the bull by the horns;" "strike while the iron is hot;" and many others that are not suitable here. It really sounds as though you're serious this time, and if you fall in love with Doris Zelter in the Hague now[7] and nothing comes of it, I will be highly disappointed. By the way, it just occurred to me that all your romances (see Rosalie Mendelssohn's unpublished works)[8] have taken place away from home, and so I've never seen you in the midst of a courtship, and yet I'm very curious about this area of your life. These are all bad jokes, but in all seriousness, I would very much like you to get married.

I held two very pleasant rehearsals of *St. Paul* while Decker[9] was here. But now everybody is scattered in all directions and so I think the event will have to be postponed until the fall. I'm truly sorry that you've had such a tough time with the piano arrangement; had you given me even one part of the job, I would have gladly worked hard on it. Furthermore, I am liking the oratorio more and more as I know it better. The weak passages, or those that appear so to me, that we have discussed[10] are few in number, and I'm very curious about the most recent changes. For example, have you really omitted the first chorus as well? I hope not "Der du die Menschen"— that aria has grown on me.[11]

The local music scene is more slovenly than ever. I'd love to know why they engaged Hauser, since he never performs.[12] At Hensel's request I've started performing again on Sundays, but the Ganzes are not here,[13] and I'm really too spoiled to let myself be accompanied by beginners. As the strict taskmaster has ordered,[14] I've continued to compose piano pieces and for the first time have succeeded in completing one that sounds brilliant. I don't know exactly what Goethe means by demonic influence that he mentioned very often near the end,[15] but this much is clear: if it does exist, you exert it over me. I believe that if you seriously suggested that I become a good mathematician, I wouldn't have any particular difficulty in doing so, and I could just as easily cease being a musician tomorrow if you thought I wasn't good at that any longer. Therefore treat me with great care.

Just as there is a Young Germany, there is a boring Germany that Beckchen is finding in Eiger, and an odious Germany that you are discovering in Scheveningen.[16] Madame Robert and Herr von Varnhagen[17] can even make one detest palm trees and oysters. But please don't lose this letter in the sea, for then one of them would be certain to find it and love me accordingly.

Adieu. Hensel sends his best. Dirichlet is leaving today and then mother will be our dinner guest. She usually listens when I read to Hensel, and that gives me great joy because lovely memories are associated with that pastime.

Farewell, and remain fond of me.

Berlin, July 9, 1846

My dear Felice, thank you for your letter with the nicest news that positioned your mention of the rice pudding at the top, naturally.[18] I could have tolerated more news, for if you imagine that Cecile wrote a great deal, you are, as they say here, under a false illusion. Cecile is too stolid to write details. I gratefully acknowledge, however, that I was the idiot upon whom you bestowed a half hour [of your time]. And why not? Am I to imagine that I'm not as worthy in your eyes as Spohr?[19] I definitely won't be such a modest rogue. In fact, we could conclude a contract with each other stating that you would write a long letter after every music festival and every important event so that one could find out about them. Whenever we get together after a long separation, too many of the details are lost, and, as Gans said,[20] it is better to hear some things twice than not at all. Now an entire oratorio of yours[21] is being introduced to the world again, and I don't know a note of it. When will we hear it? Actually I wouldn't expect you to read this rubbish now, busy as you are, if I didn't have to tell you something. But since I know from the start that you won't like it, it's a bit awkward to get under way. So laugh at me or not, as you wish: I'm afraid of my brothers at age 40, as I was of father at age 14.—Or, more aptly expressed, desirous of pleasing you and everyone I've loved throughout my life. And when I now know in advance that it won't be the case, I thus feel rather[22] uncomfortable. In a word, I'm beginning to publish. I have Herr Bock's[23] sincere offer for my lieder and have finally turned a receptive ear to his favorable terms. And if I've done it of my own free will and cannot blame anyone in my family if aggravation results from it (friends and acquaintances have indeed been urging me for a long time), then I can console myself, on the other hand, with the knowledge that I in no way sought out or induced the type of musical reputation that might have elicited such offers. I hope I won't disgrace all of you through my publishing, as I'm no *femme libre* and unfortunately not even an adherent of the *Young* Germany movement. I trust *you* will in no way be bothered by it, since, as you can see, I've proceeded completely on my own in order to spare you any possible unpleasant moment. I hope you won't think badly of me. If it succeeds—that is, if the pieces are well liked and I receive additional offers—I know it will be a great stimulus to me, something I've always needed in order to create. If not, I'll be as indifferent as I've always been and not be upset, and then if I work less or stop completely, nothing will have been lost by that either.[24] "That is the true basis of our existence and salvation."

Would it be possible to borrow the music of the dervish chorus from Leipzig sometime?[25] I don't need it now, in any case, because the next Sunday will be the last musicale for the summer. You will be receiving my chief bass, Behr, in Leipzig.[26] I believe he will become a very good comic singer, but he must tone down his excessive buffoonery a bit. He certainly has a talent for comedy. What do you think of this heavenly summer? I'm truly sorry that you have to spend it in the Königstrasse.[27] I'm enjoying the garden more than ever and love it more tenderly than ever—perhaps a premonition that we will lose it soon. All kinds of plans regarding selling the house and horrible plans about tearing it down and breaking through the street are spooked again, but Pourtalès[28] would be a real fool if he didn't buy it.

Farewell, you dear ones. Say hello to dear Cecile and all five children. Hensel also sends his best.

Your Fanny.

Just one more request. If Herr von Keudell,[29] whom you certainly know, drops by to see you within the next 2 weeks, and perhaps at a time when you're very busy, receive him warmly nevertheless, for he's here with us very often and is a close musical pal. He has the finest feeling for music and a memory that I've seen in no one except you. Works such as Schubert's Op. 150, Beethoven's Op. 130, a few numbers from Mendelssohn's Op. 60, and many other trifles he knows by heart; he also plays very well.

The above-signed.

## NOTES

1. Of July 18, 1836, in the New York Public Library (NYPL) collection.
2. Of July 24, 1836 (NYPL).
3. Johann Peter Eckermann's *Gespräche mit Goethe* (1836–48).
4. Goethe was born in Frankfurt.
5. Cecile Jeanrenaud, whom Felix was to marry in 1837.
6. Probably the servant in Cervante's *Don Quixote*.
7. Doris Zelter, the daughter of Karl Friedrich Zelter.
8. This is apparently an imaginary person.
9. Pauline Decker, celebrated Berlin soprano of opera and oratorio.
10. As in Fanny's detailed critique in her letter to Felix of February 4, 1836 (Green Brooks).
11. The first chorus was retained, but the soprano aria "Der du die Menschen" was not, although it was issued posthumously as part of Felix's Opus 112.
12. Franz Hauser, operatic baritone and collector of Bach manuscripts.
13. The violinist Leopold Ganz and his cellist brother Moritz, both close musical friends of Fanny.
14. That is, Felix.
15. Found, for example, in both Eckermann's *Gespräche* and Goethe's biography.
16. Young Germany: a liberal politico-social movement; Beckchen is their younger sister, Rebecka, married to the mathematician Peter Gustav Lejeune Dirichlet, who is cited at the close of this letter as "Dirichlet."
17. The diplomat and writer Karl August Varnhagen von Ense, husband of Rahel. The identity of Madame Robert is uncertain.
18. One of Felix's favorite dishes.
19. The composer and violinist Louis Spohr was a guest at Felix's in Leipzig.
20. Eduard Gans, student of Hegel and professor of law in Berlin.
21. *Elijah.*
22. This word appears in English in the original letter.
23. Gustav Bock, co-founder of the Berlin music publishing firm of Bote & Bock (1838).
24. Seven collections (op. 1 through 7) were prepared by Fanny for publication before she died in May 1847; four more were compiled by family members after her death and issued c. 1851.
25. Part of Beethoven's Incidental Music to Kotzebue's *The Ruins of Athens*, Op. 113.
26. Heinrich Behr, who later became a stage director at the Leipzig opera.
27. Felix and his family live at Königstrasse 3 in Leipzig.
28. Count Friedrich von Pourtalès, Berlin minister of protocol, who rented a section of the family estate.
29. Robert von Keudell, a musician friend of Fanny's.

# Women as Law Clerks:
# Catharine G. Waugh

*Nancy F. Cott*

Catharine Waugh's memoir, one of many documents of women's embattled entry into the "learned professions," reflects the particular form of the legal profession's "bars" to women. Law, unlike medicine, had no precedents for female practitioners in nineteenth-century America. To enter legal practice at that time a woman not only had to sidestep the limits on her contractual and property rights but also had to brave hostility, scorn, rejection, or neglect from most lawyers, judges, and clerks of court. On the other hand, without some male allies women could not have entered the profession at all. The early women lawyers gained their training mostly by self-education and informal apprenticeship to brothers, fathers, uncles, or husbands. Because a law degree was not requisite to practice (and would not become so until early in the twentieth century), admission to the bar rather than to law school was the first crucial hurdle. State statutes either explicitly asserted or were interpreted to allow only men's admission. Every conceivable argument from common-law constraints on wives to female disenfranchisement, from reproductive biology, supposedly inferior female intellect and rational judgment, to women's essential moral purity, was invoked to prevent women from entering the bar.

And yet gradually, after Arabella Mansfield in Iowa made the first breach in 1869, women forced changes in one state bar after another.[1] In Illinois, Myra Bradwell's famous efforts paved the way for Catharine Waugh. Bradwell, having studied law with her husband from the time of their marriage in 1852, took and passed the Illinois bar examination in 1869. When the state Supreme Court refused her admission to the bar because of her sex, Bradwell took her case to the United States Supreme Court, arguing (via her male attorney) that the "privileges and immunities" clause of the newly passed Fourteenth Amendment to the Constitution prevented a state legislature from excluding any class of citizens from the legal profession. The United States Supreme Court rejected her appeal on the ground that admission to practice law was not a right dependent on or controlled by citizenship and thus was not protected by the Fourteenth Amendment. Between Bradwell's state and federal suits, however, the Illinois legislature passed an act in 1872 giving all persons freedom of choice in occupation.[2]

Catharine Waugh, then, was not "barred from the bar," nor from law school. Having completed the course at Rockford Female Seminary in 1882, she went in 1885 to Union College of Law (later Northwestern University Law School) in Chicago, the school from which Ada Kepley, the first woman to earn a law degree in the United States, had graduated in 1870. When she finished law school in 1886, Waugh was one of approximately 100 women lawyers in the country, a member of an even smaller minority who were not wives, daughters, or other relatives of male lawyers.[3] Thus, although she had followed the modern professional route and taken a law degree, Waugh lacked the critical advantage of a guaranteed placement for the "apprentice." Her tribulations and frustrations in attempting to situate herself, a single, 24-year-old female lawyer, in the male legal establishment of Chicago in 1886, form the substance of her memoir.

Catharine Waugh wrote the memoir shortly after she returned to her hometown of Rockford, Illinois, to set up her own practice. While living there she took an M.A. at the Female Seminary and investigated women's disadvantagement in the labor market in her thesis, "Women's Wages," which was published in 1888. She exerted herself in the woman suffrage movement, raising fears among some of her contemporaries that she would desert the legal profession. "I said to myself, there's a young woman who is going to raise the credit of women in the legal profession," wrote a suffragist friend to Waugh, "and here while I'm chewing the cud of reflection you flit out of law and go off [to suffrage work]."[4] Soon acquaintances anticipated a different distraction when Waugh married a law school suitor, Frank Hathorn McCulloch, in 1890. She bore four children between 1891 and 1905. However, the marriage helped her achieve the professional aim that had been frustrated as she became a partner in her husband's Chicago law firm. Asked in 1920 how a female lawyer should "resolve the paradox" between vocation and marriage, Catharine Waugh McCulloch replied, "I don't know, tho [sic] I am used as the example of one who does both. . . . In running our home and caring for our children I believe I am a greater success than as a lawyer. My husband is the valuable one in the law firm."[5] It is hard to know whether to interpret this statement as modesty or pride in a woman who not only remained an active partner in the law firm but became increasingly involved in women's rights, led the fight for woman suffrage in Illinois (the first state east of the Mississippi River to grant women presidential suffrage, in 1913), served for years as legal advisor, frequent speaker, and national officer of the National American Woman Suffrage Association, worked avidly at the state level to remove women's civil and legal disabilities, and directed the League of Women Voters' legal department after its founding in 1920. Her efforts spanned five decades, during which she saw women admitted to the bar of every state and the proportion of women in the legal profession rise from zero to almost three percent.

In her memoir, which is dated "probably early in 1887," Waugh uses wit and irony to describe the legal profession's discrimination against women. She allows the reader to interpret the "happy ending" as a triumph of small-town flexibility over big-city provincialism. Yet her portrait of the sexism of legal practice belies that resolution. With a characteristically light yet searing touch, Waugh juxtaposes a spirited awareness of women's oppression and a pragmatic determination to forge ahead nonetheless. "The moral of her tale" emphasizes not the inevitability of patriarchy but the increment of progress.

## NOTES

"Women as Law Clerks," a handwritten document, is found in folder 98 of the papers of Catharine Waugh McCulloch in the Dillon Collection at the Arthur and Elizabeth Schlesinger Library on the History of Women in America, Radcliffe College. It is published by permission of Frank W. McCulloch and Hathorn W. McCulloch and the Schlesinger Library. The McCulloch papers and the entry on Catharine Waugh McCulloch by Paul S. Boyer in *Notable American Women 1607–1950*, ed. Edward T. James, Janet W. James, and Paul S. Boyer (Cambridge: Harvard Univ. Press, 1971), II, 459–60, provided the biographical information for the Introduction.

1. On the earliest women lawyers in the United States, see D. Kelly Weisberg, "Barred from the Bar: Women and Legal Education in the United States, 1870–1890," *Journal of Legal Education* 28 (1977), 485–502, and Joyce Antler, "The Educated Woman and Professionalization: The Struggle for a New Feminine Identity 1890–1920," unpub. Ph.D. diss., S.U.N.Y. Stony Brook, 1977, esp. p. 269.

2. *Bradwell v. Illinois*, 83 U.S. (16 Wall.) 130, 21 L. Ed. 442 (1873). As a landmark decision excluding women from professional vocation, the Bradwell case has often been discussed. See Weisberg (note 1); the entry "Myra Colby Bradwell" by Dorothy Thomas in *Notable American Women*, I, 223–25; and discussion of the case in Barbara Allen Babcock et al., *Sex Discrimination and the Law: Causes and Remedies* (Boston: Little Brown and Co., 1975), pp. 4–8. An outspoken participant in the "woman movement," Myra Bradwell helped other women lawyers and worked for woman suffrage and for the improvement of women's legal rights. She never reapplied to the bar but in 1890 the Illinois Supreme Court acted on her original motion of 1869 and admitted her. She was admitted to practice before the U.S. Supreme Court in 1892.

3. Antler (n. 1) finds 75 women lawyers in the U.S. in 1880 and 208 in 1890. Weisberg (n. 1), pp. 494–95, finds only 135 women lawyers and law students in 1890, and states that approximately one third of women lawyers at the time were married women, more than half of them married to lawyers.

4. Laura M. Johns (president of the Kansas Equal Suffrage Association) to Kittie Waugh, Dec. 22, 1888, folder 202, Dillon Collection, Schlesinger Library.

5. Questionnaire form, folder 133, Bureau of Vocational Information papers, Schlesinger Library.

Probably early 1887

Law Office
of
Catharine G. Waugh
107 East State Street

Rockford, Ill. . . . . 188-

## WOMEN AS LAW CLERKS

In the Union College of Law in Chicago from which I graduated in 1886, sex seemed no hindrance to our gaining the full benefits of all instructions. At first it certainly was quite a trial to recite before all those young men who would pause in the midst of throwing paper wads and slinging overshoes to see if either of the women knew enough to answer questions. This critical scrutiny soon changed to kindly approval and while they fought us vigorously in debate and moot court, their manly courtesy toward us made what might have been an uncomfortable place to a solitary girl so fraternally pleasant, that the Law College brings back only happy memories.

Many friends advised me to settle in Chicago and capture my share of the large fees floating about. So I decided to get a clerkship in some first class law firm and from the first support myself and most important learn the practice. Other classmates were doing the same already and why not I?

Miss Marten gave me a list of good men and firms and wrote me personal letters to several. Armed with these and letters and recommendations from two Judges friends of mine and the College of Professors I sallied forth to seek my fortune. I sailed out inflated with enthusiasm and confidence in my own abilities. I dragged myself back collapsed with chagrin and failure, and it took many days of rebuff to so quench my indomitable spirit.

Mr. F. whose sister was a friend of mine said he would have been delighted with my assistance but he already had more clerks than he knew what to do with.

Mr. W. was glad to make my acquaintance but that was the wrong season of the year to look for such a place. But on account of his fatherinlaw [sic] the Judge's kind letter he would make diligent inquiry, and carefully took my name and address so he could write me as soon as he found the place. So out I went thanking him for those exertions I imagined he would be making in my behalf, poor deluded creature that I was.

Mr. J. preferred the help of his two sons and must also confess he disapproved of women stepping out of their true sphere the home. This of course led to some discussion the nature of which you can no doubt imagine.

Pompous Judge J. never knew of anyone who needed a clerk and a dozen young men would be ready for a place as soon as vacant. This was delivered with his eyes still clinging to his newspaper and coupled with some sage reflections about the difficulty of any young person ever succeeding.

Bristly, bullet headed little Mr. B. exclaimed vehemently, "I don't approve of women at the bar, they can't stand the racket. I would prefer to find a place for my daughter in someone's kitchen and I advise you to rather go home and take in sewing. I am opposed to women practicing law." I assured him it was not in default of having opportunities to enter kitchens that I wished to do law work. That though it greived [sic] me not to be able to please everyone in my choice of a profession it seemed more properly a matter for my own decision, inwardly reflecting that only when I had defeated that pettifoger [sic] in some illustrious lawsuit would he be fully answered. Take in sewing at 60 cents a dozen for fine shirts? No thank you. He can make shirts himself. I'd never make shirts for him if he had to wrap himself in burlap instead.

Two others had advertised for law clerks and when I replied in person were dumbfounded. No objections were made to my qualifications but they wanted a man and as I was not a man and never would be they were ready to wish me a good day. I argued with them that in law school I had done everything any other student had and why not here, that any place suitable for a decent man to go on legal business would not be shunned by me. But tho [sic] I defeated them on every argument they beat me on the main point, no woman law clerk.

Kindly old gentlemen would tell me I did not look very strong and that I must not forget Miss Hulett, Miss Perry and another girl lawyer in St. Louis who died of overwork. It is amazing how many times the ghosts of those girls were resurrected to scare me away from the thought of practice.

I answered by letter every advertisement for a law clerk but a troublesome conscience always forced me to write my full name and that of course disclosed the distressing fact that I was no man.[1]

One man said, "I want a clerk who is a regular bulldozer and can blow people up hill and down and you don't look equal to it." Whether any legal knowledge would have been necessary he did not state.

But one man wrote to me stating he needed just such help. He agreed to all my modest demands, told of the large law business he would gradually turn over to me, enthused on women in the law, asked about my financial backing, whether I was engaged to be married, what my education had been and would I agree to stay five years when once he had let me into all his business. He waived all my various testimonials declaring he could read in my countenance that I would suit exactly. He was a fine looking gray-haired gentleman and I was elated at having found such a safe place, with a prospect of learning so much from my fatherly employer. Confiding my success to a friend also a friend of his I was alarmed by his advice "Don't you go near him. His law business is non est. He has been twice divorced and probably intends to raise you to the eminence of No. 3 as he has proposed to several during the past month." So I did not go even tho' he wrote several times to try it "hoping we might make arrangements that would suit *permanently* all around." So farewell to my gray haired patron.

One of my classmates who now adorns the woolsack in one of Chicago's justice courts said "Go to my old gent the Judge, I have told him about you and he will help you." So I sought Judge B. and Mrs. B who were very kind and encouraging and the first thing I knew there was a bit of an item in the Legal News telling about my qualifications.[2]

But I have reason to suppose that every reader deliberately skipped that little portion of the paper as I never heard of it except through fellow students who joked me on having a free ad.

Then I sought an influential lady who professed vast admiration for me through hearing the Professor's praises. She kissed me at a meeting and parting, called me "Dear," "My Love" and "Sweet Child" all in that first interview and knew she would find me a place at once but as I never heard of any one to whom she spoke on the subject her efforts were probably limited to the said demonstrations of affection.

Then my dear cousin the manufacturer would speak to his attorney if he could ever think of it, but alas he never thought of it.

Numbers of attorneys were very polite and hoped I would succeed but could not tell if they would need a clerk but took my name and address. Others again told me plainly they objected to having a woman.

For the smiles and kind words which perhaps they would not have wasted on a man applicant of course I felt thankful but would gladly have dispensed with them and received the clerkships they were daily giving young men classmates of mine.

When at last I gave up the search it seemed as if there was no place on earth for a young woman just graduated from law school. If she had ten or twenty years of successful practice to back her, then the world would make an exception in her favor and condescendingly allow her to continue but who would help her to begin?

It was a dreary prospect to think of.

But my fit of melancholy did not last forever, so I came back to my home in Rockford Illinois with its less than twenty five thousand inhabitants and hung out my shingle here alone. My rebuffs and discouragement in Chicago made the kind words and helpful deeds of those who had known me all my life so much of a consolation that I am again nerved up to the struggle and tho it seems like bragging to say it I beleive [sic] I will succeed.

The forty other attorneys take special pains to always say a pleasant word to me, to offer to loan me any books or blanks they have and answer any queries of mine carefully and gladly. The Judges keep a friendly eye on me, the circuit and county clerks offer their services in explaining and deciphering the books in the vaults, the sheriffs and deputies who act as bailiffs in the court and even the janitor touches his cap. I don't mean to insinuate that they all prostrate themselves at my appearance or any such nonsense but they treat me just the way I like to be treated and just as respectfully as tho [sic] my whole time was devoted to petting a poodle, embroidering purple and green cats and dogs on red, blue and yellow canvas and giving germans and card parties, and perhaps more so. Tho only in the first half year of practice I have reason to be encouraged and would now confide to you all about my first case if I had not already probably written too much. But this is a wonderfully condensed account of my sufferings and humiliation. What the moral of this tale is I can't think unless it should be, "Despise not the day of small things."

Catharine G. Waugh
Rockford, Ill's.

## NOTES

1. Madeleine Doty, who gained a law degree from N.Y.U. Law School in 1902, obtained the job of reviewing books for *The New York Times* shortly afterward by using the pseudonym Otis Notman (O, 'tis not man). See her unpublished autobiography, "A Tap on the Shoulder," Doty Collection, Sophia Smith Collection, Women's History Archive, Smith College, Northampton, MA.

2. The reference is to Myra Bradwell and her husband. Mrs. Bradwell started the Chicago *Legal News* in 1868, before she applied to the bar. For decades under her management it was the most important legal publication in the Midwest and West.

# The Female Sociograph:
# The Theater of Virginia Woolf's Letters

## *Catharine R. Stimpson*

The Virginia Woolf letters have come out: six volumes, nearly 4,000 individual letters. As the editors know, their survival is an accident;[1] they have depended on the habits of her receivers, not all of whom have had the retentive holding patterns of the archivist. Loss, then, necessarily salts our interpretations. Nevertheless, in the flair of the Woolf correspondence, we can read her writing and writing herself. Her letters exemplify a particular women's text, one that is neither wholly private nor wholly public. They occupy a psychological and rhetorical middle space between what she wrote for herself and what she produced for a general audience. They are a brilliant, glittering encyclopedia of the partially-said. Because of this, they probably cannot give us what Joseph Conrad's letters gave a critic like Edward W. Said: the materials for a full autobiography of consciousness, a mediation between life and work.[2] Rather, Woolf's letters inscribe a sociograph. They concern social worlds that she needed and wanted. They form an autobiography of the self with others, a citizen/denizen of relationships.

When young, teaching herself to be a writer, Woolf toyed with a quasi-Pateresque notion of the letter as a formed impression of consciousness, a shaped inscription of mind. In 1906, she informs her older friend Violet Dickinson: "A letter should be as flawless as a gem, continuous as an eggshell, and lucid as glass" (I, 264). The more she wrote, however, the more the letter became an act within, and of, the moment; less a steady mirror of the real than a dashing glimpse into, and from, its flux. Woolf need not care if language outruns sense and syntax; her perceptions a sense of decorum; response responsibility. She jauntily advises the composer Ethel Smyth: "Lets leave the letters till we're both dead. Thats my plan. I dont keep or destroy but collect miscellaneous bundles of odds and ends, and let posterity, if there is one, burn or not. Lets forget all about death and all about Posterity" (VI, 272).

Because middle space has value, Woolf guards it. Fearing that Smyth might print her letters, Woolf snaps: ". . . I dont understand the system on which your mind works, by nature. When you say for example that you are going to write something about me and publish parts of my letters—I am flabbergasted. I swear I couldn't do such a thing where you're concerned to save my life" (V, 86). Such a reaction suggests that the letters are to be read as intimate and honest expressions on the self. And yet, Woolf's voice is consistently undependable throughout the letters. It shifts, as do her allusions and strategies, depending on who her addressee/receiver might be. An unusually introspective letter of 1929 to Gerald Brenan, on the treachery of language, concludes: "Writing to Lytton or Leonard I am quite different from writing to you" (IV, 98). For Woolf is a performer, an actress, and the letters are bravura, burnishing fragments of performance art. She creates a series of private theaters for an audience of one, each with its own script and scenery, lights and costumes. She includes precise frames on herself at the time of writing—her house is messy, she is "tipsy" from Chianti in Italy, she had some teeth pulled. They help her audience of one enter into the play. Moreover, Woolf builds her drama, in part, on the needs and nature of that audience. Each member aids in the dictation of her lines. In France with Vita Sackville-West, her lover, she reassures Leonard, her husband, of her love for him. She can be self-doubting or confident, mocking or consoling, cajoling or demanding, rebuking (especially to Smyth) or loving, sad or buoyant and mirthful. A Woolf essay says: "A good letter-writer so takes the colour of the reader at the other end, that from reading the one we can imagine the other."[3]

Clearly, Woolf's epistolary performances are generous deeds. The letter is a gift to the other based on his or her special relationship with Woolf.[4] Even her statements of personal need are flattering because they assume that her receiver has the power to gratify them. The letters also subtly adapt the manners of the good hostess. They become the text of a drawing-room conversation. This teasing deference of the performer/hostess appears even in Woolf's earliest published letter, written in 1888, when she was six, to the poet James Russell Lowell. She pertly judges and queries the older man: "Have you been to the Adirondacks . . . You are a naughty man not to come here Good bye" (I, 2).

In the middle space, Woolf exists both with people whom she trusts and with those with whom she has reliably limited involvements. As her language reaches out to other people, she protects herself from the loneliness, the isolation, and the blank distance between human beings she recognized and feared. Through the letter, she communicates even when the physical presence of others is unavailable or unmanageable. Like any human connection for Woolf, however, epistolary performances have their risks. They can stimulate her distrust about the steadiness of the other's presence. If written out of a sense of obligation, because of the notorious pressures of the superego, a letter might distort her. She might also deform herself if she were afraid of failing in charm. Woolf believes that all letter writing involves the donning of a mask, the creation of "a kind of unreal personality." To Jacques Raverat she muses:

> The difficulty of writing letters is, for one thing, that one has to simplify so much, and hasn't the courage to dwell on the small catastrophes which are of such huge interest to oneself; and thus has to put on a kind of unreal personality; which, when I write to you for example, whom I've not seen these 11 years, becomes inevitably jocular. I suppose joviality is a convenient mask; and then, being a writer, masks irk me: I want, in my old age, to have done with all superfluities . . . (III, 136).

Even worse, any act of language can be ". . . infinitely chancy and infinitely humbugging—so many asserverations . . . are empty, and tricks of speech . . ." (IV, 97). Finally, people, deprived of guiding gestures and intonations, might misinterpret this slippery medium. The performer cannot control the audience's response, the hostess a guest's behavior. Woolf and Sackville-West disagree about *Three Guineas*. After a flurry of letters, Woolf tells her:

> Its a lesson not to write letters. For I suppose you'll say, when you read what I've quoted from your own letter, that there's nothing to cause even a momentary irritation. And I daresay you're right. I suspect that anything written acquires meaning and both the writers mood and the reader's mood queer the pitch (VI, 257).

Scarily, misreaders can become angry, and then withhold love and praise. Two strong, linked lines in Woolf's letters are witty, incisive, acerb comments about other people and apologies for having made trouble; for having been indiscreet or acerb; for having been too little of the angel in the home. Full speech and human relations are perhaps never congruent. Even today, Woolf suffers from readers' distrust of her flamboyantly cutting tongue. One of her editors, Nigel Nicolson, says of a text:

> . . . (it is) malicious beyond the point of sanity—and perhaps for that very reason the word "malicious" is inappropriate (II, xvi).

Yet, the text is hardly dreadful. Written to Strachey, in 1915, it asks for gossip and then bursts into a fantasy about her brother-in-law Clive Bell. They will buy him a parrot, ". . . a bold primitive bird, trained of course to talk nothing but filth, and to indulge in obscene caresses . . ." (II, 61). Nicolson's distress may be indicative of what Woolf feared and guessed would happen if she were too impertinent, too vicious, too often, too directly. If so, it might explain why her rhetoric can be so appealing to her immediate recipient and so amusingly nasty about a third party—a John Middleton Murry, Ottoline Morrell, or Edward Sackville-West. She asks her receiver to share her laughter at someone outside the theater of the letter. As she sets up a conspiracy to displace hostility onto such a third party, she attempts to lull her receiver into a sense of exemption from her corrosive mordancies.

The sheer bulk of Woolf's letters is proof that their benefits outweighed these risks. In the 1930s, famous and mature, she explored a rhetorical device that might enable her to be largely angry: her admonitory, often sarcastic public letters. Some went off to magazines and journals. Another was a response to a younger generation of writers, "Letter to a Young Poet."[5] Still another was *Three Guineas*. The public letter, which concerns forces (such as the patriarchy) rather than individuals, permits Woolf to be less a gossipy friend than a commentator and prophet. The letter is less the conjuring up of a small theater than the polemical venting of her personal values in a bullying impersonal world that stomps from stupidity to murder. She could be skeptical about the form. It "seems to invite archness and playfulness" (V, 83). Yet, especially in *Three Guineas,* the public letter is a forum whose architecture itself encodes protest against restrictions. Jane Marcus remarks: "Her anger and hostility at the exclusiveness of male institutions are all the more effective because 'cabin'd and cribb'd' in limited and limiting letters. Like prison journals and letters, read while we know the author is in jail, they serve their cause not only by what they say but by the very form."[6]

Woolf's deceptively casual theory about the letter as a genre, as well as her practice, assign it to my "middle space." She suggests that the letter was once a public event that fused the functions of the newspaper and conversation. It gave a group several kinds of information on multiple channels of communication. Its high century was the "unlovable" eighteenth (II, 12). Then, because of modern technology and the media it generated, the letter lost a public role. Reduced to emotional detail, it became an "intimacy . . . on ink" (II, 22). In the essay "Modern Letters," Woolf declares:

> Only one person is written to, and the writer has some reason for wishing to write to him or her in particular. Its meaning is private, its news intimate . . . it is a rash incriminating document . . . the art of letter writing . . . is not dead . . . but as much alive as to be quite unprintable. The best letters of our times are precisely those that can never be published.[7]

The style of the letter necessarily altered. It changed from being a carefully composed text that several readers would scrutinize to being a disheveled scrawl that one reader would consume.

If one wishes to conflate the feminine, the intimate, and the realm of feeling, Woolf's ideas about the modern letter label it a woman's art. However, one can doubt this hypothetical fusion and still see how deliberately Woolf's theory and practice feminize the genre. Although middle space is broad enough to include men and women, she believed that the letter had historically offered women a convention to manipulate when they were barred from others that men could enter. Reviewing Dorothy Osborne, she notes: "The art of letter-writing is often the art of essay-writing in disguise. But such as it was, it was an art a woman could practise without unsexing herself."[8] Because her precursors had pushed at and weakened patriarchal culture, Woolf could go beyond them. She could choose the letter as one of her arts, not as a compensation.

Her feminization of the letter is also much more. Despite the happiness of her marriage and despite the fact that Leonard is the co-author of some of her letters, they show—even to the most prudish of readers—how attracted she was to other women. The letters textualize how much women stirred her imagination and desire. Woolf writes of flirtations with women. Her style itself is flirtatious and seductive. Her profound relationships with women were, at the same time, surprisingly stable. The first, and perhaps most haunting, woman was her mother, Julia. In Cornwall, about as old as her mother was when she died, Woolf weeps. Her letters to women call for affectionate mothering and support. In 1929, she writes to Sackville-West: "Its odd how I want you when I'm ill. I think everything would be warm and happy if Vita came in" (IV, 9). Since Sackville-West is absent, Woolf will accept "long long letters" as a substitute.

Woolf writes consistently to Vanessa, who loved her but fled from her sister's demonstrativeness. The complexity of this relationship can be gauged by a letter to Clive Bell, written in 1908, where she asks him to transmit her love to Vanessa. So doing, Woolf taunts Vanessa by flaunting an attachment to Clive, a trick to arouse jealousy and attention that she would later use, more wryly, with Sackville-West. She plays a sexual game she repeats through the letters: she tells Clive how to kiss Vanessa. She becomes a voyeur who is simultaneously sister's lover; sister's daughter; brother-in-law's companion; brother-in-law's rival: "Kiss her, most passionately, in all *my* [italics added] private places—neck—, and arm, and eyeball, and tell her—what new thing is there to tell her? how fond I am of her husband" (I, 325)? Woolf writes to women lovers (Violet Dickinson, Sackville-West) and to serious friends (Nelly Cecil, Margaret Llewellyn Davis, Smyth). Her letters, especially to Sackville-West, can be zestful plumes of imagery, rather as *Orlando* is a rich spray of narrative. However,

Woolf's initiatives toward women and responses to them are overt and free from coding. Because the letters are in middle space, they are more explicit about personal feelings than about her feminism, her public sense of women's grievances, which friends and family shrank from.[9] She bluntly tells Jacques Raverat that she "much" prefers her own sex. She places her passion before Sackville-West plainly, but not barrenly. The salutation "Dear Mrs. Nicolson" becomes "Oh you scandalous ruffian," "My dear Vita," "Dearest Creature," and "Dearest Honey." As the fire of passion became the embers of friendship, Woolf deployed a cozy metaphor to tell Smyth about Sackville-West: "Vita was here for a night. I always fall into a warm slipper relation with her instantly. Its a satisfactory relationship" (VI, 439). When she decides that Sackville-West's desire for her has vanished, Woolf writes to her baldly. In general, the prose of her letters is austere and transparent when genuine grief is near: "And do you love me? No" (V, 376).

Such directness marks her language about Vanessa's daughter, Angelica, her "adorable sprite." To be sure, Woolf did want a child early in her marriage; she envied Vanessa hers. Her letters to Angelica are fanciful and tender, cheerful and loving. She gives Angelica jokes, checks, affection, advice, news, and games—as she did to her nephews. However, her letters about Angelica that express attraction are shocking. In 1928, Woolf writes to Vanessa: ". . . I'm showing [Angelica's photographs for *Orlando*] to Vita, who doesn't want to be accused of raping the under age. My God—I shall rape Angelica one of these days . . ." (III, 497). Later, aware of how close her lesbianism and her feeling for women in her family were, she writes to Vanessa again: "This is a very dull letter, but its been so hot . . . my wits are roasting: twice I dreamt I was kissing Angelica passionately across a hedge, from which I can only deduce that incest and sapphism embrace in one breast" (V, 417). She then moves on swiftly in an epistolary gesture that makes it impossible to know if the confession was a supportable or insupportable act of speech: ". . . neither [incest nor sapphism] come within a thousand miles of me when seeing Susie Buchan or Ethyl Smyth—both of whom came here yesterday."[10]

Homosexuality is not the only subject Woolf speaks of more openly, even raucously, in her letters than in her fiction. She mentions water closets; Leonard's wet dreams; menstruation, "the usual indisposition of my sex" (II, 360); sanitary napkins; menopause; Smyth's diarrhea. So doing, taking up the body's housekeeping functions, she adapts the frankness of Bloomsbury conversation to her letters and further demystifies herself as the ethereal loon of English letters. Yet the lesbianism is special. The relationship of Woolf's letters to her fiction in terms of her complex eroticism is parallel to the relationship between that eroticism and her marriage. The letters and the psychic life, which feed on each other, discreetly explore lesbianism. The fiction and the marriage, which also feed on each other, far more publicly investigate heterosexuality. That heterosexuality, not stringently homophobic, accepts lesbianism. Clarissa Dalloway remembers Sally Seton vividly. Miss LaTrobe, the lesbian artist in *Between the Acts,* is heroic. The Woolfs entertained what they called Sapphists and buggers.[11] Nevertheless, the fiction and the marriage shelter and conceal the volatile depths of Woolf's lesbian feelings.

No matter how forthcoming the letters are about the flesh, they are comparatively silent about two overwhelming forces in Woolf's life: her "madness" and her writing. Even with intimates she was reticent about the extremities of consciousness, whether the boundaries of creativity or oblivion. She muses to Dickinson:

> Now my brain I will confess, for I dont like to talk of it, floats in blue air; where there are circling clouds, soft sunbeams of elastic gold, and fairy gossamers—things that cant be cut—that must be tenderly enclosed, and expressed in a globe of exquisitely coloured words. At the mere prick of steel, they vanish (I, 320).

She could sardonically refer to being "mad," to going "insane," to headaches and an eccentric nervous system. She could say that her madness saved her from a rigid, chilly fastidiousness. She could tell appalling, funny anecdotes about her doctors and nurses. Yet such allusions and data and tales appear to disappear. They also mask her rage at her treatment. In 1925, she discusses *Mrs. Dalloway* and Septimus Smith with Gwen Raverat: "It was a subject that I have kept cooling in my mind until I felt I could touch it without bursting into flame all over. You can't think what a raging furnace it is still to me—madness and doctors and being forced" (III, 180). The metaphors of heat and fire consistently figure passion. Certain Woolf/Dickinson letters are "hot." Erotic passion is more detachable, however, more speakable, more writable, than rage at the consequences of madness. Woolf immediately adds to the Raverat letter, "But let's change the subject."

To Smyth, Woolf, in an autobiographical rush, praises her madness as a source of art:

> . . . And then I married, and then my brains went up in a shower of fireworks. As an experience, madness is terrific I can assure you, and not to be sniffed at; and in its lava I still find most of the things I write about. It shoots out of one everything shaped, final, not in mere driblets, as sanity does (IV, 180).

Yet, her letters are oddly superficial for someone whose life was reading, talking, and writing; who was absorbed in her work and in her own psychology as a writer; who was prodigiously productive. She could mention her schedule and its disruptions. She could wonder nervously about a new book's reception—from family, friends, reviewers, and a public that might send her "abuse or ecstasy" (VI, 267). She could be snide, rueful, or shrewd about other writers. In the beginning of her career, she rummages through the past for models; in the middle, she implicitly compares herself, often anxiously, to contemporaries; toward the end, she both supports and decries the next generation. She could declare how much her writing needs the stimulus of the noise, chaos, and color of reality. She could wonder how she might go on with her texts. For example, after her father's death, she anguishes because she cannot tell him in writing about her sorrow. (Sir Leslie Stephen, unlike his daughter, destroyed letters to him.) Simultaneously, the father personifies a blocking force. In 1908, she writes to Clive Bell:

> I dreamt last night that I was showing father the manuscript of my novel; and he snorted, and then dropped it on to a table, and I was very melancholy, and read it this morning, and thought it bad. You dont realise the depth of modesty in to which I fall (I, 325).

Despite such utterances, Woolf's letters are not her diaries. Written to others, not to the self; written for others, as well as the self, they do not reveal Woolf in her most entangled, most diving engagement with language. Indeed, they were often a distraction that permitted her to be with language, but not with its most inexorable demands and rewards. She told Smyth that she only wrote "letters when my mind is full of bubble and foam; when I'm not aware of the niceties of the English language" (V, 396).

Woolf's volumes of letters occupy still another kind of middle space: between the "literal" and the "literary," those two frayed poles with which some stake out the territories of discourse. Her letters can be literal. Sending simple information, they communicate on a flat plane. Contemporary readers may need annotations to understand a sentence. They may have to learn who "The Nun" might be, but once annotated, the letter limits its own meaning. Lunch will start at 1 p.m. Angelica is 10. The Press will reject a manuscript. Or, then, the letters are full of gossip, that discourse of exchange of details about friends and daily life. As a gossip, Woolf is conventionally, even stereotypically, feminine, but as she gossips, elsewhere, in another space, she is struggling for the different speech her novels articulated.

Even so, to borrow Roger Duchêne's terms, Woolf is an "auteur épistolaire," not a mere "épistolier." Growing in and through language, her performance can be self-reflexive. On Christmas Day, 1922, she tells Brenan: "Never mind. I am only scribbling, more to amuse myself than you, who may never read, or understand: for I am doubtful whether people, the best disposed toward each other, are capable of more than an intermittent signal as they forge past—a sentimental metaphor . . ." (II, 598). In her texts, a ludic element becomes more and more vital. She scrawls down miniature plays, with stage directions and dialogue. She characterizes some people and transforms others into characters. Her brother Thoby, before his death, is "Milford." In an 1896 letter to him, she is "Miss Jan," a helter-skelter thing. The wind has blown her skirt over her head, and her red flannel drawers have flashed before a curate (I, 2). Many images have the strength of acid: "I have had two bloody painful encounters with Middleton Murry; we stuck together at parties like two copulating dogs; but after the first ecstasy, it was boring, disillusioning, flat" (III, 115). Frequently, her tropes traverse individual letters to become conceits that provide linguistic and emotional continuity; a recurrent backdrop for the theater; furniture for the drawing room. Especially for erotically charged relationships, they can be cozily animalistic. A kindly bestiality manages eros by domesticating it and distancing it from the human body. Dickinson is a kangaroo, who offers a pouch for Virginia, her wallaby, a dear marsupial with snout and paws. Leonard is "Mongoose" to her "Mandril." To Sackville-West, she and her sexuality are "potto," an African lemur with features of an English housedog. To show her union with Sackville-West and their differences at once, Woolf transmutes her lover into another dog, but one more capable of opulence than shabby Virginia: ". . . Vita is a dear old rough coated sheep dog: or alternatively, hung with grapes, pink with pearls, lustrous, candle lit . . ." (III, 224).

Because of such tropes, because of her vast capacities for metaphoric fantasy, Woolf's letters swerve toward poetic fiction. Very occasionally, the letter constitutes a poetic or pathetic lie. One, in 1906, is poignant. To protect Dickinson, herself sick, Woolf (then Virginia Stephen) concealed the death of Thoby from her for a month. She sent a series of letters she might have written if Thoby had lived. On the day he dies, Woolf—in an act of defiance, denial, and charity—writes Dickinson to chat about illness, work, literature, gossip, and their feelings for each other. Then she ends with a broken cry for consolation. As syntactically jagged as the truth of that moment, it is unequivocal in its painful equation of death and love, equivocal in assigning the cause of pain: "Goodnight and God—have I a right to a God? send you sleep. Wall nuzzles in and wants love. Yr. AVS" (I, 248).

More commonly, Woolf imagines scenes self-consciously. She will send Elizabeth Bowen a tea caddy in magenta plush, embroidered with forget-me-nots in gold. She and Leonard will kiss for an hour. When she is dead, she will read Smyth's letters and have "many rights" (V, 178). As a dancer or athlete exercises the body, so Woolf trains her ability to poke and reassemble the materials of the day. As her letters use facts to construct fictions, they become a modern version of the epistolary novel. Time passes, but plot is fragmented. Characters arbitrarily pass before her. Perception and the phantoms of fantasy blur. In her unintended epistolary novel, Woolf also retains her impulse toward social satire. Her sociograph is a comedy of manners, as her first two novels were. The range of letters is a deposit for residual, as well as experimental, writing techniques.

Her last letters, though, are terrible, like Shakespeare's dark comedies, and heart-wrenching. A final unsigned note to Sackville-West, on March 22, 1941, is tough, compressed. Someone has apparently composed a letter to Sackville-West, but mailed it to Woolf. She declares, "No, I'm not you. No, I don't keep budgerigars." Finally, she asks, seemingly of birds, but, in retrospect, of herself:

> If we come over . . . may I bring her a pair if any survive? Do they all die in an instant? When shall we come? Lord knows— (VI, 484)

Three of Woolf's last letters belong to the last two weeks of that same month. One is to Vanessa, the beloved woman; two to Leonard, the beloved man. They echo and repeat each other, as if Woolf were drafting the chorus of her own tragedy. They have, to a painful pitch, the generosity and gratitude that most of her letters display. They tell of her absolute love for Vanessa and Leonard, and then give reasons for the suicide she was planning and would so quickly choose. For she is hearing voices, the old sign of her illness, and she refuses to fight them again. The voices are like a letter she did not write, that she cannot control, that she must receive. They are a grotesque, cruel intrusion in a middle space of consciousness; killer buffoons at loose in a theater of mind.

The Woolf letters are now a part of, and guide to, history. Her editors, serving as her historians, have added an appendix to the sixth volume. It includes letters found too late for inclusion in the earlier volumes to which they chronologically belong. The last text in this coda, though undated, may be from the mid-1930s. To Leonard, it tells him that Woolf has slept well, that she is about to begin writing for the day. She asks him to get her cigarettes. Then she concludes, in a throwaway life-line of language from Sussex to London, "Shall come back tomorrow for certain" (VI, 532). In the tomorrow in which we read, she has come back in the way she would have most preferred, as a writer. We do not exist in the middle space in which she wrote the pages of her letters. We are in the public space of reading. Though her ardent mind is language now for us, its smoke print on page, we are, too, the recipients of that language, its flare, its bright edges, its self-creating giving.

## NOTES

Versions of this paper were read at the Modern Language Association, Annual Meeting, December 1978, and at Hobart and William Smith colleges, May 1983. I am grateful to Louise K. Horowitz for sharing work on French criticism about letterwriting with me; to Elizabeth Wood for her comments; and to the body of Woolf criticism for its instructiveness.

1. I will use the United States edition of the Woolf letters, all edited by Nigel Nicolson and Joanne Trautman: *The Letters of Virginia Woolf,* I, 1888–1912 (New York: Harcourt Brace Jovanovich, 1975); II, 1912–1922 (New York: Harcourt Brace Jovanovich, 1976); III, 1923–1928 (New York: Harcourt Brace Jovanovich, 1978); IV, 1929–1931 (New York: Harcourt Brace Jovanovich, 1981); V, 1932–1935 (New York: Harcourt Brace Jovanovich, 1982); VI, 1936–1941 (New York: Harcourt Brace Jovanivich, 1982). In quoting from this edition, idiosyncracies of Woolf's spelling have been maintained.

2. Edward W. Said, *Joseph Conrad and the Fiction of Autobiography* (Cambridge: Harvard Univ. Press, 1966). My concept of "middle space" for Woolf's letters is not dissimilar to Barbara Hernnstein Smith's theory about the status of letters in *On the Margins of Discourse* (Chicago: Univ. of Chicago Press, 1978, paper 1983), but I am less concerned with the status of the letter as interpretable object.

3. "Dorothy Osborne's *Letters,*" *Collected Essays,* III (London: Hogarth Press, 1967), p. 63. She makes a related point in "Lord Chesterfield's Letters to His Son," *ibid.,* p. 84. A voracious reader, Woolf liked memoirs, biographies, and letters—in brief, the texts of self. For example, the Flaubert/Sand correspondence delighted her.

4. In "Woolf as Letter-Writer: A Reflection of the Other Person," given at the Modern Language Association, December 1978, Joanne Trautman analyzes the influence of G. E. Moore's ideal of friendship, the recognition "with precision what are the qualities of our friends," on Woolf's practice. Ms. p. 9.

5. *Letter to a Young Poet* (1932) was No. 8 in the Hogarth Press Letter Series. Dismaying a generation of the poets who had considered Woolf a friendly precursor, it was answered by Peter Quennell, *A Letter to Mrs. Virginia Woolf* (Leonard and Virginia Woolf, Hogarth Press, 1932), No. 12 in the Hogarth Series. The fact that both letters were issued by the same press shows how friendship still walled in disagreement. For more detail, see John Lehmann, *Thrown to the Woolves* (London: Weidenfeld and Nicolson, 1978), pp. 29–31. The letter series was not financially successful.

6. Jane Marcus, " 'No More Horses': Woolf on Art and Propaganda," *Women's Studies,* 4, 2–3 (1977), 274.

7. *Collected Essays,* II (London: Hogarth Press, 1966), pp. 261–62. Woolf's letters frequently close with orders to her addressee to burn the page, to hide its message, and so forth.

8. "Dorothy Osborne's *Letters,*" III, p. 60.

9. Although the editing of Woolf's letters is scrupulous, Nigel Nicolson's discomfort at Woolf's feminism betrays him into error. Introducing Volume V, he writes that Leonard Woolf was silent in his autobiography about *Three Guineas,* which "may be indicative of what he thought at the time" (V, xvii). However, Leonard did mention *Three Guineas* in his autobiography, saying that both it and *A Room of One's Own* were political pamphlets in the tradition of Mary Wollstonecraft's *A Vindication of the Rights of Women.* See *Downhill All the Way* (London: Hogarth Press, 1967), p. 27.

10. Woolf usually called lesbianism "sapphism," but Ethyl Smyth provoked her into using the more modern "lesbianism." A recent account of the Sackville-West relationship is Louise A. DeSalvo's "Lighting the Cave: The Relationship between Vita Sackville-West and Virginia Woolf," *Signs: Journal of Women in Culture and Society,* 8, 2 (Winter: 1982), 195–

214. See also *The Letters of Vita Sackville-West to Virginia Woolf*, ed. Louise DeSalvo and Mitchell A. Leaska (New York: William Morrow and Co., Inc., 1984).

11. The vocabulary of sapphists and buggers—like Woolf's racism, anti-Semitism, and cracks about the lower order—reflects undeniably, albeit unhappily, the ugly, myopic aspect of her vision.

*✒*

# Of Sparrows and Condors: The Autobiography of Eva Perón

## Marysa Navarro

Like other women who played a significant public role in periods when the feminine domain was still unequivocally domestic, Eva Perón had to defy social conventions and strong criticism, overcome lack of precedents and inexperience to enter the world of politics. In a society where first ladies were relegated to officiating at an occasional ceremony and where women were not allowed to vote in national elections, she carved out a singular dual role for herself both as Eva Perón, first lady, and Evita, the charismatic leader of the *descamisados* (the shirtless ones). In the process, she gained enormous fame but also great notoriety.

During her short political career, 1946–1952, Eva became the subject of a complex mythology that has fascinated Argentines and foreigners alike.[1] For Peronists, she was a tireless, generous, loving woman, passionately dedicated to Peronism, a dutiful wife who sacrificed her own life for the downtrodden, a veritable saint to be worshipped in flowered altars after her death. For anti-Peronists, she was a calculating, ambitious *parvenue* who had slept her way to the top; a virago who emasculated her husband and was the real power behind the throne; a hypocrite who proclaimed her love for Perón, workers, and the poor but in fact sought money and power to shower herself with jewels and satisfy her insatiable thirst for revenge against the Argentine social elite. A product of the profound ideological differences that separated Argentines during Perón's years in office, this mythology of Evita, in its official Peronist version, was also consciously shaped by Eva Perón and articulated most explicitly in the autobiographical text, *La razón de mi vida*.[2]

Published in October 1951, less than one year before Eva died of cancer at the age of 33, *La razón de mi vida* is a work of dubious literary merit but of substantial interest with respect to women's autobiographical writing. Based on conversations with Eva, it was initially ghostwritten by the Spanish newspaperman Manuel Penella da Silva and then edited by two high-ranking Peronist officials. Together with Eva, they ensured that the final version conformed to her speaking style, famous—at least in Argentina—for its awkward syntax, its passionate tone, and its frequent use of hyperbole, especially when she referred to Perón or Peronism.

In contrast with most male or female autobiographies, *La razón de mi vida* is not a retrospective or introspective account of the self. Written in the present, the narrative centers on Evita, the public persona, the woman Eva has become and her political activities. While the reasons for her entering public life and the description of her involvement with workers and the poor form the longest section of the book, the initial five chapters, which recount her life until her encounter with Perón, offer very few details about her childhood and youth. The reader is not told when or where she was born, who her parents were or what their social status was, how many sisters and brothers she had, what kind of education she received or how she became an actress. Her mother is mentioned only once but is not even named.

These omissions are puzzling in view of Argentines' lack of information about Evita's past and the rumors about her private life before she met and married Perón. By contrast, the anti-Peronist myth dwelled on the past to explain Evita, the public figure, and emphasized her illegitimacy, her questionable social origins, her limited education, and her purportedly promiscuous career as an actress. Evita does not address these and other speculations—that her mother's boardinghouse in Junín was a house of ill repute; that she had been the mistress of several military officers before meeting Perón—although she could have used her autobiography to provide her readers with a real or fictive counterversion of her past. If indeed she came from a "humble" family, as she constantly said, why did she forsake the opportunity to present an account of her childhood and thus give great credibility to her claims? Why, instead, did she describe her early years in the vaguest possible terms, thus running the risk of confirming the worst stories about her? Did she draw a curtain on her past because the rumors and speculations had some grain of truth? Does this silence overlie a keen awareness of her transgressions and thus suggest limits to her apparent defiance of social conventions?

Whatever her reasons, Evita denies the significance of her past and presents herself as a woman whose existence begins when she meets Perón, as the very first paragraphs of *La razón de mi vida* make eminently clear. Although her life, her feelings, and her thoughts are the subject of her book, she proceeds to deny their intrinsic value when she declares that her readers "will find nothing else but the figure, the soul and the life of General Perón and my profound love for him and for his cause" (p. 9). The book is dedicated to the man through whom and because of whom she exists:

> I was not, nor am I, anything more than a humble woman . . . a sparrow in an immense flock of sparrows. . . . But Perón was and is a gigantic condor that flies high and sure among the summits and near to God.
>
> If it had not been for him who came down to my level and taught me to fly in another fashion, I would never have known what a condor is like, nor ever have been able to contemplate the marvelous and magnificent immenseness of my people.
>
> That is why neither my life nor my heart belongs to me, and nothing of all that I am or have is mine. All that I am, all that I have, all that I think and all that I feel, belongs to Perón.
>
> But I do not forget, nor will I ever forget, that I was a sparrow, nor that I still am one. If I fly higher, it is through him. If I walk among the peaks, it is through him. If sometimes I almost touch the sky with my wings, it is through him. If I see clearly what my people are, and love them and feel their affection caressing my name, it is solely through him" (p. 10).

Evita's autobiographical style achieves a rare dignity in this passage and gives us a glimpse of her effectiveness as a public speaker who professed her unending and grateful love to Perón. While the metaphor of the sparrow and the condor might be dismissed as a rhetorical device, yet another example of her tendency to exaggerate, it nevertheless conveys the distance Evita wants to emphasize between the person she was when she met Perón, a struggling movie actress of questionable social background, and the then charismatic Colonel Perón, minister of labor, soon-to-be minister of war and vice-president. At the same time, it underscores her notable transformation since her marriage to him: A "humble" woman, she would have always remained a "sparrow," lost in anonymity or perhaps remembered as one actress among many others. Her union to Perón wiped out her past, gave her a new identity, separated her from all others, men and women, rich or poor, because it transformed her into the only being who, next to him, "almost touches the sky."

While the metaphor of the sparrow and the condor is designed to accentuate Perón's superior qualities, it clearly also exalts Evita. Because she is his creation, his wife, the closer she is to him, the more she shares his attributes, and the further they both are from all others. Moreover, her insistence that she has never ceased to be a sparrow, that she is a "humble" woman, cannot simply be read as yet another rhetorical device or a complete denial of her taste for jewels and Parisian clothes or her desire for power. It is a reminder of Evita's political role as mediator within Peronism, the only person who partakes of both the leader and the *descamisados* and thus serves to unite the two.[3] Finally, acutely conscious of her self as a powerful, famous and exceptional woman, Evita marks her separation from Perón when she speaks of "her" people and their affection when they pronounce her name "among the peaks."

In this perspective, one can understand how Evita, a self-described woman without family, home, friends, or past, can claim to have had since childhood a "fundamental feeling of indignation" in the face of social injustice. Her enemies may not understand her actions, she admits, but her passion, her energy, and her constant efforts on behalf of the downtrodden are genuine and deeply felt. That feeling, she insists, "is the force which had led me by the hand, since my earliest recollections, to this day . . ." (p. 20). Once again, she does not offer details of how she discovered this feeling; she simply recounts that when she was eleven, she "heard for the first time from the lips of a workingman, that there were poor because the rich were too rich . . . that revelation made a strong impression on me" (p. 18). Her indignation, which she feels acutely to the point of physical suffering is, she confesses, perhaps the only inexplicable aspect in her life: "I think that just as some persons have a special spiritual predisposition to feel beauty differently and more intensely than do people in general, and therefore become poets, painters, or musicians, I have a particular spiritual disposition to feel injustice with unusual and painful intensity" (pp. 19–20). She searched and failed to find solutions for her preoccupation with injustice; as a woman, therefore "weak," she resigned herself "to be a victim" until the "marvelous day" when her life coincided with Perón's. Recognizing in him an extraordinary man "I put myself at his side. . . . He accepted my offer" (p. 35).

Eva does not disclose how or when she met Perón, but she presents her marriage as the union of two radically different human beings with similar ideals. "We got married because we loved one another and we loved one another because we both wanted the same thing. In different ways we had both wanted to do the same thing: he, knowing what he wanted to do, I with intuition; he, with intelligence, I with my heart; he, prepared for the struggle, I, ready without knowing anything; he, cultured and I, simple; he enormous and I small; he master and I pupil. He the figure and I the shadow" (p. 63). This marriage, then, represents the coming together of two unique human beings. He was exceptional because he wanted to eradicate social injustice but so was she, because she had suffered from it all her life and was ready to help him in his cause. In this instance, her eulogy to Perón is a vehicle for emphasizing that she is his equal. Thus, while comparing him favorably with Alexander the Great, Columbus, and Napoleon, she simultaneously asserts that Evita, the leader, owes her identity not only to Perón but also to her own "particular spiritual disposition," a kind of divine election. "Chance," she writes, "is not the cause of all that I now mean to my country and to my people. I firmly believe that I was shaped for the work I perform and the life I lead" (p. 49).

Evita explains that she entered public life because Perón's election to the presidency prevented him from maintaining a close contact with the people. She denies having any personal ambitions of her own or playing a political role independently of Perón. When she describes her activities with trade unions in the ministry of labor, she sees herself as only "the shadow" of the Leader: "Where he gave a masterly lesson, I hardly babble. Where he solved a problem in four words, I am sometimes stuck for weeks at a time. Where he decided, I only suggest. Where he saw light, I hardly see a glimmer. He is the guide, I am only the shadow of his superior presence" (p. 114). She is careful to explain that in her role as the only intermediary with labor she does not interfere in governmental matters. Perón, she says, imposes limitations on her actions and she accepts his orders willingly.

Evita confesses to wanting to be included in the history of Argentina. She insists, however, that she would be satisfied with a footnote in the chapter on Perón, a footnote that should read: " 'There was at Perón's side a woman who dedicated herself to conveying to the President the hopes of the people he later converted into realities' . . . 'All we know about that woman is that the people called her, fondly, *Evita*' " (p. 95). And yet, she also states that she "chose" to become "Evita." She affirms her personal decision to acquire a dual personality, boasting that as Eva Perón, the president's wife, she represents a role that many other women have played but that as Evita, she lives "a reality which perhaps no woman has lived in the history of humanity" (p. 94).

Throughout *La razón de mi vida,* Evita couches her audacious claims to self-importance and her achievements in a language of self-denial, humility, and subordination. She seems intent on proving that despite her power and her defiance of social conventions, she is not an anomaly, she is still a woman in the most conventional sense. Her rhetoric of self-denial is not only designed to attenuate the transgression that her entry into the realm of politics represents; it is also an implicit answer to her enemies who accused her of behaving like a man. As Ezequiel Martínez Estrada was to put it after her death: "he [Perón] was the woman and she was the man."[4] Thus she describes her actions as nothing more than the behavior of a dutiful and loving wife who does everything in her power to enhance her family's well-being. She compares Argentina to a home that is happy because Perón, the father, "transformed the hopes of our people in realities with his wonderful hands" (p. 311). Like all "humble" women, she is "the head of a home, much larger, it is true, than they have made, but in the final analysis, a home" (p. 311). She depicts herself as a wife who, while fond of jewels and clothes, freedom and fun, forsakes them all for the welfare of her family, a mother who wakes up every morning "thinking about my husband and my children" and who, like all good mothers, prefers her weakest children, those who need her most. Evita thus becomes the embodiment of the moral virtues traditionally ascribed to women: ever-loving, duty-bound, self-sacrificing, generous, a model of abnegation. Her perfection is not even marred by her own lack of children, since the workers, the old, the poor, and the underprivileged are in fact her children. Self-denying, virginal, pure in spirit, Evita emerges as a paradigmatic mother comparable only to the Virgin Mary. In Catholic Argentina, this vision of the self found throngs of willing believers. Before she died, a special session of Congress declared her *Jefa Espiritual de la Nación* (Spiritual Leader of the Nation), and after her death, a workers' union of newspaper distributors sought her canonization. Although the Vatican did not respond, Argentina was flooded with pictures of Evita, dressed like the Virgin Mary, her head covered with a veil and surrounded by a halo.

Evita's distinct sense of destiny, her narcissism and self-glorification are unusual among women who have played a significant role in public life. In this instance, as well as in others, she departs from the pattern exhibited by other political women. In her study of Emmeline Pankhurst, Dorothy Day, Emma Goldman, Eleanor Roosevelt, and Golda Meir, Patricia Meyer Spacks finds that such women tend to emphasize the hidden costs of public life, shy away from claims of self-importance, refrain from self-assertion and "use autobiography, paradoxically, partly as a mode of self-denial."[5]

For Evita, however, the very act of autobiography represented a daring form of self-assertion. Until *La razón de mi vida* was published, autobiography in Argentina was essentially the exclusive purview of the intellectual and political male elite. Since the mid-nineteenth century, they had written numerous memoirs, subjective accounts of their struggles to create an independent nation. Adolfo Prieto has pointed out that "the history of Argentine autobiographical literature condenses beyond the shadow of a doubt, the history of the power elite in Argentina" and that it must be included in any study of that class.[6] Being a woman, barely educated and a newcomer to politics, Evita, despite her substantial power, therefore lacked legitimacy to write in the accepted autobiographical tradition. She not only invaded a male realm but also transgressed rigid sociocultural demarcations and, by writing about her self, her feelings, especially her love for Perón, subverted the established rules of the genre. Her book was her defiant answer to those who ridiculed her lack of education, sneered at her speeches, questioned her social background, and devalued her actions as a political figure. It was an arrogant symbol of her power and she rev-eled in it, proclaiming the unparalleled rewards she had found in her "mission." She told her story as she wished, censoring all aspects of her life that might tarnish her vision of herself, and reduced significant historical events to backdrops on a stage dominated by Perón and herself, the divine father and the mother of Argentina.

Ironically, the publication of *La razón de mi vida* marked the beginning of the end of Evita's meteoric political career. Her candidacy to the vice-presidency, proclaimed in August 1951, was opposed by the military, and she had to withdraw it. In October 1951, her health was so frail that she could not attend the ceremony marking the publication of her book. In this text, however, Evita created the idealized self-image she wanted to perpetuate, a myth so powerful it still haunts Argentina today.

## NOTES

1. The myth of Evita has even taken the form of a Broadway musical hit. See: Andrew Lloyd Webber and Tim Rice, *Evita, The Legend of Eva Perón, 1919–1952* (London: Elm Tree Books, 1978); J. M. Taylor, *Eva Perón: The Myth of a Woman* (Chicago: Univ. of Chicago Press, 1979); and Marysa Navarro, "Evita and the Crisis of 17 October 1945: A Case Study of Peronist and Anti-Peronist Mythology," *Journal of Latin American Studies,* XII, 1 (May 1980), pp. 127–38.

2. Eva Perón, *La razón de mi vida* (Buenos Aires: Peuser, 1951). Translated in several languages, it was published in the United States as *My Mission in Life* (New York: Vantage Press, 1953). In this essay I have used the Peuser 1951 edition. My translation. All subsequent references to this edition are given in the body of the text.

3. See Miguel Murmis y Juan Carlos Portantiero, *Estudios sobre los orígenes del peronismo* (Buenos Aires: Siglo Veintiuno, 1972); David Rock, ed., *Argentina in the Twentieth Century* (Pittsburgh: Univ. of Pittsburgh Press, 1975); Marysa Navarro, *Evita* (Buenos Aires: Corregidor, 1982); and Frederick C. Turner and Juan José Miguens, eds., *Juan Perón and the Reshaping of Argentina* (Pittsburgh: Univ. of Pittsburgh Press, 1983).

4. Ezequiel Martínez Estrada, *¿Qué es esto? Catilinaria* (Buenos Aires: Editorial Lautaro, 1956), p. 241.

5. Patricia Meyer Spacks, "Selves in Hiding," in Estelle C. Jelinek, ed., *Women's Autobiography* (Bloomington: Indiana Univ. Press, 1980), p. 132.

6. Adolfo Prieto, *La literatura autobiográfica Argentina* (Buenos Aires: Editorial Jorge Alvarez, S. A., 1966), p. 21. In this survey of autobiographical texts written by authors born before 1900, Prieto mentions (but does not analyze) only one woman, Mariquita Sánchez.

# "Difficult Journey— Mountainous Journey," The Memoirs of Fadwa Tuqan

## *Donna Robinson Divine*

Fadwa Tuqan was born in 1917, but her line of descent extends far back into Muslim history. During the Ottoman Empire, 1517–1918, when imperial rule in provincial areas like those of Palestine depended on the service of local landholders, Fadwa Tuqan's ancestors were among the most influential residents of Nablus. The Tuqan family's political power, religious authority, and cultural preeminence rose from its economic dominion over vast tracts of agricultural land. In an era often marked by economic uncertainty and political disarray, families like the Tuqans provided Palestinian Arabs with a crucial element of cultural and political continuity.

From this perspective, the beginning of Fadwa Tuqan's memoirs[1] evinces a strong ambivalence toward her family legacy. She mentions the impoverished traditions that sustained her family and its position and seems disposed to deny the value of her material and cultural legacy. Elsewhere, she notes ironically how many people claim to be descended from the family of Muhammad but then proceeds to speak with pride of her family lineage and its connections to Muhammad. These contradictions may be contextually related to the upheavals that Palestinian Arabs, such as Fadwa Tuqan, have experienced in this century, radical changes that may account for the troubling light in which the "I" of these memoirs casts her family's history.

First among these upheavals was that a world ordered by the personalism of the urban patriarch, warrior village shaykh, or local religious leader, disappeared with the defeat of the Ottoman Empire in World War I.[2] At the time, the Empire was reconstituted into several independent nation-states with the Arab population no longer citizens of a large Muslim community, but rather subjects of smaller territories under the tutelage of

© 1984 by Donna Robinson Divine

one Western power or another.[3] This dismantling of the Ottoman Empire required that power be exercised in the name of new values and that it be obeyed on the basis of new criteria. For Palestinian Arabs, the shift in political discourse was followed by a substantial increase in the non-Arab population, resulting from Britain's sponsorship of a Jewish National Homeland in Palestine.[4] The British policy of encouraging Jewish immigration and Jewish land purchases compounded the awareness of abrupt and strange governmental and geographic changes.

As her memoirs indicate, Fadwa Tuqan witnessed a devastating war in 1948–1949 and the subsequent dispersal of her people into several Arab countries. The majority of Palestinian Arabs, like Fadwa Tuqan, lived in the parts of Palestine controlled by Jordan. Determined to prevent rebellions or agitations from what was perceived as a restive Palestinian-Arab population, the Jordanian regime restricted political activity and refrained from economic development in this area, thereby subjecting its Palestinian population to harsh economic crises and severe political repression.[5] The Jordanian rule, itself, ended abruptly in war. The Israeli military occupation of the West Bank, which began in June 1967, caused Palestinian Arabs to undergo yet another major change. Control of land and water resources was now threatened by the expansion of Jewish settlements. West Bank Palestinian Arabs were forced to abandon agriculture for more lucrative employment as wage laborers.[6] Through all of these upheavals, Palestinian Arabs, as a community, have had to live in political suspension unable to establish independently their own political priorities.

Fadwa Tuqan found her own poetic voice only after the loss of Palestine in 1948 and the simultaneous death of her father (Chapter ii, p. 29). In the many volumes of poetry for which she is primarily known,[7] she sought to give meaning to the upheavals that Palestinian Arabs have endured and to commemorate the belief that the inner resources of her people are beyond the reach of any political or military rule. Although disenchanted with the traditions and organization of her society, Fadwa Tuqan wrote of a bright future out of solidarity with the oppression and subordination of Palestinian Arabs. From the poetry of her brother, Ibrahim, she had learned to see connections between economic inequalities and the self-interest of the political leadership.[8] But her own poetry, as an act of writing, became a way of establishing links to other forms of oppression. She wrote less as a Palestinian-Arab artist than as a Palestinian-Arab woman speaking of a meaningless oppression she experienced, thereby defining herself as a spokesperson for all victims (Chapter iv, p. 12).

To be sure, in the aftermath of World War I and with the rise of nationalist movements, a new view of the role of women emerged in Arab societies, especially within educated circles.[9] And yet what appeared as a profound transformation in Cairo or Beirut barely affected the con-sciousness of Arab women in Palestine who, as Fadwa Tuqan states in her memoirs, did not discard their veils until 1948 (Chapter iv, p. 14). Indeed, and despite the dramatic changes recorded for men in this period, the lives of the women continued to be restricted by traditions, and discrimination against them appeared unchanging.[10]

Thus, although the gradual improvement in the quality of education was not shared equally by all Palestinian Arabs, it served to accentuate gender-based differences. Muslim women were often educated at home by tutors, and if sent to school, they attended for much less time than their brothers, male cousins, or even female Christian friends.[11] As she states in her memoirs, Fadwa Tuqan was forced to leave school at the age of eleven or twelve because she engaged in what was construed as shameful conduct when she accepted a flower from a sixteen-year-old boy; her parents pre-ferred to sacrifice her education than risk public dishonor. By contrast, Fadwa's brother, Ibrahim, was educated at the finest schools and gradu-ated from the prestigious American University of Beirut (Chapter iv, p. 15). The disjunction between her own desires and the way she was forced to live engendered the markedly ambivalent feelings toward members of her family that her memoirs recorded. In the pages of this text she often refers to the strained relationship with her father. Ironically, though she chose not to marry, she has lived her life as a poet faithful to the poetic goals her father set for her.

Twentieth-century writers and politicians have published autobiogra-phies in Arabic, and some Arab women have written of their own lives.[12] But the memoirs of Fadwa Tuqan, which appeared serialized in 1978–1979 in the journal of the Israel Arab Communist Party, *el-Jadida,* represent an unprecedented conjunction of politics and personality because of the can-dor and self-scrutiny with which feminist impulses are inscribed. Beyond the historical and familial strains she describes, and the emotional turmoil that must necessarily result from them, the memoirs emphasize the impor-tance of struggling on, and above all, of living without despair.

## NOTES

1. Fadwa Tuqan, "Memoirs: Difficult Journey—Mountainous Journey," *el-Jadida* (1978–1979), chapter iii.

2. Moshe Ma'oz, ed., *Studies on Palestine during the Ottoman Period* (Jerusalem: Magnes, 1975).

3. *Palestine, A Study of Jewish, Arab and British Policies,* Volume I (New Haven: Yale Univ. Press, 1947).

4. J. C. Hurewitz, *Struggle for Palestine* (New York: W. W. Norton, 1950); and Yehoshua Porath, *The Emergence of a Palestinian-Arab National Movement, 1918–1929* (Lon-don: Frank Cass, 1974).

5. Shaul Mishal, "Conflictual Pressure and Cooperative Interests: Observations on West Bank–Amman Political Relations, 1949–1967," in *Palestinian Society and Politics,* ed. Joel S. Migdal (Princeton: Princeton Univ. Press, 1980), pp. 169–84; Amnon Cohen, *Political Parties in the West Bank under the Jordanian Regime, 1949–1967* (Ithaca: Cornell Univ. Press, 1982); A. Plascov, *Refugees in Jordan 1948–1957* (London: Frank Cass, 1981).

6. Mark Heller, "Politics and Social Change in the West Bank," in *Palestinian Society and Politics,* ed. Migdal, pp. 185–211; Salim Tamari, "The Palestinians in the West Bank and Gaza: The Sociology of Dependency," in *The Sociology of the Palestinians,* ed. Khalil Nakhleh and Elia Zureik (New York: St. Martin's Press, 1980), pp. 84–111.

7. Fadwa Tuqan's poetry collections include: *Wahdi ma' al-Ayyam* (Alone with Days, 1955); *Wajadtuha* (I Have Found It, 1957); *A' tina Hubban* (Give Us Love, 1960); *Amam al Bab al-Mughlaq* (In Front of the Closed Door, 1967); *al-Layl wa'l-Fursan* (Night and the Knights, 1969); *al-Fida', Wa-l-Ard* (The Freedom Fighter and the Land, 1968); *'Ala Qimmat al-Dunya Wahidan* (Alone, On Top of the World, 1973); and *Kabus al-Layl Wa'l Nahar* (The Nightmare of Night and Day, 1974). Some of her poems have appeared in translations. See Issa J. Boullata, ed., *Modern Arab Poets 1950–1975* (Washington, D.C.: Three Continents Press, 1976); A. M. Elmessiri, *The Palestinian Wedding* (Washington, D.C.: Three Continents Press, 1982); Kamal Boullata, ed. and trans., *Women of the Fertile Crescent: Modern Poetry by Arab Women* (Washington, D.C.: Three Continents Press, 1978); and Naseer Aruri and Edmund Ghareeb, eds., *Enemy of the Sun: Poetry of Palestinian Resistance* (Washington, D.C.: Drum & Spear Press, 1970).

8. Salma Khadra Jayyusi, *Trends and Movements in Modern Arabic Poetry,* Volume I (Leiden: E. J. Brill, 1977), pp. 284ff. More broadly, see M. Peled, Annals of Doom, Palestinian Literature—1917–1948," *Arabica,* Vol. XXIX, Fascicule Z (1982), pp. 142–83.

9. Thomas Philipp, "Feminism and Nationalist Politics in Egypt," in *Women in the Muslim World,* ed. Lois Beck and Nikki Keddi (Cambridge: Harvard Univ. Press, 1978), pp. 277–94.

10. Bertha Spafford Vester, *Our Jerusalem* (Garden City: Doubleday, 1950); M. E. T. Mogannam, *The Arab Woman* (London: Herbert Joseph, 1936).

11. See Donna Robinson Divine, "Palestinian Arab Women and Their Reveries of Emancipation," in *Living Change: Cross Cultural Perspectives on Women and Social Change,* ed. Susan C. Bourque and Donna Robinson Divine (Philadelphia: Temple University Press, 1985).

12. The Egyptian writer and educator Dr. Taha Husayn wrote his autobiography, the first volume of which, published in 1926, was described by the noted historian H. A. R. Gibb as, "the finest work of art yet produced in modern Egyptian literature"; see his "Studies in Contemporary Arabic Literature—III," *Bulletin of the School of Oriental Studies,* V, 3, p. 458. Other autobiographies of Palestinians are Ahmad al-Shuqayri, *'Arbu 'un 'Aman Fi-l-Hayyat al-Arabiyya wa-l-Dawliyya* (Beirut, 1969); Khalil al-Sakakini, *Kadha Ana Ya Dunya,* ed. Hala al-Saka-kini (Jerusalem, 1955); among the autobiographies published by Arab women are Inbara Salam el-Khalidi, *Joula fi al-Dhikrya Bein Lubnan Wa-Filastin* (Beirut, 1978); Ramonda Hawa Tawil, *My Home, My Prison* (New York: Holt, Rinehart and Winston, 1979); Nawal El-Saadawi, *The Hidden Face of Eve* (London: Zed Press, 1980); Leila Khalad, *My People Shall Live* (London: Hodder and Stoughton, 1973).

DIFFICULT JOURNEY—MOUNTAINOUS JOURNEY:
The Memoirs of Fadwa Tuqan

When I was young, I was incapable of describing life as forcefully as a poet does. My world—the world of writing—was frightening and emotionally empty. I lived amidst thoughts sown in writing, but I was isolated from the world itself. As I matured into a woman, I was like a wounded animal, sterile in its cage. Although confined and deprived of a homeland, I was asked by my father to write political poetry. He wanted me to follow in the footsteps of my brother, Ibrahim,[1] and publish for the good of the nation and its politics. Through writing, my father wanted me to respond to our national despair, but his demand made me miserable. I was unable to compose poetry; my inner voice was weak in protest against everything that had caused my silence. I was expected to create political poetry while the corrupt laws and customs insisted that I remain secluded behind a wall, not able to attend assemblies of men, not hearing the recurrent debates, not participating in public life. Oh, my nation, I want you to know the face behind the veil when I was forbidden to travel freely. I only knew Jerusalem because Ibrahim had invited me when he worked there for the Palestine Broadcasting System. He had wanted me to know a city other then Nablus,[2] my birthplace.

The home environment in which I was raised did not nourish an interest in the outside world, but encouraged me rather to turn away from the struggle.[3] Nevertheless, my father demanded that I realize the lofty aspirations he had for me. And yet, he never allowed me to establish a connection between his aspirations for me and my own inner emotions. For that reason, I was unable to compose poetry and instead sought refuge under a cover of tearful submission.

When we come of age, we are expected to concentrate our energies no matter what the personal cost, the obstacles and difficulties which preoccupy us. My father believed it was possible to solve any problem. My past had been deeply rooted in poetry, but my emotions had taken a very different direction from the course my father was urging me to follow. The poet must know the world before it can be healed through poetry. How else can the political issues be weighed? Where was I to find an intellectual atmosphere in which I could write political poetry? From the newspaper my father brought home at lunch every day? The newspaper is important, but it doesn't have the power to inspire poetry in the depths of one's soul. I was enslaved, isolated in my seclusion from the outside world, and my seclusion was imposed as a duty—I had no choice in the matter. The outside world was taboo for women of good families, and society didn't protest that seclusion; it was not part of the political agenda.

My mother, as I recall, was one of the first members of the Society for the Welfare of Women. And yet, nothing changed for her. She did not participate in social gatherings, and unlike other members of the Society, she was not allowed to travel at all unless accompanied by a member of the family. This women's organization was founded in Nablus in 1921 by Miriam Hashem, a teacher (who died in 1947). Many outstanding people were members. In 1929, it became affiliated with the General Union of Arab Women, founded in Egypt by Huda Sharawi.[4] This affiliation stirred Palestinian women into being involved in their own political struggle.

The women in my family left the house only on rare occasions, such as family celebrations in the houses of relatives and close friends. Although my father permitted my mother to join Miriam Hashem's organization, he restricted her activities to those associated with fundraising. If conferences were held in Egypt or in other cities in Palestine, my mother was not allowed to attend. Seclusion from the outside world deprived the home atmosphere, which women breathed, of any political or social consciousness.

Given the many prohibitions imposed on women, their movements in the home strongly resembled those of domesticated poultry who can come and go freely until they find fodder and then suffer constant temptation. But this particular domesticated poultry confined its energies to hatching the young. Women exhausted their lives with the big, copper cooking pots and gathering firewood for the stove in all seasons. As in other societies where the lives of women make no sense, the lives of Palestinian women, in every epoch and in every house, seemed devoid of significance. Such an environment had a stifling grip on me, which intensified as I approached sexual maturity.[5]

My journey through life was filled with the misery of acute emotional and intellectual struggles. During the early years, I hated politics. I tried to realize my father's wishes in order to gain his love. I was not socially liberated but in my heart I justified rebellion and rejection. How could I possibly struggle for the sake of political liberation and for my own national convictions? Just as our society needed strong political action so too did I need political activity. And while our cultural needs were not as pressing, we were also deprived in this area as well.

I was conscious of my talent but I knew it could not mature except in society. This society created barriers to restrict me. The world of the harem stood between me and society. A spirit of impotence prevailed, and I could not write poetry. I was idle. I stopped exercising my poetic talents. In my difficult journey, I concealed the gift of my poetry. The strong awareness of what I had repressed and what I could potentially express left its traces on my spiritual and bodily existence. I became very thin and my brain felt fragmented. The weariness of my soul burdened all my limbs and during the night my body felt as if it had drowned.

Let me talk about the meaning of my life, its purpose and the particular poet's anxiety which I bear. My afflictions tore me apart, but if my wretchedness increased my tears, it also expanded the sensitivity of my soul. I found relief when I thought of the wisdom of the ancient saying, "If I am not for myself, who will be for me? And if I am only for myself, who am I?"

My commitment to life weakened as I remained secluded from the outside world. My soul was tormented because of this seclusion. My father's demands may have initiated my turmoil, but the pain always stayed with me, taking different forms throughout the journey of my life. Ultimately, at the source of my struggle was a tradition whose laws and customs constantly tested me. The process of maturing was a most painful experience in body and soul. I was oppressed, crushed; I felt bent out of shape. I could not participate in any aspect of life unless I pretended to be another person. I became more and more distant.

When I recovered, the words which intensified my feelings of subjugation and suppression also enriched the individuality and quality of my poetry. My work is existential, but it also penetrates the life of the harem which is narrow and constricted like a long-necked bottle. The talent, which I seemed initially to lack, had been blocked from view by this narrow long-necked bottle. My only bridge to society was the political poetry which I occasionally published in newspapers. I felt increasingly alienated and sensed that my poetic gifts were being plundered. I was aware of my ambition, but in those circumstances of seclusion, it appeared pathological. In the midst of my journey, my misery deepened, and one of my protectors, Nadim Salah, our family doctor, saved me from death and delivered me from my torture.

In 1948, during the Palestine War,[6] my father died. With the loss of Palestine, my writing problems also ended. I began to write the nationalist poetry my father had always wished me to write. I began to devote myself to the nationalist cause, as had Ibrahim during his lifetime. I wrote poetry spontaneously and now with no complaints from the outside world.[7] I was convulsed by the Palestine problem, the tragic situation of the refugees and the difficulties of the Arab world whose armies fought the war. I did not expect miracles from a politics which was then in its earliest stages, but I did not despair or abandon political activity. Politics gave me the will to persist in a struggle against the fragmentation and poverty of our war-torn nation. My immobility ended.

## The Enclosed Environment of Women in Nablus
### during the 1930s and 1940s

Because of my family's status and position, my feelings about my-self were strongly affected by the opinions of others. Even when I was angry at the outside world, my emotions were strongly affected by its views of me. My emotions were so volatile that I never questioned the need to disguise them. This disguise was my defense against criticism.

Men and women in Nablus have particular social customs which they impose by designating certain people as the city's "watchdogs." The authority these people enjoy does not stem from their special knowledge, but rather from their hateful pretentiousness. It has often been said that people from Nablus disapprove of everything. Unlike other citizens of Nablus, I do not impose on others customs alien to their own, nor would I deprive anyone of free discussion. For the most part, however, people in Nablus are civil to one another without being especially warm or close.

During the 1930s and 1940s, I could not leave the house unless accompanied by another family member, such as my mother or aunt or sister or cousin. It was impossible to breathe freely during these visits. I was forced to join members of my family on their visits occasionally, although the atmosphere was hostile. I yearned for any situation in which my mother or the other women in my family would be allowed to go out more than once or twice a month. At the time, women were usually illiterate or had the most rudimentary skills of literacy. Their meager education could be furthered only at the government high school in Jerusalem (dar-al-mu'alamat)[8] where they received a secondary school education.

However, there was a group of schoolteachers in Nablus and in other Palestinian cities who had a distinct social status. These women teachers distinguished themselves by their education and material possessions. They demanded and received deference from the common people. The women teachers had established a network of philanthropic societies which distributed pittances to people who were overwhelmed by what they considered extraordinary generosity. From these teachers, I learned the meaning of economic independence. In fact, my sisters and I began to support a woman enslaved by family and custom. This woman could not count on support from her family. Not that she was liberated from social customs and constraints. In fact, because her education was very limited, she could not change her personality and instill confidence in her own abilities and talents. In blind imitation of custom, she continued to consider male sponsorship and female subordination the rule. She believed that the power of men to make all the decisions in society was nothing more than brotherly compassion. But when the men in her family were unemployed, this woman was forced to turn to society for sustenance.

The situation for women teachers was not much better than the situation for other women in society, for they too had to abide by society's rules, which constrained their behavior. The rules were shaped by arrogance, conceit, and pomposity. Despite their knowledge, these teachers did not have any special regard or appreciation for the books or articles published at the time. They were not cultured, nor did they engage in serious reading. Rather, the importance of this group stemmed from their fastidious dress. The money they earned as teachers enabled them to satisfy their desires for fashionable clothes. They never altered the rules and practices that existed among common people.

This educated class read in a destructive, hostile spirit. Only one woman was different. She alone possessed a craving for knowledge and culture. Mrs. Fakhriya Hajawi was my former teacher in a school attended by the daughters of prosperous families in Nablus. She was very concerned with my life in and out of school. Sitt Fakhriya[9] loved to read the newspaper to me or to read from the Egyptian journal *Al-Risala*. She was bursting with knowledge and would urge me to pursue my poetic journey. When I met her, I began to speak to her about writing, reading, and about the structure of *qasida*.[10] She responded by giving me her attention, which made me profoundly happy.

With the exception of Sitt Fakhriya, I could not respect the privileged position of educated women. In turn, they made their negative feelings clear in unpleasant and haughty encounters with me. They would say sharply: "Her brother, Ibrahim, composed the poetry and appended her name to it." They directed their negative comments at me until Ibrahim's death. Their hostility was painful, and I was aware of the pain even though I was very young. Once I reached the age of puberty, I began to realize that every success achieved by a woman has its price both for her and her family. It is not even possible to laugh at the antics of clowns without being criticized. But I realized this only later; at the time, I merely suffered in silence.

During the 1930s and the 1940s, I was secluded in female society. Because urban society strove for outward appearances which would distinguish it from village society, it maintained an isolated and inhospitable existence for women. But the breach between me and female society grew wider. While I kept my disdain secret, I could neither contribute to society nor accept anything from it. Female society was consumed by idle chatter. The chatter manifested the illiteracy of women who had no access to the beautiful and fertile writing appearing in the larger world around them. Unable to join them in their illiteracy, I was forced into a breach with the society in which I was born.

## I See; I Hear; I Suffer

I didn't show my father any emotions. My feelings toward him were almost neutral: I neither loathed nor loved him since I didn't matter to him. I felt for him only when he was sick, imprisoned, or banished for political reasons. His temper cast a shadow over us; in the morning we scarcely noticed it until it would explode like a storm. I was afraid he would die and abandon us. This outweighed any other feelings I had about him, feelings of alienation or indifference. I was not aware of the significance of this until I reached adolescence when I feverishly began to scrutinize my youth.

My burdens made me suffer. Seeing this, Ibrahim compensated for my father and always showed me great tenderness, affection, and goodness. When Ibrahim died, my father still imposed shackles on my life. But when my father passed on to the next world, I was freed from the frightening duty which had stifled my emotions and which I had endured for so many years. Even though I was sharply critical of his legacy I tried not to betray it. I considered his death an attack against the family itself. From that day on I was empowered. I no longer kept my distance from controversies: I saw, I heard, and I suffered. Earlier, I had written a *qasida* called "Life," but my true feelings had been distant, absent.

## The Narrow Long-Necked Bottle

I was much more attached to my aunt than to my mother, and my attachment to my paternal uncle, el-Hajj Hafez, was stronger and deeper than my attachment to my father. Because of the warmth of his heart, his joking and laughing, I felt he truly loved me. My memories of my uncle continue to be clear and vivid, although my thoughts are fragmented and muddled. My uncle was involved in many enjoyable quarrels and controversies. One dispute between him and my father concerned my uncle's participation in family councils. The men of the city, considering my father too rigid in his views, would approach my uncle instead and meet constantly with him. I would often run to him during his meetings and he would take me in his arms and set me on his lap. My father would never do this.

During the first quarter of the year, the men of Nablus would celebrate the birthday of the Prophet Moses—Nebi Musa. The idea for this holiday began during the Ayyubid period[11] in an effort to attract large numbers of Muslims to Jerusalem when many Christians were there celebrating Easter. This presumably would put Muslims on their guard against a surprise attack by the Crusaders. Muslim youth would arrive in the holy city in huge numbers from cities and villages all over Palestine. They would meet at the tomb of Nebi Musa, which is located between Jerusalem and Jericho. During the holiday, the young men of Nablus would go out with the religious dignitaries who were in charge of the rituals. The procession began with the religious men beating on drums and cymbals and singing popular songs. The parade continued to the city's limits, then turned to Jerusalem to join a procession of religious dignitaries of Hebron and Jerusalem. The singing continued throughout the Easter celebration.

In the Nebi Musa procession, just as in the procession of a bride and groom where the Quran is recited, the parade would stop in front of our house and look for the family "jester." The shouting and calls for my uncle would rise higher. My uncle would leave his office chamber to join the holiday procession near the government offices. The young men would mount him on their shoulders. They would all draw weapons. My uncle would wave his sword imploring the enthusiastic crowd to reply to his words: "We are men of the mountain of light." In the parade, orange-blossom water would drip from the pitchers or from narrow long-necked bottles.

I was very proud of my uncle. Eventually, I recognized the reasons for his popularity. In 1925, the National Party was founded in Nablus to support the candidacy of el-Hajj Amin el-Husayni[12] to the Supreme Muslim Council.[13] Other parties, like the National Democratic Party, opposed the National Party in the elections. My uncle was one of the founders of the National Party. After his own success in the municipal elections, he distanced himself from party rivalries and from the factions in both the local council and the country. Of the two parties, the National was connected to el-Hajj Amin el-Husayni and the National Democratic was led by Ragheb el-Nashashibi,[14] mayor of Jerusalem. These two parties created damaging divisions in the country. Unlike my uncle, my father did not avoid this political battlefield. He belonged to various political organizations and was imprisoned several times by the British mandatory authorities. Still, my uncle continued to be more popular and prominent.

When my uncle died of diphtheria in 1927, at the age of fifty-two, I began my encounter with death. As if struck by lightning, I fell into confusion and a whirlpool of inconsolable sadness. For the first time, I experienced loss, and I grieved. Man's life is a chain of distinct losses, starting as a separation from the mother's breasts and ending with his own death. My uncle's death deprived me of a loving guardian. After his death, he lay still, shrouded on a bed. I was confused by the lack of worry on his pale face, his unawareness of a crying family and friends. I concealed my sadness, trying not to think of the loss of the family member I felt closest to. We deceive ourselves in thinking that we can preserve the memory of the deceased by placing little stones on his grave. That ritual doesn't compensate for the loss. To tell children that it does is only to deceive them as they are forced to confront death. I hid my own grief and drew near to it only at night, crying myself to sleep.

I am not a philosopher. As a child, I reasoned simply as children do. But I was preoccupied by the dread which death inspired. I wondered about the external appearance of death since the dead seem absolutely isolated and indifferent. Even Julia my childhood friend, who was distantly related to me, could not share my feelings of death for she, herself, died before my eyes in the seventeenth year of her life. She struggled alone and had to struggle alone, for no beholder can partake of another's death. When I think about Julia's death, I do not remember how she looked, but rather how I felt about her. I became angry when people said that death carries our loved ones to paradise in reward. The death of my uncle marked the end of my childhood. Julia's death appeared so unjustifiable that I thought only about death for a time. I was obsessed with the questions of why people died and why they left me. I was a child. I asked these questions simply and clearly.

## SHAYKHA

Among my earliest memories are those of an aunt we called "Shaykha."[15] I knew her as a master of intimidation, the person who controlled all the women in the family. She also reported on the activities and behavior of the boys in the family, serving as a sort of police, transmitting accounts surreptitiously to my uncle.

Societies in which supervision is arbitrary and repressive engender dual reactions: submission and revolt. But these reactions, in turn, intensify the repressive power and create a hegemony in family and society. In my family, it was Shaykha who not only laid the foundation for this sort of power, but who also encompassed the qualities of submission and revolt.

When she was only sixteen, Shaykha returned to her father's house divorced from a marriage which had lasted a few months. She became a follower of the Sufi Order of Shaykh Abd al-Kadir al-Kaylani.[16] For Shaykha the religious order served as an escape from the frustrations of a failed marriage. In the religious community of this blind Egyptian shaykh, there was a polarization between female members who were divorced and those who were widows. The group assembled in the house of the treasurer who, with his wife, had the authority to dispense *baraka*[17] and facilitate ritual purity. The shaykh proclaimed his *baraka* in a way that aggrandized his own importance. So doing, he deprived his followers of their own capacity to reason. By sharpening sensations with the fragrance of musk, the shaykh could convince his followers to see what was not visible, to hear what did not exist.

The account of the shaykh's *baraka* brings to mind a story about my old Turkish grandmother, "Mother Azziza." One day she was present at one of the shaykh's demonstrations. In tears, she renounced what she saw and launched a devastating attack against the shaykh. From that day, an enmity was firmly established between Shaykha and my mother, whose modern outlook, especially on the subject of death, was at odds with Shaykha's religious piety. Shaykha attacked my mother, my brother Ahmad, and me for opposing her views.

As she aged and grew weaker, Shaykha was constantly engaged in praying, fasting, or proclaiming revelations. She would fast for three months—Rajjab, Shabban and Ramadan—and pray and perform sacrifices at night.[18] Her prayer beads[19] were huge and always by her side. They consisted of a thousand individual beads, and as she touched each one she would pronounce one of the names of Allah.[20] Her personality was like that string of prayer beads, displayed for public and private devotions; the beads were a concrete manifestation of her piety.

As a child, I used to love to watch people engaged in prayer especially because of the theatrics involved. I would often stop at the gate of the Al Bek Mosque facing our house in the old market area to watch the different ways in which the worshippers prayed. While their facial expressions were quite different, they all began at a speedy pace, then humbled themselves without paying attention to anything but God. My heart and spirit were moved as I watched the worshippers pray firmly and slowly.

I noticed the hand movements. They were raised behind the ears, then brought instantly above the head and finally to the right side as prayers were whispered in undertones. Body movements began: bowing the torso to the front; raising the body and lifting the head to the sky, kneeling down, prostrating themselves while placing their hands on their legs. Raising two index fingers, the assembled group would testify to the existence of God. They would pronounce praises to God aloud and turn their heads from right to left.

Only much later did I discover why it was important to express religious submission through prayer. I learned of a continuity in religious rituals from the period of peasant paganism. All modern religions try to evoke a mysterious environment through their theatrics and expressions, which are similar to the devotions and activities of the early natural religions.

Shaykha's call to religious prayer was exaggerated and artificial. Occasionally, she seemed to imitate the rituals of Dervishes.[21] She would begin vehement, trembling motions, moving her head fiercely right and left while repeating the name of Allah . . . Allah . . . Allah . . . Allah . . . , etc. She pronounced the name rapidly, without pause, foaming at the sides of her mouth.

Because of Shaykha, my faith changed. Occasionally, it was said that her religious rigidity dissolved in gatherings of women visitors. I did not find that to be true. She loved to issue decrees for the women in the family and to censure them for religious impiety. Shaykha would insult people simply because they were poor or unsuccessful. Thus did Shaykha believe.

In most circumstances, she took the particular behavior of individuals as a general commentary on all humanity. She would permit one of the girls in the family to become friendly with a relative, a school friend or a neighborhood girl. Then seeing the two together in the courtyard she would fume with rage. This used to drive every school friend or neighborhood companion away from the house. When I did Shaykha a favor or buy her a gift from the *suk*,[22] she would insinuate that I was trying to buy her love. Even when she smiled or showed some gentleness, her affection always stopped like a cold wall which cannot nourish green plants. In a way, I combined traits of my mother and those of Shaykha, and yet the two were very different. On the one hand, there was my mother's warmth, gentleness, and softness, and on the other, Shaykha was like a desert without trees or water. She was a harsh goddess who aimed her breath at an invisible throne.

Proud and haughty, Shaykha was in control of an entire stratum of women who blindly obeyed her. This "pious" Shaykha would lead the simple women by her example. She would sit with them during their children's illnesses. The women would hold pitchers of water while Shaykha stood near the sick babies reading passages from the Quran. The women believed Shaykha could purify and bless the water as she exhaled into the pitchers. Given her devotion to God, this "pious" Shaykha held an astonishing view of the upper class, which she expressed arrogantly: "We are above and you are below. This is God's Wish." During the 1930s and 1940s, this view was commonly held by the classes which benefited from the established order. They legitimized their positions of authority through the name of God. One could always hear the words: "Sayyids, Ladies, At Your Service, Sayyid; At Your Service, Ladies; At Your Service, Sons of Sayyids."[23]

Ideas are effective as long as people accept them and do not revolt against them. We must reject Aristotle's saying, "that the slave resembles the beast," even though this idea was consistent with the venerated thought of Athenian society and not questioned at that time.

I remember what a woman once said to Shaykha: "Honor us, oh lady, with a visit during the holidays, for we visit you often and you do not visit us." But Shaykha stared at her and said in her haughty way: "Listen, you will visit us always and forever and we will not visit you in order to emphasize the significance of the day of our departure."[24] What has happened to the world! How inverted things are! The woman was ashamed and my heart filled with sympathy for her. I left the room, rushed to my mother to tell her how Shaykha had shamed this poor woman. I was young. I did not understand the meaning of cruelty, but I distanced myself instinctively from Shaykha's views. My feelings overwhelmed me, and I fell ill.

Although it may have been unconscious, I considered class pride improper. In my home, criticism of Shaykha's haughtiness was tolerated until it affected the family as a whole. Shaykha would say to us in utter simplicity: "We are all Creations of the Lord and our fate is in God's hands," but this harsh woman turned away from all else. It is not right to turn from suffering in order to honor important men who hold esteemed social positions. Because she believed it was, God punished her and afflicted her with the hostility of the poor. My mother told us about democracy simply, and she could explain spontaneously how the demise of democracy affected all people at all social levels. My mother could teach us in a practical way the true meaning of the phrase, brotherly unity is no burden.

I saw Shaykha as a symbol of the hardness of society, and I did not find my efforts to destroy that symbol absurd. Ultimately, I was unable to put an end to Shaykha's religiosity and to convince her that her feelings were inhuman. She never could accept my beliefs that the true meaning of religion had been distorted and that Allah's attributes of love, mercy, and goodness had produced illiteracy and ignorance for most men and women. What Shaykha considered permissible and forbidden, proper and improper was a strange, soggy mixture. She would cry to me for help but considered me an apostate. "Come on up weak one. Buckle down. Submit more or you will enter Hell and so will your mother who sewed those disgraceful clothes for you." Shaykha's views undermined any serenity I had in my childhood. Her simplicity confused my young mind. Peace returned only when I began to imagine that it was the God of Hell who visited with my mother. I imagined Allah himself as a harsh and fearful ruler without compassion.

Once, when I had raised my voice in song—"how secure is the breath of fresh air for the beautiful beloved everywhere . . ."—Shaykha entered the room like a storm and said: "Silence, close your mouth or you will perish and awaken in Hell. Hinkiyan . . . Hind . . . Surena. . . ." My voice was suddenly broken; the song, broken and incomplete, stuck in my throat. Hind and Surena were professional singers in Nablus whom Shaykha called Hinkiyan or harpies, a term she derived from the Persian word for God.

Shaykha hurt me deeply during those days by condemning the desires I satisfied daily through music and dance. I regarded music and dance as desirable and liberating activities. I, alone, possessed the power to control music and dance; the world in which I lived did not. Shaykha could not impose her power over song, and I did not believe her when she said that song and dance were ugly.

My mother used to hum softly with her sad, tender voice. I would hum and sit on her lap listening attentively. Resting from time to time and comforting me—at family gatherings and with my friends—in warm soft light—she would make me content, which she loved to do as she would remind me of the words and music of a song. Singing delighted me and made me happy. To fulfill an ambition, my mother had learned to play the violin. But she was so devoted to that ambition that the instrument was forbidden in our house. Playing an instrument and singing represented outlets and then, at a later phase of my youthful journey, symbols of the sentimental yearnings I had suppressed. In harmony and song—both in listening and in practicing—I found a release of tension. Like poetry, this release served as a means to realize my talents and liberate my imprisoned capacities.

One of the strongest of my depressing memories of Shaykha began in the girls' room. This room, in the front of the house, did not belong to her, for each of the upstairs rooms had a different name. She entered unexpectedly and came upon my older brother, Ahmad, who was answering some of my questions on poetic meter and form. Shaykha stopped silently and looked over our heads. Then she said to Ahmad reproachfully, "Even you, then what more? For girls, words are opponents who collapse in battle." Ahmad joked with her, using some meaningless words. Then he turned his attention once again to me and to my questions about poetry.

"Even you. . . ." A terrifying expression for me which Ahmad understood with indulgence and which made a loving impression on him. In contrast, Ibrahim, whom I always loved, was emancipated from family traditions and from Shaykha's harsh shackles. From that day on my attitude to Shaykha was completely hostile. I no longer hoped for anything different in the future. Shaykha was the nightmare of my childhood and adolescence, and she left her harsh traces on many years of my life.

Those who thought little of their role in my life were often the ones who, in retrospect, penetrated it most deeply.

## NOTES

1. During the period of the British mandate, Ibrahim Tuqan (1905–1941), Fadwa's brother, was considered the most prominent poet of the Palestine-Arab community.

2. Nablus, a Palestinian city of modest size, is located in what is now called the West Bank. During the last decades of the Ottoman Empire (1517–1918) many men from Nablus held high administrative positions. In the course of British rule, Nablus served as the center of a local Palestinian-Arab cultural revival. Known as "Jabal al-Nar" (the mountain of fire), Nablus has a reputation as the site of rebellion and resistance to government.

3. Fadwa Tuqan is referring to "the struggle" against the Zionists in their efforts to establish a Jewish state in Palestine.

4. Huda Sharawi (1882–1947) was one of the founders of the equal rights movement for women in Egypt and in the Arab world.

5. Upon reaching puberty, an Arab girl in urban areas was normally veiled and forced into the strictest seclusion if her family could afford to be deprived of her labor outside the house. In a later chapter of her memoirs, Fadwa Tuqan says that at the age of puberty, she was not even permitted to attend school.

6. In 1947 the British decided to withdraw from Palestine, and on December 1, 1947, the United Nations voted to partition the country into a Jewish and an Arab state. These two decisions were among the factors that transformed the protracted communal violence between Jews and Arabs into full-scale war. On May 15, 1948, as the Jewish leadership proclaimed the establishment of Israel, the regular armed forces of Egypt, Trans-Jordan, Syria,

Lebanon, and Iraq crossed the boundaries of Palestine to help Palestinian Arabs in their ultimately unsuccessful efforts to block the creation of a Jewish state.

7. According to Fadwa Tuqan, people often said that Ibrahim had written the poetry and had signed her name to it. See *Memoirs,* p. 30.

8. *Dar al-mu'alamat* literally means "the house of female teachers" and refers to a teacher-training school in Jerusalem.

9. *Sitt* means "Mrs."

10. *Qasida,* sometimes translated as "ode," is a poem of praise consisting of twenty-five to one hundred verses with rhymes arranged in a particular pattern. The meter and subject matter are determined by convention.

11. "Ayyubid" refers to the dynasty founded by Salah al-Din ibn Ayyub, known in Europe as Saladin. Salah al-Din led the assaults against the Crusader kingdoms in Palestine and Syria, crushing them at the Battle of Hattin in 1187.

12. El Hajj Amin el-Husayni was the single most prominent leader of the Palestinian Arabs during the period of the British mandate. For generations, members of this landholding family had held important religious and administrative positions in Jerusalem. During the period of British rule, el Hajj Amin el-Husayni, Grand Mufti and president of the Supreme Muslim Council, often served as the chief spokesman of the Palestinian Arabs.

13. The Supreme Muslim Council was newly constituted by the British in 1922 and given wide discretionary powers over the disbursement of sums of money collected for the development and maintenance of Muslim educational and charitable institutions. It became a significant vehicle for exercising political and economic power in the Palestine-Arab community.

14. Ragheb Bey Nashashibi was the leader of another economically and socially prominent Jerusalem family. Ragheb Bey headed a group of families opposing el Hajj Amin el-Husayni's leadership and Husayni family hegemony.

15. *Shaykh* is an Arabic word for "leader," usually of a tribe or clan. *Shaykha* is the feminine form of the word.

16. Fadwa Tuqan probably refers to 'Abd al-Qadir al-Jilani (d. 1165/66), a founder of one of the four major Sufi orders. The blind Egyptian shaykh mentioned later was probably the leader during Shaykha's time.

17. *Baraka* means "blessing." Muslims believe that God instills this power in the persons of his prophets and saints.

18. Shaykha fasted two months longer than necessary according to Muslim law and performed rituals required only during the month of Ramadan.

19. Prayer beads consist of a chain of thirty-three or ninety-nine beads used to enumerate the various names of God or to help in remembering various prayers.

20. From the Quran, and subsequent tradition, Muslim piety has carefully taken ninety-nine names called the "most beautiful names," which believers are supposed to memorize and use in meditation.

21. Dervishes, derived from the Persian word for "poor," is applied to the Muslims who consider themselves mystics, more commonly called sufis, and who distinguish themselves by dress and style of prayer.

22. *Suk* means "marketplace."

23. *Sayyid,* a term describing the descendants of the prophet Muhammad, represents a type of nobility.

24. To emphasize the piety of Arab women and their deep commitment to tradition, it is commonly said that they leave their houses only on the day of their death, when they are taken out to be buried.

## CHAPTER FIFTEEN

# Women and Autobiography at Author's Expense

## Philippe Lejeune

*Have you ever written a novel, a poem, a comedy, an essay? Why keep your manuscripts in a drawer? Did you know that an important publisher is looking for writers, famous or unknown? Send him your manuscripts immediately.*—A suave voice makes this announcement every evening on the radio.—I've got a manuscript in a drawer. Why not try? I open the newspaper and see that this same publisher promises to promote the books chosen for publication "in newspapers, on radio, and television." He's serious. He says, moreover, that the contracts are bound by article 49 of the copyright law. It's legal then. With pounding heart, I send off my manuscript. The name of the publisher is La Pensée Universelle, 4 rue Charlemagne, Paris 4ème. That has an impressive ring. So I wait, without much hope: my manuscript has already been rejected by other publishers, and no one at home encourages me. Miraculously, in less than three weeks, I have an answer from La Pensée Universelle: my book has been accepted by the editorial board! They're going to print 3000 copies!

That's where the miracle ends: I have to *pay*. That is the first disappointment, but ignorance of the law is no excuse (article 49 governs publishing contracts labelled "at author's expense"). The book itself is gray and dull, and if you aren't used to correcting proofs, it will be full of misprints and mistakes: the publisher can't waste his time. But the promise of publicity is duly kept: three times a year, on one or two pages of the *Monde des livres* or the *Magazine Littéraire,* the publisher prints a list of 150 books. This unreadable advertisement serves not to recruit readers (in any event, the publisher has already been paid for his work) but to attract new authors. At this point, the author realizes woefully that no bookstore is stocking the book. If you try to distribute it alone, 500 or 600 copies may be placed at best, but more often, only 100 or 150. After two years, the publisher threatens to pulp the 2000-some remaining copies. The author can do nothing but come and take away the books by the carton and stack them in the cellar where the rats and mice will read them.

Self-publishing has always existed discreetly. What is new is the systematic use of publicity to seek out consenting victims at all social levels, exploiting most people's ignorance of the mechanics of publishing and distribution. The result is startling. In order to study the autobiographical genre, I have been reading books from La Pensée Universelle for a year. I have bought the most recent publications and read others at the Bibliothèque Nationale; this "corpus," unique in its genre, can shed light on a number of issues, including women's autobiographical writing.

First and foremost, there is the sheer number of texts. From 1974 to 1981, there has been an average of 440 books published per year; that is, more than 3,500 books for the eight-year period—an enormous amount. From a quantitative and sociological perspective, we see that the proportion of women authors varies by year (20 percent in 1975, 28 percent in 1981) and averages about 24 percent. The proportion of women authors also varies according to genre. Here is, for example, the breakdown by genre in the 1981 catalog:

| *Genre* | *Number of Books* | *Percent of Women Writers* |
|---|---|---|
| Essays | 82 | 11 |
| Narratives (nonfiction) | 53 | 26 |
| Novels | 195 | 32 |
| Short stories, novellas | 23 | 30 |
| Plays | 15 | 17 |
| Poems | 290 | 30 |
| Total | 658 | 28 |

The publisher's catalogs do not use the same classification every year, but one can still see that over these eight years, for 1535 books of fiction (novels, short stories, novellas), 27 percent are written by women, and for 1071 books of poetry, 25 percent are written by women. It's more difficult to tabulate autobiographical writings, which fall under several rubrics (narratives and essays, most notably), but the proportion of female-authored writings seems to be about 25 percent.

As they stand, these figures mean nothing. They must be compared to others, but interpretation of the figures remains problematic. For example, if women writers account for *only* 25 percent of self-published autobiographies, wouldn't this be because women have fewer economic resources and less financial autonomy than men? A tempting but tenuous hypothesis. Looking at the *Répertoire Livres Hebdo 1981,* which records all books published in France (including translations), I found that under heading 921 (Memoirs, Autobiographies, "Souvenirs"), there are 332 works, 73 of which are authored by women (24 percent). Of these 332 works, 41 were published at La Pensée Universelle, 17 of which were written by women (41 percent). This would lead, however, to an opposite but equally tenuous conclusion: less well received than men in regular publishing channels, women must rely on their own financial backing. Indeed, to reach a proper conclusion, one would have to know the number and proportion of men and women who *write*—but nobody knows that. In France there are reading surveys periodically, but no one has thought (nor found the means) of asking people about their writing practices. For lack of information, we might compare present figures with analogous figures from 50 to 100 years ago. We would find, I suppose, that the proportion of female autobiographies published (at author's or publisher's expense) has increased enormously.[1] Before examining the possible specificity of female autobiography, then, it would be helpful to know the historical modalities of its emergence, to see to what extent access to autobiography is tied to changing social roles.

Beyond statistics, the interest La Pensée Universelle holds is that it opens a window onto an unknown world: the underside of the publishing system. It represents an unheard-of situation: *publishing without a publisher.* The principal function of a publisher is legitimizing texts that are chosen and in which money is invested.[2] The reading of a printed book today is founded on the premise: "this work has value since it has been selected." Although we may not concur with the choice, we know it exists. At La Pensée Universelle, the book is a printed object, but no one has legitimized it: everyone knows that La Pensée Universelle publishes anything and everything. It refuses manuscripts only if the client won't pay or if the book is pornographic or slanderous. So here I am confronted by a portion of those unknown books rejected by all publishing houses, the submerged part of the iceberg. Faced with this spurious publication, I as a reader face responsibilities that have, in fact, always been mine (responsibilities of choice) but that I usually disregard. However, this very spuriousness makes me see the visible part and the whole of the system in a new light. Publishers often say that there is no such thing as unrecognized genius and that books without publishers are mediocre or bad—a statement that ignores the fact that the great majority of books that do find a publisher are mediocre as well. What are the criteria? Since reading the books of La Pensée Universelle, I often find myself reading other books as if *they* too were published there—discovering, as it were, that the Emperor has no clothes. But the real question here is a social one: what is the purpose of the publication of autobiographical (or biographical) texts? Autobiography is an instrument for reproducing the dominant ideology or for questioning it. Therefore, there are markets (with supply and demand) and strategies of distribution. The appreciation of the *quality* of texts is certainly one of the factors in publication; but by insisting on this factor, one must leave the other criteria of choice in the shadows where they seem so obvious they aren't ever questioned.

Here are accounts of the lives of twelve women, excerpted from autobiographies published at La Pensée Universelle. I have chosen them for the greatest possible diversity in order to gain a representative sampling. One of the charms of La Pensée Universelle is the unexpected; each book resembles a grab-bag prize, for the reader is not already inured by a preprinted list of the books in the series. I confess to having often been astonished, bewildered, overwhelmed by reading the texts of La Pensée Universelle as if they had been placed in bottles and thrown into the sea. No doubt that's because I was reading them in the second degree, as if I were a confessor listening to the world's miseries, or as if I worked for S.O.S. Courrier.[3]

In the following accounts, I have briefly described the author and her life. Then a few sentences are meant to give a sense of the voice speaking in the text. You should read these accounts as though they were part of the plot of a single novel. Twelve women from the four corners of France want you to understand their lives and to validate them. They do not know one another. Each shouts her plea without hearing that of the others: writing is deaf. But *you* can hear everything, as if you were reading one of those contemporary works of sociological investigation that juxtapose testimonies on various aspects of the female condition.[4] But the difference is that these women *write*. They have taken the initiative of producing a book, often without previous writing experience. Apart from the two youngest (Joyce Avila and Anne Moutte), who are addressing women and who are trying to create an intimate and lyrical resonance in their prose, the problems these women face are not "secondary" stylistic problems (how to escape from the existing model of discourse to create a women's writing), but primary problems of communication: how to reproduce the existing model. While I did not discover any unrecognized genius, nor any level of subversive writing, I was astonished by the strength of these women's desire for self-expression. There are, of course, a number of functional stumbling blocks. Some of the authors imitate academic styles. Others write as if they were speaking to intimates, leaving too much unsaid. Or else they misjudge the reader's possible reactions, as in the case of Jeannine

Lavigne or Rolande Debray. But there are successes as well. G. Beaufort's and Emilie Crisimily's narratives are enthralling. The dairy shop owner's autobiography hits its mark: after reading it, I no longer see tradespeople in the same light. Perhaps that's because one has a better chance of being inspired when speaking directly of the self. I would suppose that the novels, poems, and essays published by La Pensée Universelle, although I haven't read them, fall more easily into cliché than do these singular life accounts, motivated by an urgent desire to convince.

Who are these women? Ages: 30 to 77. Autobiography is in no sense an activity reserved for old age. Of these twelve texts, only two are family chronicles of the traditional type, corresponding more or less to American how-to books such as *How to Write Your Autobiography*.[5] On the other hand, almost all the texts share a desire to write that stems from a crisis situation, agony, or failure. The three texts that seem to be written by women satisfied with their lot (Laure Cans, Anne Moutte, and Jacqueline Barret) are also texts of crisis, sometimes full of violence. Laure Cans's grudge against Simone de Beauvoir gives the reader the impression that the life of wife and mother, which she champions so, has not, perhaps, fulfilled all her hopes, and that she is trying to convince herself it has. Anne Moutte is settling the score with her husband, who cheated on her when she was pregnant. Jacqueline Barret was subjected to the most petty financial control, whose injustice sickened her: she pulled out of business and began to write. Geneviève Beaufort started to write after contemplating suicide. Christiane Saint-Pierre wrote because she could not adapt to life in Canada. Joyce Avila was depressed, but the reader suspects she may be slightly mythomaniacal (did she succeed as well as she says?). So life is hard. And no one understands you. It struck me that there was not a single male figure positively represented in any of these books. Men are absent, dead, or erased. The Proprietess never speaks of the Proprietor, her husband, a dairy shop owner like herself with whom she works. Jeannine Lavigne's vine-grower is so egotistical and miserly that one wonders how she could have loved him. Rolande Debray's husband is an unbeliever; all we know about him is that he doesn't believe in her visions.

The dominant tone of these narratives then is a discourse of persecution (but such is often the case for male-authored narratives published by La Pensée Universelle). This raises two questions for possible exploration that I shall simply mention. How can one interest readers (unknown) in the injustice you have suffered at the hands of fate or of men? For when they are not legitimized by external factors (publisher, preface writer, militant group) nor sustained by artful writing, the claims of the persecuted can seem crazy. And when persecution fails, when identification does not occur, the paranoid side of autobiography (and the construction of any "I") becomes visible. This in turn raises the question of the reader's identity: I am a man and read these texts as one; women will read them as women. No doubt a second mode of explanation in these and similar texts could be offered: the various types of unhappiness or crisis prompting women to express themselves and the strategies of discourse they use in dealing with their crises. Some of these texts are openly militant in the most diverse ways: in favor of traditional marriage (Laure Cans), the modern liberated couple (Anne Moutte), or homosexuality (Joyce Avila). In other texts, the crushing weight of recorded facts is striking in contrast to the apparently resigned ideological discourse that overlays them (Simone Salzard, Rolande Warnesson). It also happens that the reactions of her women readers lead an antifeminist narrator, Jacqueline Barret, to become aware of a feminist dimension to her narration.

Coming back to the group's composition, let's consider geographic origin. There are three native Parisians (Jacqueline Barret, Rolande Warnesson, Joyce Avila), and two with parallel destinies, who went to Paris to find work (Emilie Crisimily and Geneviève Beaufort). The other seven are from the provinces. Here, my sample is not perfectly representative: by claiming to be an important Parisian publisher, La Pensée Universelle recruits its authors from the provinces much more overtly than other Parisian publishers. La Pensée Universelle is thus much closer to the heart of France. This is also true of the cultural and social status of the authors. Among the twelve women, six have had a secondary education, high school or beyond; the six others only completed the elementary grades. As for their professions, two were housewives and mothers (Laure Cans, Anne Moutte). The others are or were: cleaning ladies, concierges, workers, employees (Beaufort, Crisimily, Salzard, Warnesson), grade school teachers (Debray, Françoise, Saint-Pierre), secretaries (Avila), and tradeswomen (Barret, Lavigne). Nine were married and had children, one is homosexual, and the last two are single or alone (Salzard, Françoise). All of them are unknown: no notoriety, not even a local reputation. On every level, then, these narratives are more representative of the real lives of French women than are the sensational commercial novels (*Have You Seen the Pilot? It's a Woman,* by Danielle Décuré, a bookstore bestseller in 1982) or the feminist texts of the avant-garde.

In every corner of France today women's words and images are being indexed and recorded. At L'Institut d'Histoire du Temps Présent a group is working on an "oral history of women." The Centre Audiovisuel Simone de Beauvoir has just been created to record and disseminate feminist video productions and other kinds of images produced by women.[6] Here, then, I have tried to become a part of this survey of women's activities. Although the most conventional means are used, and although even their discourse may be deemed alienated, these women have nevertheless taken the initiative to write. Our response should be to read them.

I will conclude this brief presentation by setting forth, without any pretensions at solution, three kinds of problems. To begin with: what is the relation between a spontaneous and "unsorted" production and the books published by real publishers, duly distributed and read? There are two possible hypotheses (which are in no way contradictory).

First, there might be a homology between the sorted and the unsorted. Perhaps some kind of narratives exist at La Pensée Universelle as in traditional establishments, but the quality may be inferior. Apparently Françoise Prévost's book about breast cancer, *My Leftover Life,* published by Stock, sold well. Editions du Seuil published a testimonial of a mother whose child was psychotic, *The Impeded Mother,* by Françoise Giron (a more optimistic account than that of G. Beaufort). What about a young lesbian's autobiography? Some excellent ones, such as *Play Us España* by Jocelyne François, have already appeared. Perhaps a Pensée Universelle author is one who has always come too late.

To be profitable, publishing inevitably aims at wide circulation: one good book that sells tens of thousands of copies, rather than ten books that won't sell even a thousand. The selection process is pitiless. But if all the women who had a troubled love life, an unhappy childhood, or breast cancer were to publish accounts of their trials—what a bottleneck there would be! Amateur authors who want to express themselves—strengthened by their suffering and their writing travails—are all the more hurt by rejection because they feel it is their right to be read by their contemporaries: they don't understand the law of the system that they want to penetrate. There, too, it's a struggle to survive. Writing—the means they thought would solve their problems and end their loneliness—earns them, finally, despite some satisfactions, nothing but a new sense of failure.

Second, there might be a discrepancy between supply and demand. People love notoriety and experiences that are outside the ordinary. Books are solicited and sometimes created quite artificially in order to respond to this demand (collected interviews, books written by ghostwriters, translations), while the narratives of people who have led ordinary lives are discarded. Miserable lives, like those of Emilie Crisimily or Rolande Warnesson, are "interesting" only when they have been recorded and reproduced by an ethnologist; otherwise they would have to be stylistic masterpieces to overcome the existing hurdles of publishing. Moreover, real life has its vogues; it has to be the right time. In 1973–74, nurses' lives were in fashion; in 1975–76, prostitutes' experiences. Usually, however, the right time never comes. Jacqueline Barret, the dairy shop owner whose book is interesting and entertaining, took her manuscript to Laffont, a specialist in the real-life genre, then to Editions des femmes; it was rejected, no call for dairy shop owners. Yet in 1982, a mediocre book, *The Woman Farmer,* by Anne-Marie Crolais, based on tape recordings, enjoyed great success. It espoused the same cause as Jacqueline Barret: the right of wives of artisans, merchants or farmers who work with their husbands to claim professional status.[8] Farming is in crisis, peasants are blocking roadways, and Anne-Marie Crolais is a well-known trade unionist. As for the lives of dutiful women and family chronicles, who, outside the family circle, is going to be interested? The gap between the supply of written lives and the public's supposed demand demonstrates (if there were a need to do so) the mythological character of the taste for the real-life narrative.[9]

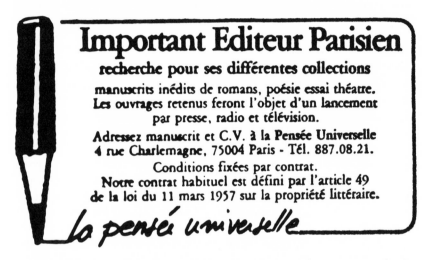

ii. An advertisement in *Le Monde des Livres* (September 24, 1982) for *La Pensée universelle*.

What can be done, then? La Pensée Universelle lures its authors by promising a huge printing and by inducing them to believe they will be read by a real public.[10] But if La Pensée Universelle succeeds, it's because it fulfills a need no one else satisfies. There's no reason to be indignant when nothing else is available.

The solution would undoubtedly be to develop more modest and decentralized networks of distribution. This would assume a certain awareness among would-be authors, who should not all be dreaming of national or "universal" distribution, but be better able to weigh their options. This has already been done by men and women who choose self-publishing in a responsible way and take complete charge of manufacturing and distributing their books. One woman who took this route is Marie-Antoinette Dugué-Monclin. For her eightieth birthday, instead of a fur coat she had her husband give her the money to print her memoirs at a local printer. Wisely, she had 200 copies printed of ther book, entitled *80 Years of Hap-*

*piness . . . In Spite of Everything.* Then there's Louise Vanderwielen, hairdresser and manager of a bar who on her own had an autobiographical narrative in the third person printed called *Lise of the Flat Country,* which recounts her struggles against emotional and material misery as a workman's daughter. The book was circulated by hand, appealed to certain readers, and has just been reedited and widely distributed by Presses Universitaires de Lille. The development of local publishing and cultural networks could provide a testing ground or a first readership for those who want to communicate their experiences. A slightly utopian example of this: in two provincial towns (Macon and Epinal) there is a Library of Undistributed Works (LUW); you can go there to deposit manuscripts, or self-published texts, and read those other people have deposited; there's a notebook for readers' remarks, and meetings are arranged between writers and readers. But do authors ever read one another?

Last but not least. Can one discern the specificity of feminine autobiographical writing by reading these texts? One can easily guess that the answer is no, but also that "this doesn't prove anything" since one can always argue that these women write in a language imposed on them by men. I can only say that reading the narratives from La Pensée Universelle, it is easy enough to see, in the use of language, the strategy of discourse, and the organization of the narrative, the cultural and social differences of the authors but in no way their sexual difference. Of course, this would be more apparent if I described narratives by men alongside those of women. While they are not written differently, these male-authored texts are more numerous and varied because of the social roles open to men. There are, for example, many war stories. To give some indication of their character, here is a list of eight books, chosen from many others, that tell the lives of ordinary men.

(1)   Marcel Chabrol, *My Life,* 1981, 52 pp. The career of an assistant accountant who worked for fifteen bosses.

(2)   André des Chaintres, *Eternity Like the Sea,* 1981, 219 pp. Literary self-portrait of a priest from Lyon.

(3)   Doctor Bernard Deleu, *The Misunderstood Homophile,* 1980, 280 pp. Militant autobiography of a homosexual doctor.

(4)   Philippe Hanssens, *Alone Among Others,* 1981, 195 pp. Born in 1953, physically and mentally handicapped. The story of a successful rehabilitation in spite of social workers.

(5)   Henry Hirsch, *The Life Behind,* 1981, 254 pp. Book of revenge against an oppressive father. A conjugal memorial dedicated to his wife, who died in 1965.

(6)   Joseph Liebe, *Who Am I?,* 1980, 218 pp. A young delinquent considers his past.

(7)    Victor Martin, *Eighty Years of Memories*, 1980, 362 pp. Work and integrity lead to success. An engineering career and accomplishments in public works.

(8)    Albert Mauler, *Joys and Sorrows of a Child from a Big Family*, 1981, 157 pp. A happy childhood in spite of poverty. Was first a pastry apprentice, then managed to become a schoolteacher.

I had the same reactions to these books as I did to the women's narratives: surprise at the varied pallette of situations and the candor of discourse impervious to the conventions of literary communication. I also felt overwhelmed by the distress that all of these books manifest more or less openly. Perhaps male narratives are on the whole less bleak, possibly because of the professional satisfactions men can claim. And yet even this is not certain. At La Pensée Universelle there are hardly any happy autobiographies—but are there anywhere? What women are undoubtedly trying to gain through the tool of autobiography is equality in the expression of unhappiness. And so I will conclude by dedicating this essay to Emilie Crisimily, whose narrative moved me deeply and whose naive pseudonym[11] is a sort of stammer that says it all.

Translated by Katharine A. Jensen

## NOTES

1. I say this on the basis of my research at the Bibliothèque Nationale (Paris, catalog number Ln27), which lists biographies and autobiographies. In the nineteenth century, the proportion of female autobiographies is infinitesimal, well under 10 percent.

2. See Pierre Bourdieu, "La Production de la croyance: contribution à une économie des biens symboliques," *Actes de la recherche en sciences sociales,* no. 13 (February 1977).

3. "S.O.S. Courrier," founded in May 1981, aims "to establish by mail friendships between single or solitary individuals." It also personally answers letters of distress (see *Le Monde,* 11–12 October 1981).

4. For example: Christiane Germain and Christine de Panafieu, *La Mémoire des Femmes, sept témoignages de femmes nées avec le siècle* (Paris: Sylvie Messinger, 1982), 285 pp.; or Charlotte Le Millour, *La Maternité singulière. Avoir un enfant sans père. Récits de mères célibataires* (Paris: Robert Laffont, collection "Réponses," 1982), 296 pp.

5. I have indexed and described these manuals in "Apprendre aux gens à écrire leur vie," *Moi Aussi* (Seuil, 1986).

6. Institut d'Histoire du Temps Présent (CNRS), 80b rue Lecourbe, 75015 Paris. Centre Audiovisuel Simone de Beauvoir, 32 rue Maurice Ripoche, 75014 Paris.

7. Françoise Prévost, *Ma Vie en plus* (Stock, collection "Elles-mêmes," 1975); Françoise Giron, La Mère empêchée (Seuil, collection "Libre à elles," 1978); Jocelyne François, *Jouenous Espana,* Mercure de France, 1980 (Prix Femina 1980). In 1964 the first large feminine (and feminist) series was created ("Femmes") at Denoel-Gonthier, and in the 1970s, other publishers followed this example. In 1973 Les Editions des femmes was established, which, in addition to publishing activities, opened women's bookstores in Paris (74 rue de Seine, 75006 Paris), Marseille, and Lyon.

8. Ségolène Lefébure, *Moi, une infirmière* (Stock, 1973); Jeanne Cordelier and Martine

Laroche, *La Dérobade* (Hachette, 1976), a story of a prostitute; Anne-Marie Crolais, *L'agricultrice,* in collaboration with Nicole du Roy (Ramsay, 1981).

9. See my study of "Le Document vécu," in *Je est un autre, l'autobiographie de la littérature aux médias* (Seuil, 1980).

10. For example, the monthly journal *Lire,* edited by Bernard Pivot, sent to La Pensée Universelle a novel that contained insults addressed to the president of the republic and a collection of poems that La Pensée Universelle had itself already published. The two manuscripts were accepted! Once published, the collection of poems sold *no* copies. So the books are neither read by the publisher himself, nor sold. To read the story of this experiment, see "Les Pièges du compte d'auteur," in *Lire,* No. 87 (November 1982), pp. 40–43.

11. The name "Crisimily" is a combination of "crise" (crisis) and "Emilie."

## SUMMARIES

(1) Emilie Crisimily, *Traumatisme psychique* ("Psychic Trauma"), 1981, 223 pp.
Born in 1904 in Corrèze, daughter of peasants. Unhappy childhood. Goes to Paris, works as a maid, then as a concierge. Marries a militant Communist. Is deported to Ravensbruck. Depicts lucidly her bleak oppressed youth and the horror of concentration camps. "Ever since I was born, I've been marked; I've never felt good about myself. It's psychic. I've always suffered. I take everything to heart. Life is too hard. It's brought me nothing but torture; I have no love for it."

(2) Laure Cans, *Mémoires d'une femme rangée* ("Memoirs of a Dutiful Woman"), 2 vols., 1975–80, 254 and 250 pp.
Born in 1912. Part of the Protestant Bourgeoisie of Mayenne. In 1937, marries an agronomical engineer. Four children. Gives an account of her youth, then a family chronicle intended to defend the joys of family life and the virtues of marriage against the attacks of Simone de Beauvoir. "It is essential that we, decent women, wives and mothers, know how to remember the profound pleasure, the shared confidence, and the incomparable joys that our little ones have given us. That's what happiness is."

(3) Rolande Debray, *Et la Lumière fut* . . . ("And Then There Was Light . . ."), 1981, 90 pp.
Born in 1920. Retired schoolteacher in Picardie. Recounts neither her life nor her career, but in 25 chapters, the stages of her relationship with Jesus Christ, God, and the Virgin Mary. In 1960, God

made the sun spin counterclockwise for her. "I told my family about this extraordinary event and naturally, no one took me seriously. They spoke of illusion, suggestion, hallucination, a wandering imagination, and a lot of other things. But *I* knew that in spite of their mockery, God, in his infinite goodness had simply answered me, as he did Joshua."

(4)   Jacqueline Barret, *La Patronne* ("The Proprietress"), 1977, 158 pp.
Autobiography of a dairy shop owner born in 1922 who spent all her life in the region of St.-Ouen. She concisely tells about her career, her shops, and all the joys of the dairy business. She wants to break down the prejudices that victimize tradespeople. Trade has been a game, a passion for her. "The pleasure of selling which sustained me! Making money? I never thought of it, I assure you. It was lively, it was hard, there were big responsibilities: all this gave me pleasure."

(5)   Rolande Warnesson, *Les Obstacles de ma vie* ("The Obstacles of My Life"), 1977, 75 pp.
Daughter of Parisian tradespeople, born in 1927. Dream: to be a singer. Reality: employee. She marries a mill worker and has two children. She describes all the obstacles of her life: her husband's professional defeats, constant moving, giving birth, illness, mourning. One struggles, one survives. A very precise account, moving and resigned. "I want my book to be read and re-read, so that people will not lose courage. If you slide down the hill, you can pull yourself up again by holding on to all your powers, and accepting what nature wanted you to be: to be born, to live, and to die."

(6)   Jeannine Lavigne, *Mon Heure de gloire* ("My Hour of Glory"), 1980, 81 pp.
Love story of a 47-year-old woman grocer in a village in Beaujolais. A 59-year-old vine-grower whom she had met through a matrimonial advertisement abandons her after a three-year affair. "After he had his pleasure ["après s'être diverti sur mes côtelettes"] he up and left." Alternating between prose and poetry, she tells about her betrayal. "Here is a woman who is still beautiful at the age of fifty and can still love an older man and lose her mind. I've decided to take up the pen to find relief, not to avenge myself, no, but to do justice: a great love must be known the world over, for it is so rare."

(7)   Geneviéve Beaufort, *Vivre avec un enfant psychotique, est-ce vivre?* ("Is Life with a Psychotic Child Living?"), 1981, 152 pp.

Born in 1930. Abandoned as a child. Goes to Paris, makes her living as a cleaning woman and concierge. Raises her psychotic son, now 28 years old. Bleak book about the long ordeal of this "education." Appeal for solidarity among parents of the handicapped, warning doctors who don't know what it is to live with a psychotic. "When I happen to pass certain people on the street who have been hit harder than my son, I say, 'Thank God he's not like that.' I've always lived by the principle that it's the only way not to be too unhappy."

(8)   Christiane Saint-Pierre, *Du sirocco au blizzard* ("From the Sirocco to the Blizzard"), 1980, 123 pp.
Born in Algeria in 1935. Daughter and then wife of farmers. Two children. In 1962 her family returns to France, then in 1967 emigrates to Canada. Family chronicle meant for her children "in order for them to understand better why they are Canadian, although born in Algeria of French parents."

(9)   Simone Salzard, *La Mauvaise Etoile, histoire d'une vie* ("The Unlucky Star, Story of a Life"), 1978, 95 pp.
A life of sacrifice. Born in 1940, working-class family, Christian. When she was 18, her mother died. She broke off her engagement to raise her six small brothers and sisters. Works as a gatekeeper at the SNCF. She recounts her exemplary life in the third person. Bitterness pierces the resignation. She has spent her life on the sidelines. She consoles herself by thinking of the rich and unhappy people she knows. In the end, "money doesn't make happiness.

(10)   Marthe Françoise, *Ça vous tombe dessus* ("Everything Falls on You"), 1980, 91 pp.
Forty years old, single, grade school teacher, Béarn, southwest France. Breast cancer, mastectomy. "To my family, to my friends who were so supportive, to the doctors who cared so well for me. To anyone for whom these pages will be helpful."

(11)   Joyce Avila, *Jardins divers* ("Different Gardens"), 1980, 250 pp.
Born in 1950. Vibrant and dominant. Describes her homosexual love life: her initiation, her conquest, her numerous affairs. Her professional life as a legal secretary. She has driven race cars. She has just formed the first female group to encourage encounters among women. A militant book. And yet: "I'm twenty-nine years old and feel as if I've ended my life. Nearly thirty years of struggle without making myself heard. Today, I'm tired of desperately lashing out,

my throat is raw from explosive cries, my body which strained toward the future now seeks its becoming. I am no longer me. I don't belong to myself any more, then again. . . . I don't belong to anyone. I feel alone."

(12) Anne Moutte, *Candice, ou le ventre rond de sa Maman* ("Candice, or Her Mama's Round Belly"), 1981, 60 pp.
Born in 1950. This book gives a lyric account of two pregnancies: the birth of a stillborn boy, then after much anxiety, the birth of a girl, Candice. Anne will raise her to make her into a free woman like herself: "As for me, I'm a real fox, a flirt, feminine, a feminist for the women who don't know how to protect themselves and who give in to what's macho. That's not for me, I've learned to protect myself, to satisfy myself, to demand equality in relationships. I've fought my battles and not without pain. . . . It's all rot, my love. No penis in your head, I'll make sure of that. I'll protect you, child of mine, from the terrible maternal hold. I will give you freedom."

# My Memory's Hyperbole

## Julia Kristeva

*Hyperbole! from my memory . . .*

*Mallarmé,* "Prose pour des Esseintes"

When the *New York Literary Forum* asked me to contribute an auto-biographical text for this special issue, I had just finished reading *La Céré-monie des adieux* by Simone de Beauvoir. One must surely be endowed with the naive cruelty of this exceptional woman to create such a myth or, at the very least, to make it exist by giving it a narrative thread. In spite of the legend that surrounds the author of *Mandarins,* I am convinced that she has still not been properly evaluated as a chronicler who knew how to construct an entire cultural phenomenon. And isn't it the same austere and cutting pen of this feminist in search of rationalism that gave *Les Temps modernes* its true erotic consistency? Before Marxian rationalizing turned this journal into an idol for the international Left, from the postwar period to today, Beauvoir's cold account of a sexuality more contained than un-veiled gave the publication its well-known aura.

My own history, and perhaps most of all, the disturbing abyss that the psychoanalytic experience shapes between "what is said" and undecidable "truth" prevent me from being a good witness. Moreover, *making history* now appears to me, as I will try to show in the course of this essay, a task that, if it has not become impossible, has now been displaced. Rather than compiling "archives" or "annals," other questions make us stretch mean-ing into fiction. I say "us" because it seems to me that a profound turmoil has occurred in the last few years, still barely visible but operating in all spheres of culture.

What follows, then, will be an autobiography in the first person plural, a "we" of complicity, friendship, love. This "we" is the setting commonly recommended by the social contract for illusions, idealizations, errors, constructions. To write the autobiography of this "we" is surely a paradox that combines the passion for truth of the "I" with the absolute logical necessity of being able to share this truth only in part. To share it, first of all, between "us," so that this "we" survives. To share it also with you, so that an account, a report, a scheme remains (autobiography is a narration), rather than have speech fall into the fervor of dreams or poetry. Being hyperbolic, this "we" will retain from the problem-ridden paths of "I"s only the densest image, the most schematic, the one closest to a cliché. Should I shy away from it? I think of Canto III of Dante's *Paradisio* where the writer, having had visions, hurries to push them aside for fear of becoming a new Narcissus. But Beatrice herself shows him that such a denial would be precisely a mistake comparable to the narcissistic error. For if an immediate vision is possible and must be sought, then it is necessarily accompanied by visionary constructions that are imperfect . . . fragmentary, schematic. . . . Truth can only be partially spoken. And it is enough to begin. . . . Common sense not withstanding, this hyperbolic "we" is, in effect, only a part of "me." It is merely a temporary stability in which projections and identifications are settled among some and allow the history of a perpetually changing whole to be written. A "we" is alive only if it is never the same. As the chief locus of the image, it thrives only on the change of images. What the "I" loses in delegating itself to the group is partially regained in the metamorphoses of the "we." It is by transforming itself, by changing itself totally that the collective image, the group portrait, proves it is a momentarily fixed passion. To speak of "us" is not an analysis, it is a history that analyzes itself. But isn't any autobiography, even if it doesn't involve "us," a desire to make a collective public image exist, for "you," for "us"?

If you watch newsreels from World War II through the Algerian War on French television, you will find the same rhetoric of the image (technical improvements don't really affect the televised aesthetic of this period). The same verbal rhetoric lasts until 1962–1963: romanticism, bombast, bathos doled out by the slightly nasal voice of an anchorman adept at intoning war bulletins. In the shadow of political events, a fundamental change of outlooks was necessary for us to regard this verbal edema as obsolete, to realize it belonged to another era. I see the written trace of this change in the austere pairing down of the *nouveau roman,* in its obsession with precision and details, for example, as well as the whole intellectual trend centered on the study of forms. This formalism was the purging of that subjective or rhetorical edema that our parents had set up to protect themselves against the devastating suffering of wars, or that they had used to construct their martyrdom. Fundamentally, May '68, despite its romantic airs, functioned like the fever of this process. An *analytic* process (in the etymological sense of the term, that is, dissolving, abrasive, lucid), which leads us to a modernity that is, of course, mobile, eccentric, and unpredictable, but that breaks with the preceding years and that, or so it seems, must leave its mark on the end of our century.

In short, an account of the intellectual path of this period should primarily be an account of change—and for some it was an explosion—of bodies, of discourses, of ways of being. A sexuality freed from moral constraints, an image of the body no longer merely captured in a fine narcissistic surface but vaporized and sonorized with the help of drugs or rock or pop music if need be. . . . These mutations, these revolutions, contained as many delights as dramas, which had to be confronted, displaced and sublimated at each bend. Women with the pill, free love in broad daylight, assaults on the family, but also, the quest for complicity, tenderness, the security of a childhood always begun anew. . . . The adventure of ideas should be read against the background of a revolution in the reproduction of the species that attacks the classic conception of the sexual difference, makes women emerge aggressively, and finally leads to erotic ties around a new calm and civilizing secular cult of the child. . . . Political demands, of course! But also something beyond demands, with their explosiveness integrated into the fabric of time, of ethics.

## The "Tel Quel" Experience As It Was

During Christmas '65, in a bleak and rainy Paris, I would have been completely disappointed with the "city of lights" had I not attended midnight mass at Notre Dame, the ultimate meeting place for tourists. When I arrived in the French capital, I met people who were rather poor, whereas the elegant little restaurants and the chic little boutiques seemed to me to belong to a prewar movie. Between the technical brilliance of America and the leveling radicalisms of East European societies (which embodied, for me, two aspects of "modernity"), France seemed stuck in a pleasant archaicness, attractive and unreal. However, the social discontent that was brewing reached me through newspapers and conversations I overheard—even among people who seemed to be well off. I then realized that this country of shopkeepers wished to become the most developed of East European countries, as if its occult, unspoken goal was transforming itself into a society such as the one I had just left, a society that was criticized in Paris, only in fascinated, hushed tones.

My scholarship, in the framework of Franco-Bulgarian cultural agreements, encouraged my meeting writers and academics. I was, therefore, immediately immersed in an intellectual universe that both partook of this climate (by its interest in critical Marxism, in détente, in what was to become "socialism with a human face," etc.) and, at the same time, was wholly outside of it. I saw intellectuals as forming a real citadel within the state, without, however, burning their bridges to politics. They seemed to be engaged in a unique task: a subtle (even esoteric) and generous task, which not only was specifically French in its refinement and predisposition to formulas but also had universal aims and stakes. Having come to France under the auspices of the Gaullist dream of a "Europe from the Atlantic to the Urals," I felt I had found in this territory that stretched from the publishing house of Le Seuil to the E.H.E.S.S. (then E.P.H.E.) a cosmopolitanism that transcended the socialist and the European domains and that constituted a continent of thought, speculation, and writing corresponding to the high points of the universalistic legend of Paris.

I had received a francophile and francophone education. Since I had been trained as an intellectual in the French sense of the word, the *Marseillaise,* and Voltaire, Victor Hugo, Anatole France—authors in no way incompatible, so it was said, with Marxist-Leninism—had been my language but also my moral textbooks. I was then in no way out of my element in the intellectual climate of Paris. I even had the impression, when I wasn't viewed as a more or less monstrous anomaly, that people saw in me, aside from my Stalinism, a perfect product of the French system projected into the future. Moreover, the Hautes Etudes was the ideal place for me: a structure of meeting and greeting similar to the one that served wandering scholastics in the best periods of the Middle Ages.

As soon as I arrived, I found in this environment a hospitality that, though cold and suspicious, was nonetheless functional and reliable; besides which, it never contradicted itself. Despite the xenophobia, antifeminism, or anti-Semitism of one person or another, I maintain that French cultural life, as I have known it, has always been marked by a curiosity, discreet but generous, reticent but essentially receptive to nomadisms, oddities, to graftings and exogamies of all kinds. The great tolerance of the English or the enormous capacity for assimilation among Americans surely provides more existential opportunities. But they are, finally, because of their lesser *resistance,* less conducive to the production of new thoughts.

The particular climate of France at that time can be understood in sociological terms. The chasm between social archaism and intellectual advances gave the latter an autonomy that helped them grow. Furthermore, the independence of Gaullist nationalism gave freedom of thought a power unequalled elsewhere: outside of France, there was nowhere else in the world where one could, in the heart of the most official institutions and in the spotlight of the media, draw simultaneously on Marx, Saint Augustine, Hegel, Saussure, and Freud. Finally, the genius of French institutions knew how to accommodate safety valves or precarious loopholes alongside bureaucratic or bureaucratized bastions: the Ecole des Hautes Etudes counterbalancing the Sorbonne, *Tel Quel* developing despite the *N.R.F.* or *Temps Modernes*. It is banal to say that this universalistic cosmopolitan climate belongs to a tradition, one that probably dates back to the eminence of clerks and that established intellectuals of the eighteenth century as an autonomous force, beyond but not outside the city-state. However, this tradition also has an intrapsychic, sexual basis.

When thought admits its indebtedness to language—which was the case of the French "essayist" tradition long before structuralism—the speaking being is thrown into the infinite conceived as the power and cunning of the verb. From this locus, the intellectual acquires a transpolitical and transmoral function. Without belonging to any particular group or sect, yet giving the appearance of belonging to one, he thus reaches, by the very range of his search, the key zones, the most sensitive areas of social understanding. Modern art, madness, subjective experience, various marginal phenomena then became not mere objects of observation but actual fields of *study,* as well as of *implication,* which allow for an oblique grappling with "the social." In this way, the dilemma of "engagement" was reworked and displaced for us. It had become an implication, wholly comprised within the intellectual adventure that we lived as a *practice,* subverting the distinctions between the individual/society, subject/group, form/content, style/meaning. With Michel Foucault and Jacques Lacan we didn't have to attack Jean-Paul Sartre's walls. The labyrinths of the *speaking subject*—the microcosm of a complex logic whose effects had only partially surfaced in society—led us directly toward regions that were obscure but crucial, specific but universal, particular but transhistorical, far from society's policed scenarios.

In any event, at the end of '65, I landed at Lucien Goldmann's and Roland Barthes's doors at the Hautes Etudes. Lucien Goldmann welcomed me to his seminar on the "sociology of the novel" with fraternal distraction, convinced that I was a congenital Marxist, since I came from Eastern Europe. At the time, he was settling scores with existentialism, which was of little interest to me (I had arrived in Paris with two modern authors, Maurice Blanchot and Ferdinand Céline, in my suitcase), but the immeasurable practical help he gave me ensured my survival in France in the beginning. It was a kind of help that only those exiled from any country know how to give. With much liberalism and understanding, he directed my thesis on the origins of novelistic discourse, a thesis I defended, not without insolence, amid the generalized commotion of May '68. The atmosphere of a Goldmann seminar was very cosmopolitan: Marxism had already become a Third World matter, but it was also a refuge for young Germans and Italians rebelling against the legacy of families that had been more or less accomplices of the nazi or fascist regimes. . . . In addition, the

Vietnam War was raging, and it simply seemed natural for us to side with the victims, that is, with the Marxists. Invoking this war, I thus refused René Girard's invitation to work in an American university. I found Goldmann's objection to my decision candid at the very least: "one has to go there in order to defeat capitalism from the inside," he said to me.

At the same time, at the Hautes Etudes, located in the same C section of the Sorbonne, the teaching of Roland Barthes attracted me because of its capacity to make formalism, which I had found reductive, extremely appealing. His audience, which was more exclusively French in those days (except for a few, Todorov among them who had come to France before), was astounded by the suicide of Lucien Sebag, which remained a mystery beyond all words, all comments. On my arrival, the only topic of conversation was the presentation on Stéphane Mallarmé that Philippe Sollers had just given. I thus read a few issues of *Tel Quel,* and I met Sollers in May '66 through Gérard Genette, who was then attending the same seminar though he was an established literary critic.

Our first conversations with Sollers, in the office at 27 rue Jacob, at the Deux Magots, later at the Coupole, and at the Rose-Bud (Montparnasse soon became our neighborhood) were full of intellectual passion. I can still see us discussing *l'Expérience Intérieure* of Georges Bataille, a still vilified author whom Sollers had helped me discover. We also spoke of nationalism, for a quarrel divided East European intellectuals: should Sovietization be resisted with cosmopolitanism or nationalism? Lastly, there was feminism: "We women, like the proletariat, have nothing to lose but our chains," I used to say, with a simplicity that could only have been disarming. Soon after, our friend Sarah George Picot, who was later in the Psychépo group with me, filmed an interview on this theme—a precocious feminist document that I believe is lost . . .

These details would have a personal meaning only if they did not reveal an important aspect of a period soon labeled "structuralist."

For us, structuralism (insofar as one can make generalizations about studies that range from Roman Jakobson's to Claude Lévi-Strauss's, or to certain works of Emile Benveniste, as well as of Barthes or Algirdas J. Greimas) was already accepted knowledge. To simplify, this meant that one should no longer lose sight of the real constraints, "material," as we used to say, of what had previously and trivially been viewed as "form." For us, the logic of this formal reality constituted the very meaning of phenomena or events that then became structures (from kinship to literary texts) and thus achieved intelligibility without necessarily relying on "external factors." From the outset, however, our task was to take this acquired knowledge and immediately do something else.

For some, the important task was to "deconstruct" phenomenology and structuralism as a minor form of a hidden metaphysics. Among these

was Jacques Derrida, whose "Introduction" to Husserl's *Origins of Geome-
try* had been discovered by Sollers, and who was involved in *Tel Quel* for a
time, when he already considered literature the privileged object of desire
and analysis. For others, among whom I place myself, it was essential to
"dynamize" the structure by taking into consideration the speaking subject
and its unconscious experience on the one hand, and on the other, the
pressures of other social structures. I seized upon Saussure's *Anagrammes,*
parts of which Jakobson and Starobinski had published. From this starting point, I tried to establish a "paragrammatical" conception of the literary text as a distortion of signs and their structures that produces an
infinitesimal overdetermination of meaning in literature. From the same
perspective, I reinterpreted a writer just republished in the U.S.S.R.,
whom we often read in Eastern Europe, seeing in his work a synthesis of
formalism and history: Mikhail Bakhtine. A post-formalist, he had introduced, through the carnaval, Rabelais, Dostoievski, and the polyphonics
of the modern novel, the notion of *alterity* and *dialogism* into the arsenal of
studies inspired by formalism. My conception of dialogism, of ambivalence, or what I call "intertextuality"—notions heavily indebted to
Bakhtine and Freud—were to become gadgets that the American university is now in the process of discovering.

This compelling interest in the outer limits of a structure or subjective
identity was stimulated by contact with modern literary texts: Bataille first,
Mallarmé, Lautréamont, Artaud, Joyce, as well as the publications of my
friends at *Tel Quel.* In their writings they aimed at reworking and enrich-
ing the technique of the *nouveau roman,* to make it incorporate a painful,
dramatic, or ecstatic internal experience, which its somewhat protestant
austerity had rejected. Bataille, Joyce, or Artaud were the initiators of this
writing technique, which we often reread and discussed. Soller's *Requiem,*
with its traces of the military hospital and the Algerian War, is a good
indication of the change of direction imposed on the formalist legacy.

Concern with style as experience or as subjective symptomatology was
to lead me to an increasingly *clinical* way of viewing language: acquisition
of language by children, on the one hand, dissolution and pathology of
discourse, on the other. Little by little, my "semiolotic" mode of thinking
(which I already called "semanalysis") expanded to include a truly psychoanalytic approach.

Psychoanalysis—as the locus of extreme abjection, the refuge of private
horror that can be lifted only by an infinite-indefinite displacement in
speech and its effects—represents for me today the logical consequence of
my initial questioning, which it still allows me to pursue. Leaving aside the
uncertainties or the perversities of analytic institutions, I see psychoanalysis as the lay version, the only one, of the speaking being's quest for
truth that religion symbolizes for certain of my contemporaries and

friends. My own prejudice would lead me to think that God is analyzable. Infinitely . . .

My friendship with Emile Benveniste holds an important place in this period dominated by my participation in *Tel Quel*. This austere scholar, who used to read to me from the *Rigveda* directly from Sanskrit into French and whose name appears below a *Surrealist Manifesto,* borrowed the "Rodez Letters" from me so he could read them during the constitutional congress of the International Semiology association, held in Warsaw in 1968. He secretly confided in me his belief that there were only two great French linguists: Mallarmé and Artaud. I can see him, some time later, at the hospital in Saint-Cloud, then later in Créteil, stricken with aphasia but surprisingly warm toward me, tracing with a trembling hand on a white sheet of paper the enigmatic letters T-H-E-O.

. . . *Tel Quel* became, I think the privileged link where the structuralist advance turned into an analysis of subjectivity. For the first time in modern history, except for the very brief futurist-formalist alliance shattered by the Stalinist regime in the U.S.S.R., a kind of thought was emerging that had as its foundation—as its object of analysis but especially its primary stimulant—the practice of writing in the process of production. A devaluated or simply ornamental zone, also far removed from the large art market that benefits painting, film, theater, and music—*l'écriture limite* became the symptom around which a new theoretical discourse on language as subjective experience was constituted. This was not a mere "theory of literature" that remains, by its imaginary uncertainties, the weak link in the social sciences, but a testing point for psychoanalysis, one that is called upon to measure itself against a social creation, the text, rather than a private delirium. Finally, this writing is a site where the "sacred" is subverted, insofar as it is the discourse of a crisis in identity.

As I see it, this latter point, fundamental because of the breadth of the tradition it touches on (in France, largely Catholicism) and because of the interest it holds for the post-May '68 generation, is often misunderstood. It is interpreted as a manifestation of distress, the fad of a generation bereft of revolutionary ideas, even a joke. If it is true that Maurice Clavel ostensibly waived the post-'68 banner of this movement, then *Tel Quel* bears the responsibility for its nocturnal emergence, like that of an old mole gnawing through the basements of mechanistic rationalism. Without the flair of the "nouveaux philosophes"—who are, all in all, fellow travelers closer to the media than to our research—our own thoughts on writing and the various mythemes of the sacred (from the sacrificial rite that institutes the symbolic to the Virgin, and the topos of the incarnation) have had a swift and artful dissemination whose toughness and corrosiveness have not always been appreciated. In short, these thoughts, as various articles and works of fiction published in *Tel Quel* demonstrate, have nothing to do with religious psychology or ideology but rather with certain phantasmic and linguistic knots on which the power of the sacred is built.

I remember the visit to the offices of *Tel Quel* of an editor from the Soviet journal *Voprossi Filosoffi*. A specialist, I think, in aesthetics and modern literature, she was shocked by the formalism of the novels published in the series and by critics who left no room for the "soul," for the *doucha,* as she said. This provoked great hilarity on Sollers' part, who was astonished to hear a "dialectical materialist" express herself in such a way. I am convinced that this laughter lives on in the author of *Paradis* and *Eloge à Jean Paul II.*

The plurality, the diversity of these orientations—literature, psychoanalysis, history of religions—is disconcerting. Some readers have exhibited a tendency to see decided reversals in this phenomenon. It is true that the dominant concerns have not always been the same. "Semantic materialism" may have been overtaken by the "subject on trial," but it was never eclipsed. The names of Bataille, Sade, Artaud, and Joyce have remained fixed references, attesting not only that our aim has not been principally, even exclusively, literary, but that an experiment was involved even though personal or circumstantial limitations led to highlighting only one aspect of a palette of possibilities.

Obviously, each person who has worked, or who does work with, for, or against *Tel Quel* has his or her own profile, his or her own limit. From Barthes, Todorov, Genette, Derrida, from Deguy, Hallier, Faye, Ricardou, Baudry, Henric, etc., to those—such as Sollers, Pleynet, Risset, Devade, Houdebine, and Scarpetta, who continue to be involved or, more indirectly, B.-H. Levy first of all but also Benoist, Muray, and Jambet—the epistemological, ideological, stylistic options clearly vary (even diverge) among the writers. Is public opinion wrong to associate these irreducible diversities, somehow and in spite of everything, to the myth of a poststructuralism or to *Tel Quel?* It seems to me that the common denominator among this divergence, which perhaps hinges on a question of generation or "the spirit of the times," nevertheless lies in a post-phenomenological or post-analytical vigilance. We set forth as pioneers—some of us cautiously, others recklessly—against what must be termed the phobic discretion of phenomenology and analysis before the contemporary aesthetic experience and what we have called the modern religion, that is politics. One day, we will have to accept, or dare to think, that we are responsible for a certain position in language from which the meaning of the human adventure, bordering on the insane, is deciphered with an involvement that is decidedly risky (this has nothing to do with neutral "scientific" description).

In fact, a future historian of ideas will be able to discern the harbinger of the present insurrection against political reductionism in a specific lecture at a Milan colloquium when we criticized "politics as common measure." That historian will be able to decipher in our readings of Hegel, during our memorable "theoretical groups" at 44 rue de Rennes not simply "the only initiation to speculative philosophy appealing to today's youth" (as a journalist recently said) but also, and above all, the never abandoned effort to take transcendence seriously and to track down its premises in the innermost recesses of language. We will also be able to see, for instance, how certain brilliant students from my courses on Céline became journalists expert in the subtleties of right-wing aesthetics, or in the diffuse spirituality of our times.

I am not trying to have laurels bestowed upon us as precursors of the movement of vulgarization peculiar to contemporary cultural life. I would rather reestablish differences. Whether we came from a Catholic education or a frankly atheist one, or from an exquisite blend of the two, familiarity with Freud and with style in modern art and literature modified for us the enigma of Faith as well as the omnipotence of universal reason. Without rejecting their appeal, their economy was transformed into an inquiry on the dynamics of the speaking Subject and of Meaning. More than the convivial embroidery of Heidegger on the canvas of Logos, it was Lacan's insolence in daring to introduce the "great Other" into the very heart of the speaking structure that propelled us on this course. We are attempting, in our own fashion, to circumscribe the unavoidable necessity of this Other and to analyze its crises, which determine the transformations, the life, and the history of discourses. That there is meaning, which is "One" and polyphonic nevertheless; that it exists but only in the irreducible multiplicities, that it follows the whims of desires and games of languages— these are surely views common to artists and analysts. In holding to these views, we necessarily felt far removed from both the anti-oedipals and the "deconstructionists." In a margin, irreducible and constructive, such as it is: *tel quel*.

## What's the Use of Politics in Times of Distress?

*Clarté,* the journal of communist students, had published, at the end of 1965, I think, a large picture of Sollers along with a text in which he explained, in essence, that only the socialist Revolution could provide a social setting propitious to avant-garde writing. This was, before the mediation of Genette, my first encounter with *Tel Quel.* And the first seduction. The theme Sollers elaborated had struck me. Not that the Romantics or the Surrealists hadn't proclaimed it before him. But it seemed to me completely unrealistic from the standpoint of the socialism I had experienced. I knew to what extent a regime born of a Marxist social mutation rejected not merely all aesthetic formalism deemed individualistic or antisocial, but also all individual stylistic experience that could question or explore the common code and its stereotypes in which ideology must seek shelter in order to dominate. Nevertheless, the logical firmness and the existential assurance of this young star in a *nouveau roman,* rewritten by the painful adventure of the Algerian War and the Bataillian mystique, led me, as well as those who were to become my friends at *Tel Quel,* to think that "in France, it would be different." In addition, hadn't Louis Althusser, whom we met soon after, taken the toughest (for me, the most "Stalinist") points of Marxism in order to instill new hope in the French Communist Party and all of French society, the harbinger of a worldwide Marxist spring? I remained, then, less sensitive to the arguments of the director of studies of the rue d'Ulm than to the revolutionary aestheticism of *Tel Quel,* which seemed, after all, to bode well for the success of the futurist utopia.

Our attitude, which many termed scandalous at the time and which I now regard as illusory, still constitutes the national wager in France today. Were we, then, in the avant-garde on this level as well?

An important point must be emphasized to understand our boarding the Communist Party vessel. The French Communist Party (P.C.F.) was, and still remains to a large extent, the only French party to have a cultural politics. The fact that today this party has lost its intellectuals of national and international renown does little to change its impact upon the cultural workers at the base. Even more—and in my mind this is essential—the P.C.F. is the only party in France to have drawn a lesson (often machiavellically subtle thought for the most part clumsily and dogmatically applied) from having closely witnessed the great adventures on twentieth-century thought and art. The Socialist Party has only followed this course somewhat belatedly. Scorched by Stalinist social realism and shaken by détente, the Kremlin, with Aragon (like the Vatican with Mauriac), had already hailed the work of the young Sollers. But starting in 1966, the entire machine of the P.C.F. awakened to the experiments of the avant-garde. Let's not forget that in France, institutional recognition of Russian formalism, futurism and, by analogy, of contemporary writing, with literary theory as one of its facets, first came with the publications of the P.C.F., *Les Lettres Francaises* and the *Nouvelle Critique,* and the colloquia it organized (Cluny I and Cluny II). In facf, I recently saw Japanese academics in Kyoto initiated into semiology through the published acts of these colloquia.

It is clear that without the fomentation of the militant base (schoolteachers and professors), the "social sciences" in their structuralist hue, and this includes Lacanian psychoanalysis, would not have invaded the university. Although the Edgar Faure reform provided a helping hand in this assault, these disciplines and methodologies nevertheless get their clientele from the audience of the P.C.F.—notwithstanding the protests of leftists declaring "war unto death against the Communist Party." This may seem paradoxical on the part of a party devoted—if one is to believe its programs—to Marxist-Leninism. Those were times for "revisionism," however, and I'll always remember the words of comrade Juquin, during a luncheon of the *Nouvelle Critique* colloquium, explaining to my companions, young bourgeois recently interested in the doctrine, that "Leninism is obsolete." The P.C.F. was trying to take a social-democrat turn which, as we know, failed. The Socialist Party profited from this failure and gained ground, thus pushing the Communist Party toward its present decline.

But to remain on the cultural level, the narrow-minded battle of Mme. Saunié-Seite against all forms of noninstitutionalized thought was nevertheless correct on this point: the Communist Party certainly appropriated, on behalf of the establishment, those currents of thought and aesthetic creation that would have remained marginal without it. From the moment of institutionalization, however, we ceased to believe in the permanent subversiveness of the Community Party and ceased to see ourselves in what we had briefly believed was fated to mark the explosive beginnings of a revolutionary party.

Before coming to this moment of divorce, though, I cannot help but emphasize the scandal that our attitude caused in the moderate intelligentsia. I will pass over the first greeting I received from French public opinion: an insulting article in the magazine *Minute,* claiming to unmask me, on the basis of an article on Bakhtine I had published in *Critique,* as a Soviet spy. It was brought to me at Cochin hospital, where I was suffering from viral hepatitis in the spring of 1967, and I think it aided my recovery.

More spectacular in my view were articles in the *Nouvel Observateur,* in which, after publication in the *Tel Quel* series of a book by Pierre Daix, then still a member of the French Communist Party, we were labeled "Jdanovians" and "catatonics." I admit that I still find the connection between the rigidity of Jdanov and our baroque readings of Sade, Bataille, Freud, or the materialism of Lucretius to be rather tenuous. What I think I understand, however, is the feeling of betrayal, of a truly narcissistic injury, that an essentially Trotskyist—as it should be in the West—left must have felt in seeing our rapprochement to the Communist Party.

What, in fact, were we doing on this galley? Can one discern a general reason, a common denominator in this provisional attraction to the P.C.F. beyond our very diverse psychological motivations, linked to each of our personal histories?

The generation of our elders, which should reproach itself for its dogmatic words and deeds and the more or less tragic consequences that occurred during its stint in the Communist Party, typically explains or, better yet, stigmatizes our behavior as "religious." As if religion were unanalyzable, the fascinating and indescribable enigma before which reason must lay down its arms.

For us, on the contrary, religion, I repeat, was not an enemy to flee, a target for reinvestment beneath the facade of a lay institution. It had already become a discourse for analysis. Since we were neither guilty of terrorist words and deeds, nor even secretly religious, what were we looking for in the P.C.F.? My hypothesis, I think, far from exempting us, casts a less violent but more cruel light on the cynicism that binds the individual to politics, on the perversion that lies at the heart of the political institution, regardless of its nature.

As a state within the state, having considerable powers of dissemination and propaganda distinct from the traditional circuits saturated with more conventional products, the P.C.F. was the best mouthpiece for experimental literary or theoretical work. To make this work public, in order to continue it, seemed to us imperative in an era of mass media. Indeed, an interview with Jean Paulhan, published at the time, compared the surrealists to *Tel Quel,* emphasizing that we were a "mass movement." It was true, and to a large extent thanks to the Communist Party, not to be used by it.

To be sure, we did not deliberately exploit this misunderstanding. If there were any cynicism on our part, it can be derived from what must rightly be called our exaggerated regard for theory. Dialectical materialism, which, in our view, represented Hegel overturned by Lucretius, Mallarmé, and Freud (to cite only three parameters of a nonmechanistic materialism), gave us some hope, if not of modifying the bureaucratic defects of an oppressive machine—we didn't have the pragmatic soul of law-enforcers or founders of morally pure communities—at least of bracketing them.

I identify as political perversion a coherent structure determined by an ideal (this ideal was *theoretical* for us; perhaps it has been *moral* for others), which nevertheless uses the abjections of a reality, one that is neglected or even foreclosed, on behalf of libidinal or sublimated gratifications. (Our own gratification was essentially the development and appreciation of our work.) During the anarchic eruptions of May '68 (in which we participated around the clock), we kept from the beginning a foot on the barricades (that romantic intoxication corresponded to our erotic rhythms and our thoughts, which had broken with convention) and an eye in search of something that could ensure cultural transmission, something in the party that could be useful (to us).

Does this mean that I consider the intellectual essentially ambivalent, torn, treacherous? Not at all. Not only because others were, at the time, greater anarchists or conformists, depending on the logic of their own history. Not only because the principal result of May '68 was to accelerate the revisionism of the P.C.F., leading to a general social-democratization of French society—a process during which communist sensibility swerved to the center-left, while Gaullist sensibility engendered a powerful center-right, creating a bipartyism in the face of which any revolutionary stance was, ipso facto, transformed into an archaicly oedipal attitude. But most of all, because this shift to the outskirts of the P.C.F. gave us a clear view of the reality of a machine, of a group of human beings constituting itself to serve as the conveyor between, on the one hand, the ideal (be it murderous) and, on the other, the individual (whatever that person's value).

Rejected by both the perverted and the "political" animal, this machine is the killer mechanism of individual difference. "Society is a crime committed in common": in congresses and articles, in courses and theses, we have never ceased observing the truth of Freud's famous statement.

Because I brushed against this perverse experience in its cultural manifestation, I still cannot discard the idea that it is the central problem of modern social life, one we still need to analyze. My *Essai sur l'abjection* is probably indirectly linked to this notion. One thing is certain: it is because we saw what was perverse in our relation to the Communist Party that we kept aloof, from then on, from any other political perversion, even a left-wing one. Our Maoism was an anti-organizational, anti-partisan antidote, a utopia in pure form, which had nothing to do with the sects of the left (which were wary of us, and rightly so), proletarian or not, all of whom were rejects fascinated by or love-hating the Communist Party. In this light, the P.C.F. itself does not appear an oddity. More radically, more sombrely, it is the essence of the political tie: popular common sense, radical rationalization, the banal hideout, the orthodox lining of perversion.

What about the schisms, anathemas, persecutions, exclusions that checkered our game with these intrinsically perverse institutions? When they did not grow out of individual psychoanalysis, they were based on the wounds that our child's play with the (red) fire of politics reopened in the flesh of phobic adults. At times, reading articles in which some Parisian writer labeled me a Bogdanov, enemy of the wise Lenin, along with metaphors unleashed from the cellars of Bolshevism, I felt immersed in the universe of *The Possessed*. The sleepwalking fascination exerted by the clichés of the October Revolution on intellectuals weaned on the French Revolution seemed to illustrate a demonic and inevitable eternal return, in which it is impossible to distinguish between cause and effect, living spark and apocalyptic debacle.

As this period was ending, at least for me personally, my Czech friend Antonin Liehm arrived in Paris. An editor of the journal *Literarni Listi,* Liehm was at the center of the "Prague spring" and had been expelled from his country after the arrival of Soviet tanks. He and I resumed our conversational on "liberty and Marxism" in jest, with an irony that only the phoenix people of Central and Eastern Europe can keep alive. About the same time, Louis Althusser, a leader with a great following, was proclaiming the necessity of maintaining the "dictatorship of the proletariat" but in a state of tension that seemed on the verge of breaking down. For the liberal press, however, the myth of the "Stalinist dogmatism" of *Tel Quel* was in full swing. It was time to flee.

## PEKING-SHANGHAI-LOUOYANG-NANKING-XIAN-PEKING . . . NEW YORK

When we left, in the spring of 1974, for the first great voyage of Western intellectuals to China after the Cultural Revolution, many considered the trip a pilgrimage to the Mecca of dogmatism. It was impossible for me to make French intellectuals and my friends from Eastern Europe recognize that the China of the Cultural Revolution represented hope for national and libertarian socialism. For some of us, this gesture of friendship and adherence to the Chinese revolution was a way of associating with a left-wing political movement devoid of the Communist Party legacy. For others such as myself, who were not interested in political discourse, it was a means of finding another set of social and historical roots for "internal experience."

What we were looking for in the spasms of Chinese anti-bureaucratism at a moment when the party machinery had exploded and women, after the young, were suddenly pushed to the front line, was Taoist culture, Chinese writing, and poetry, like jade, bland but subtle.

Joseph Needham, whom I had met in the chapel of Caius College, in Cambridge, and to whom we owe the monumental *Science and Civilisation in China,* had no trouble convincing me that Mao, poet and writer, was the most faithful modern version of ancestral Taoism. I loved—I still love—to lose myself, as in a dream, in the characters of Chinese texts that my professor at Jussieu had rudimentarily taught me. In short, it was classical China, dressed in the worker's blue suit of socialism, that we had gone to find, more interested in Ming tombs or Buddhist steles than in the stories ("bricks, as information theory uses the term," said Roland Barthes) of the friendly Chinese activist comrades. I myself was alarmed by the profound, unflagging, sly presence of the Soviet model, the only sign of the twentieth century in this land of peasants, and all the more evident because it was violently resisted. This led me to write an awkward book, *Des Chinoises,* in which I tried to convey the strangeness of China and to explain the fascination we Occidentals feel for it, a fascination unquestionably involved with our own strange, foreign, feminine, psychotic aspects.

Politically, I saw nothing that might possibly prevent the Cultural Revolution from becoming a national and socialist variation, whose basic reference point remains the province of the Soviets. It marked my farewell to politics, including feminism.

The eruptions, encounters, loves, passions, as well as the more or less liberated or controlled eroticism that have shaped each person's biography constitute, I am convinced, the deepest influences on an individual path. In this essay, I simply present visible surface effects. Only a diary, a novel, could perhaps one day restore the wild indecency of it.

I can say, however, that for most of the Paris-Peking-Paris travelers (Roland Barthes, Philippe Sollers, Marcelin Playnet, François Wahl, and myself), this arduous journey, one that from the outset was more cultural than political, definitively inaugurated a return to the only continent we had never left: internal experience.

The psychoanalytic adventure on which my inquiries into infantile language, psychotic discourse, and style had started me finally led me to the Institute of Psychoanalysis. Lacan, whose seminar I attended until 1974 and whose baroque genius sometimes upset me as much as an actual session with an analyst, had not managed to free himself of the constraints his entourage imposed on him to follow us to China, as he wished to do. Even then, I thought I could discern signs of age in him—and signs of imposture in his school. I therefore avoided following him to his painful end.

The psychoanalytic experience struck me as the only one in which the wildness of the speaking being, and of language, can be heard. Political adventures, against the background of desire and hate that analysis openly unveils, appeared to me the way distance changes them: like a power of horror, like abjection. The sublime and horribly compromised work of Céline gave me the opportunity to speak of this.

*Tel Quel*—never a whole, but rather a provisional association of individuals as they were, *tel quels*—continued to develop, more than ever emphasizing the irreducible nature of writing, style, passion. Barthes's *Fragments d'un discours amoureux* became the best-seller of a formalism altered in its very core: the pleasure of the text. Sollers, after *Nombres* and *Lois* and *H,* which explore oneiric and vocal writing, published the first part of *Paradis,* a saga in which the impact of sexual and political reality is bound to an apocalyptic lyricism that he was able, like a bard, to voice and stage in an excessive, magical performance that traveled from Beaubourg to Greenwich Village.

An unavoidable stage of our journey was our discovery of America. Pleynet, who sought out all forms of modern painting, had for some time been a frequent visitor. Since the early 1970s, I had been, in turn, warmly welcomed by a generous American university, free and encouraging in its curiosity and intellectual naiveté. The Alexandrine, cosmopolitan, decadent climate of New York City always gives me (this despite the archaisms of the American left) the impression of a latter-day Rome; I find nothing more stimulating to my work than those sojourns across the Atlantic. It seems to me that the Western individual, whose "hecceite" we, with Duns Scott, unearthed in the last few issues of *Tel Quel*, simultaneously enjoys, in the United States, a barbaric youth and an exquisite exhaustion.

To view my skeptical appreciation for this state of mind—of which the United States is clearly only an emblem—merely as a fad would be to ignore the individualist and universalist, desperate and jubilant aloofness, with its solitary atomism and its neutralized polyglotism, which substitutes for a community in this country of immigrants. They are traits specific to this *fin de siècle* culture; jazz and rock are their popular manifestations. The United States is a culture in which you write a novel as though you were playing jazz or rock, where you can hear or think discourses, beginning with the convulsive excesses of individuals in the modern megalopolis, whose words seem to be mere provisional and inessential masks. It could be that they represent inordinate ambitions that often disturb editors, analysts, and academics alike. What is clear is that in this inordinacy there is no adherence to a culture, be it local, regional, French, Latin, or Mediterranean. It is perhaps a quest, in form and meaning, for these limits, which have become the reality, the *tel quel*, of our time.

While the Latin American or Arab Marxist revolution is brewing on the doorstep of the United States, I feel closer to truth and liberty when I work within the space of this challenged giant, which may, in fact, be on the point of becoming a David before the growing Goliath of the Third World.

I dream that our children will prefer to join this David, with his errors and impasses, armed with our erring and circling about the Idea, the Logos, the Form: in short, the old Judeo-Christian Europe.

If it is only an illusion, I like to think it may have a future.

Translated by Athena Viscusi

# Bibliography

SELECTED WORKS

*I. Feminist Criticism*

Bloom, Lynn Z. "Heritages: Discussions of Mother-Daughter Relationships in Women's Autobiographies." In *The Lost Tradition: Mothers and Daughters in Literature*. Ed. Cathy N. Davidson and E. M. Broner. New York: Ungar, 1980, pp. 291–302.

Brée, Germaine. "Le Mythe des origines et l'autoportrait chez George Sand et Colette." In *Symbolism and Modern Literature: Studies in Honor of Wallace Fowlie*. Ed. Marcel Tetel. Durham, N.C.: Duke Univ. Press, 1978, pp. 103–12.

Dehler, Kathleen. "The Need to Tell All: A Comparison of Historical and Modern Feminist 'Confessional' Writing." In *Feminist Criticism: Essays on Theory, Poetry and Prose*. Ed. Cheryl L. Brown and Karen Olson. Metuchen, N.J.: Scarecrow Press, 1978, pp. 339–52.

Didier, Béatrice. *L'Ecriture-femme*. Paris: Presses Universitaires de France, 1981.

Hoffman, Leonore and Rosenfelt, Deborah, eds. *Teaching Women's Literature from a Regional Perspective*. New York: Modern Language Association, 1982.

Jelinek, Estelle C. "Teaching Women's Autobiographies." *College English* 38 (1976): 32–45.

———, ed. *Women's Autobiography: Essays in Criticism*. Bloomington: Indiana Univ. Press, 1980.

Juhasz, Suzanne. "'Some Deep Old Desk or Capacious Hold-All': Form and Women's Autobiography." *College English* 39 (1978): 663–68.

Luna, Marie-Françoise. "L'autre lieu du moi: Etude sur trois journaux de jeunes filles." In *Le Journal intime et ses formes littéraires*. Ed. Vittorio Del Litto. Geneva: Droz, 1978, pp. 299–318.

Marks, Elaine. "'I Am My Own Heroine': Some Thoughts about Women and Autobiography in France." In *Teaching about Women in the Foreign Languages*. Ed. Sidonie Cassirer. Old Westbury, N.Y.: The Feminist Press, 1975, pp. 1–10.

237

Mason, Mary G. "The Other Voice: Autobiographies of Women Writers." In *Autobiography: Essays Theoretical and Critical.* Ed. James Olney. Princeton: Princeton Univ. Press, 1980, pp. 207–35.

Mason, Mary Grimley, and Carol Hurd Green, eds. "Introduction." *Journeys: Autobiographical Writings by Women.* Boston: G. K. Hall, 1979, pp. xiii–xvii.

Miller, Nancy K. "Women's Autobiography in France: For a Dialectics of Identification." In *Women and Language in Literature and Society.* Ed. Sally McConnell-Ginet, Ruth Broker, and Nelly Furman. New York: Praeger, 1980, pp. 258–73.

Smith, Sidonie. "The Story of a Caged Bird: Maya Angelou's Quest after Self-Acceptance." In *Southern Humanities Review* 7 (1973): 365–73.

Smith-Rosenberg, Carroll. "The Female World of Love and Ritual: Relations between Women in 19th-Century America." *Signs* 1, no. 1 (Autumn 1975): 1–29.

Spacks, Patricia Meyer. "Reflecting Women." *Yale Review* 63 (1973): 26–42.

———. "Stages of Self: Notes on Autobiography and the Life Cycle." In *The American Autobiography.* Ed. Albert E. Stone. Englewood Cliffs, N.J.: Prentice-Hall. 1981, pp. 44–60.

———. "Women's Stories, Women's Selves." *Hudson Review* 30 (1977): 26–46.

## II. General Theory

Anderson, Howard, and Irvin Ephrenpreis. "The Familiar Letter in the Eighteenth Century: Some Generalizations." In *The Letter in the Eighteenth Century.* Ed. Howard Anderson et al. Lawrence: Univ. of Kansas Press, 1966.

"L'Autobiographie." *Revue d'histoire littéraire de la France* 75, no. 6 (1975).

Beaujour, Michel. *Miroirs d'encre: Rhétorique de l'autoportrait.* Paris: Seuil, 1980.

Blanchard, Jean Marc. "Of Cannibalism and Autobiography." *Modern Language Notes* 93 (1978): 654–76.

Blanchard, Marc Eli. "The Critique of Autobiography." *Comparative Literature* 34 (1982): 97–115.

Blasing, Mutlu Konuk. "Introduction: The Form of History and the History of Form," *The Art of Life: Studies in American Autobiographical Literature.* Austin: Univ. of Texas Press, 1977, pp. xi–xxviii.

Brée, Germaine. "The Fictions of Autobiography." *Nineteenth-Century French Studies* 4 (Summer 1976): 438–49.

Bruss, Elizabeth W. *Autobiographical Acts: The Changing Situation of a Literary Genre.* Baltimore: Johns Hopkins Univ. Press, 1976.

Burt, E. S. "Poetic Conceit: The Self-Portrait and Mirrors of Ink." *Diacritics* 12, no. 4 (Winter 1982): 17–38.

Butterfield, Stephen. *Black Autobiography in America.* Amherst: Univ. of Massachusetts Press, 1974.

Cooke, Michael G. "'Do You Remember Laura?' or, The Limits of Autobiography." *The Iowa Review* 9, no. 2 (1978): 58–72.

*Les Correspondances: Problématique et économie d'un genre littéraire.* Nantes: Presses de l'Université de Nantes, 1983.

Cox, James M. "Autobiography and America." In *Aspects of Narrative.* Selected

Papers from the English Institute. Ed. J. Hillis Miller. New York: Columbia Univ. Press, 1971, pp. 143–72.

Didier, Béatrice. *Le Journal intime*. Paris: Presses Universitaires de France, 1976.

———. "Ecrire sa vie," *Stendhal autobiographe*. Paris: Presses Universitaires de France, 1983, pp. 5–50.

Donato, Eugenio. "The Ruins of Memory: Archaeological Fragments and Textual Artifacts." *Modern Language Notes* 93 (1978): 575–96.

Downing, Christine. "Re-Visioning Autobiography: The Bequest of Freud and Jung." *Soundings* 60 (1977): 210–28.

Fleishman, Avrom. *Figures of Autobiography: The Language of Self-Writing in Victorian and Modern England*. Berkeley: Univ. of California Press, 1983.

Foucault, Michel. "L'Ecriture de soi." *Corps écrit* 5 (1983): 3–26.

Genette, Gérard. "Le Journal, l'anti-journal." *Poétique* 47 (September 1981): 315–22.

Girard, Alain. *Le Journal intime*. Paris: Presses Universitaires de France, 1963.

Goldknopf, David. "The Confessional Increment: A New Look at the I Narrator." *Journal of Aesthetics and Art Criticism* 28 (1969): 13–21.

Gossman, Lionel. "The Innocent Art of Confession and Reverie." *Daedalus* 107 (1978): 59–77.

Gunn, Janet Varner. "The Autobiographical Situation," *Autobiography: Towards a Poetics of Experience*. Philadelphia: Univ. of Pennsylvania Press, 1982.

Hedin, Raymond. "Strategies of Form in the American Slave Narrative." In *The Art of Slave Narrative: Original Essays in Criticism and Theory*. Ed. John Sekora and Darwin T. Turner. n.p.: Western Illinois Univ., 1982, pp. 25–35.

Hipp, Marie-Thérèse. *Mythes et réalités: Enquête sur le roman et les mémoires (1660–1700)*. Paris: Klincksieck, 1976.

Horowitz, Irving Louis. "Autobiography as the Presentation of Self for Social Immortality." *New Literary History* 9, no. 1 (1977): 173–79.

"Individualisme et autobiographie en Occident," Actes du Colloque de Cerisy, *Revue de l'Institut de Sociologie* fasc. 1–2 (1982).

Jay, Paul. *Being in the Text: Self Representation from Wordsworth to Roland Barthes*. Ithaca: Cornell Univ. Press, 1984.

Landow, George P., ed. *Approaches to Victorian Autobiography*. Athens, Ohio: Ohio Univ. Press, 1979, pp. xiii–xlvi.

Lang, Candace. "Autobiography in the Aftermath of Romanticism." *Diacritics* 12, no. 4 (Winter 1982): 2–16.

Lejeune, Philippe. *L'Autobiographie en France*. Paris: Colin, 1971.

———. "Autobiography in the Third Person." *New Literary History* 9, no. 1 (Autumn 1977): 26–50.

———. *Je est un autre: L'Autobiographie de la littérature aux médias*. Paris: Seuil, 1980.

———. *Le Pacte autobiographique*. Paris: Seuil, 1975.

———. *Moi Aussi*. Paris: Seuil, 1986.

"La Lettre au 17ᵉ siècle." *Revue d'histoire littéraire de la France* 78, no. 6 (November-December 1978).

Litto, Vittorio Del, ed. *Le Journal intime et ses formes littéraires*. Geneva: Droz, 1978.

Man, Paul de. "Autobiography as De-facement." *Modern Language Notes* 94 (1979): 919–30.

Marin, Louis. "On the Theory of Written Enunciation: The Notion of Interruption-Resumption in Autobiography." *Semiotica,* spec. suppl. (1981): 101–11.

May, Georges. *L'Autobiographie.* Paris: Presses Universitaires de France, 1979.

———. "Autobiography and the Eighteenth Century." In *The Author in His Work.* Ed. Louis L. Martz and Aubrey Williams. New Haven: Yale Univ. Press, 1978, pp. 319–35.

Mazlish, Bruce. "Autobiography and Psycho-Analysis: Between Truth and Self-Deception." *Encounter* 35 (1970): 28–37.

Mehlman, Jeffrey. *A Structural Study of Autobiography: Proust, Leiris, Sartre, Lévi-Strauss.* Ithaca: Cornell Univ. Press, 1971.

Misch, George. *Geschicte der Autobiographie,* 4 vols. Frankfurt am Main: Schulte und Bulmke, 1946–1969. First two volumes translated as *A History of Autobiography in Antiquity.* London: Routledge and Kegan Paul, 1950.

Neumann, Bernd. *Identität und Rollenzwang: Zur Theorie der Autobiographie.* Frankfurt: Athenaeum, 1970.

Niemtzow, Annette, "The Problematic of Self in Autobiography: The Example of the Slave Narrative." In *The Art of Slave Narrative.* Ed. John Sekora and Darwin T. Turner. n.p.: Western Illinois Univ., 1982, pp. 96–109.

Olney, James, ed. *Autobiography: Essays Theoretical and Critical.* Princeton: Princeton Univ. Press, 1980.

Pascal, Roy. *Design and Truth in Autobiography.* Cambridge: Harvard Univ. Press, 1960.

Pike, Burton. "Time in Autobiography." *Comparative Literature* 28 (1976): 326–42.

Rosenfeld, Alvin H. "Inventing the Jew: Notes on Jewish Autobiography." *Midstream* 21 (1975): 54–67.

Rousset, Jean. "Le Journal intime, texte sans destinataire?" *Poétique* 56 (November 1983): 435–43.

Ryan, Michael. "Self-Evidence." *Diacritics* 10, no. 2 (Summer 1980): 2–16.

Sayre, Robert F. "Autobiography and Images of Utopia." *Salmagundi* 19 (1972): 18–37.

Schultz, Elizabeth. "To be Black and Blue: The Blues Genre in Black American Autobiography." *Kansas Quarterly* 7, no. 3 (1975): 81–96.

Shapiro, Stephen A. "The Dark Continent of Literature: Autobiography." *Comparative Literature Studies* 5 (1968): 421–54.

Shumaker, Wayne. *English Autobiography: Its Emergence, Materials, and Form.* Berkeley: Univ. of California Press, 1954.

Silverman, Hugh J. "Un égale deux, ou l'espace autobiographique et ses limites." *Revue d'esthétique* 33 (1980): 279–302.

Smith, Sidonie. *Where I'm Bound: Patterns of Slavery and Freedom in Black American Autobiography.* Westport Conn.: Greenwood Press, 1974.

Spacks, Patricia Meyer. *Imagining a Self: Autobiography and Novel in Eighteenth-Century England.* Cambridge: Harvard Univ. Press, 1976.

Spengemann, William C. *The Forms of Autobiography: Episodes in the History of a Literary Genre.* New Haven: Yale Univ. Press, 1980.

Stone, Albert E., ed. *The American Autobiography: A Collection of Critical Essays.* Englewood Cliffs, N.J.: Prentice-Hall, 1981.

Sturrock, John. "The New Model Autobiographer." *New Literary History* 9 (1977): 51–63.

Vance, Christie, ed. *Genre* 6, nos. 1 and 2 (March and June 1973).

Vance, Eugene. "Le Moi comme langage: Saint Augustin et l'autobiographie." *Poétique* 14 (1973): 163–77.

Wu, Pei-yi. "Self-Examination and Confession of Sins in Traditional China." *Harvard Journal of Asiatic Studies* 39 (1979): 5–38.

# About the Authors

RICHARD BOWRING is professor of modern Japanese studies at the University of Cambridge, and currently engaged in a study of *The Tale of Genji*.

MARCIA J. CITRON, associate professor of music at Rice University, has written articles on women composers for *Music and Letters, The Musical Quarterly, Current Musicology,* and *The New Grove Dictionary of Music and Musicians.* She is author of the recent book, *The Letters of Fanny Mendelssohn Hensel to Felix Mendelssohn* (1987), and completing a study of Cécile Chaminade.

NANCY F. COTT is professor of history and American studies at Yale University where she has also chaired the Women's Studies Program. She is the author of *The Bonds of Womanhood: 'Woman's Sphere' in New England, 1780–1835* (1977) and of *The Grounding of Modern Feminism* (1987).

DONNA ROBINSON DIVINE is a professor in the department of government at Smith College and cofounder of the Smith College Research Project on women and social change. Author of articles on Zionism, Israeli, Egyptian, and Palestinian Arab politics, she is currently completing a social history of Palestinian Arabs from 1839–1939.

FRANCES SMITH FOSTER is professor of English and comparative literature at San Diego State University. She is author of *Witnessing Slavery: The Development of the Ante-Bellum Slave Narrative* (1979). Her articles on slave literature, autobiography, and science fiction have appeared in such journals as *Extrapolation, Black American Literature Forum, CLA Journal,* and *Journal of American Culture.* She is currently working on a study of nineteenth-century Afro-American women's literature.

MARY D. GARRARD is professor of art history and chair of the art department at the American University. She has published articles on Artemisia Gentileschi and has recently completed a book on the artist's work to be published by Princeton University Press. Her articles on Renaissance art include a study of Michelangelo, Raphael, and the liberal arts (*Viator: Medieval and Renaissance Studies,* 1984). With Norma Broude she edited *Feminism and Art History: Questioning the Litany* (1982).

SANDRA CARUSO MORTOLA GILBERT, a professor of English at Princeton University, and SUSAN DREYFUSS DAVID GUBAR, a professor of English at Indiana University, coauthored *The Madwoman in the Attic: The Woman Writer and the Nineteenth-Century Literary Imagination* (1979) and coedited *Shakespeare's Sisters: Feminist Essays on Women Poets* (1979) as well as *The Norton Anthology of Literature by Women: The Tradition in English* (1985). At present, they are working on a sequel to *The Madwoman*, to be entitled *No Man's Land: The Place of the Woman Writer in the Twentieth Century.*

ELIZABETH C. GOLDSMITH is assistant professor of French at Boston University. She has published articles on Sévigné, Bussy-Rabutin, and Madeleine de Scudéry and is the author of *Exclusive Conversations: The Art of Interaction in Seventeenth-Century France* (1988). She is currently editing a volume of essays on women and letter-writing that will be published in 1988.

ELAINE DOROUGH JOHNSON received her Ph.D. in Spanish from the University of Wisconsin and is assistant professor of Spanish at Augustana College in Illinois. She has lectured and published on a variety of topics including Mercè Rodoreda's novels and short stories, the Chicano narrative, and the teaching of Spanish to native Spanish speakers.

AMY KATZ KAMINSKY is associate professor of women's studies at the University of Minnesota. She has published essays on Spanish and Spanish-American literature and is currently completing an anthology of Spanish women writers from 1400–1900.

JULIA KRISTEVA, a practicing psychoanalyst and professor of literature at Paris VII, is the author of several works of literary theory and criticism, the most recent of which is *Soleil Noir: Mélancolie et dépression* (1987).Her translated works include *Desire in Language, Powers of Horror,* and *Revolution in Poetic Language.* The autobiographical text included in this volume was written for *The Female Autograph.*

PHILIPPE LEJEUNE is maître de conférences of French literature at the University of Paris-Nord. His works focus primarily on the theory and history of the autobiographical genre in France. His publications include: *L'Autobiographie en France, Le Pacte autobiographique, Lire Leiris, Je est un autre,* and *Moi aussi.* A selection of his essays—*On Autobiography*—is forthcoming from the University of Minnesota Press.

JANEL M. MUELLER, professor of English and humanities at the University of Chicago, has published on various aspects of Renaissance and earlier literature. Her recent major work, *The Native Tongue and the Word: Developments in English Prose Style, 1380–1580* (1984), includes further discussion of Margery Kempe, Julian of Norwich, and other early female authors. She is currently at work on a book-length study of nature, culture, and gender in Milton's major poems.

MARYSA NAVARRO teaches Latin American history and women's studies and is Associate Dean for the Social Sciences at Dartmouth College. Her articles have appeared in *Les Temps Modernes, Signs, Journal of Latin American Studies, The Nation,* and *Ms Magazine.* She has written a biography of Eva Perón and is presently working on women and labor unions in Argentina.

DOMNA C. STANTON is professor of French and women's studies at the University of Michigan. The associate editor of *Signs* from 1975–80, she is the author of *The Aristocrat as Art: A Comparative Study of the 'Honnête Homme' and the Dandy* (1980), as well as of articles on seventeenth-century French literature, women writers, and critical theory. Her anthology of French feminist poetry, part of a four-volume series entitled *The Defiant Muse,* was published in 1986.

CATHARINE R. STIMPSON, professor of English and Dean of the Graduate School at Rutgers University, is the author of fiction and essays. The founding editor of *Signs: Journal of Women in Culture and Society,* she is editor of the Women in Culture and Society series at the University of Chicago Press.

MARY FLEMING ZIRIN is an independent researcher-translator of Russian literature currently engaged in writing a book focussed on the lives and works of prerevolutionary Russian women writers.